The Best of
Holidays & Seasonal Celebrations
Issues 5-8

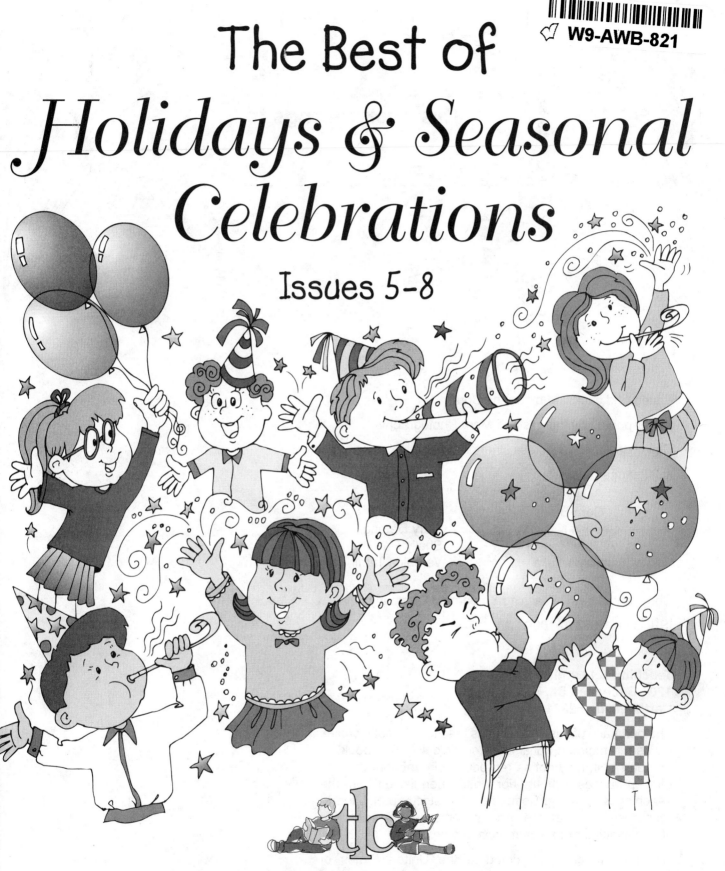

Teaching & Learning Company

1204 Buchanan St., P.O. Box 10
Carthage, IL 62321-0010

This book belongs to

_____

Edited and compiled by Donna Borst

Cover photos by Images and More Photography

Cover designed by Teresa Brierton

Illustrations by:

Becky Radtke	Janet Armbrust
Cara Bradshaw	Luda Stekol
Chris Nye	Mary Detring
Gary Hoover	Shelly Rasche
Gayle Vella	Veronica Terrill

Copyright © 1997, Teaching & Learning Company

ISBN No. 1-57310-100-1

Printing No. 987654321

Teaching & Learning Company
1204 Buchanan St., P.O. Box 10
Carthage, IL 62321-0010

At the time of publication every effort was made to insure the accuracy of the information included in this book. However, we cannot guarantee that agencies and organizations mentioned will continue to operate or to maintain these current locations.

Table of Contents

Fall 7

Winter 93

Spring and Summer 199

Dear Teacher or Parent,

We've done it again! Our first compilation of *Holidays & Seasonal Celebrations* was such a success, we knew it was time for another edition. The result: *The Best of* **Holidays & Seasonal Celebrations:** *Issues 5-8*.

The criteria was the same—take the very best materials from the past year's issues of the magazine and turn them into a single, easy-to-use classroom resource. We think you will be quite pleased with what we've come up with and we want to thank every author, illustrator and teacher who contributed to our success. Without you, none of this would be possible.

Our second year at *Holidays & Seasonal Celebrations* has been just as exciting and just as rewarding as our first. We continue to be amazed at the creative and talented teachers who grace the halls of schools everywhere. We feel very lucky to have the opportunity to present just a sampling of these ideas to you. Judging by the response to our magazine, we feel certain that you continue to need and want new ideas and activities for all of your holiday celebrations. Therefore, we will continue to do our best to provide you with the most creative resource possible.

Thank you for allowing us into your classroom and for giving us the chance to be a part of your teaching process. We're all in this together and together we can make a difference.

Sincerely,

Donna

Donna Borst

If you would like to contribute to future issues of *Holidays & Seasonal Celebrations*, please direct your submissions to:

Teaching & Learning Company
Holidays & Seasonal Celebrations
1204 Buchanan St., P.O. Box 10
Carthage, IL 62321-0010

My Favorite
Season

I love the autumn
With its red and gold leaves,
Crisp days and cool nights,
Sweaters and long socks,
Baked apple and pumpkin pies.
Autumn is my favorite season . . .

Until winter comes.

I love the winter
With its snowmen and sleds,
Ice skating on frozen ponds,
Crackly fires and toasted marshmallows,
Sleep-in mornings.
Winter is my favorite season . . .

Until spring comes.

I love the spring,
With its rain showers,
Scents from fresh flowers,
Tall, green grasses,
Kite-flying winds.
Spring is my favorite season . . .

Until summer comes.

I love the summer
With its long, barefoot days,
Backyard barbecues and cold lemonade,
Camping trips,
Warm, lazy nights.
Summer is my favorite season . . .

Until autumn comes.

by Paige Taylor

An Autumnal Question

It's cool in the mornings,
And hot after school.
Long pants, short pants,
What is the rule?

A jacket works great
When the weather is cold.
I just take it off
When the sun gets bold.

But what for my legs?
What about them?
Long for the morning,
Then roll up the hem?

Do I freeze in the morning,
Or melt later on?
Autumn's confusing.
Where's summer gone?

by Elizabeth Giles

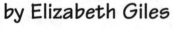

Count Your Blessings

An Autumn Celebration of Rhyme and Reason

One, two, three, four,
Fall is knocking at the door.
Colored leaves that seem to blaze,
Count the blessings of autumn days.

Five, six, seven, eight,
Fall is pressing at the gate.
Squirrels gather instead of laze,
Counting their blessings on autumn days.

Nine, ten, eleven, twelve,
Fall moves books onto our shelves.
Getting ready for schooltime plays,
Teachers count the blessings of autumn days.

Thirteen, fourteen, fifteen, sixteen,
Fall is a season for weather mixing.
Sometimes chilly, with wintry gaze,
Count the blessings of warm autumn days.

Seventeen, eighteen, nineteen, twenty,
Fall brings in a harvest of plenty.
Corn and pumpkins boldly gaze,
As farmers count the blessings of autumn days.

Twenty-one, twenty-two, twenty-three, twenty-four,
Fall follows summer in a windy roar.
Soon winter creeps in, and cold weather stays.
A warm coat is a blessing on autumn days.

Twenty-five, twenty-six, twenty-seven, twenty-eight,
Fall changes clocks, now early seems late.
It is dark in the street, the sun barely stays.
Light is a blessing on dark autumn days.

Twenty-nine, thirty, thirty-one, thirty-two,
Fall skies are bright, a glaring blue.
Hear the birds calling out as they raise
Their wings to fly South on autumn days.

Thirty-three, thirty four, thirty-five, thirty-six,
Fall brings a day of treats and of tricks.
Dressing in finery, the pumpkins ablaze,
Halloween is a blessing of autumn days.

Thirty-seven, thirty-eight, thirty-nine and forty,
Can you count more blessings that rhyme so smartly?
Fall or autumn, the seasonal name
For a time of blessings too many to tame!

Note: This rhyming story can be read aloud as a set for the enrichment activities which follow. This piece is also suitable for a choral reading with students in grades 2 or 3. It makes a nice PTA or Parents' Night presentation, when adorned with props and perhaps some creative movement.

by Dr. Linda Karges-Bone

Enrichment Activities

Language Arts

1. Create a language comparison chart by drawing a line down the center of a sheet of chart paper. Label one side *Autumn Things* and the opposite side *Other Seasons*. Guide children in sorting words and phrases into the two categories. Example: *schooltime* would be an Autumn Things word; *hot* would be on the Other Seasons' side.

2. As you read the poem aloud, ask older children to write down pairs of rhyming words. Younger children can give a hand signal as they hear pairs of rhyming words.

3. Create a glossary of Autumn Words. Children can put the words in alphabetical order and write original definitions of the words. These words can become spelling and handwriting assignments for the next few weeks.

4. Children can copy a portion of the poem as a handwriting sample. Place the sample in each child's language arts portfolio. Be sure to date it. Then continue the process of doing a handwriting sample during each season of the school year, using a seasonal poem for continuity.

5. Tell the children that poems and rhymes are shorter than stories but have interesting ways of putting big ideas into small places. Ask them to listen for the answers in these excerpts from the poem:

   a. How could a season "knock at the door"? Is it a real knocking? Answers: It could be the wind. It could be leaves falling against the ground. It could simply be a way of saying "I'm here. I'm a new season."

   b. Do leaves really blaze? Answers: Yes, if you rake and then burn piles of leaves. They could blaze. No. You could say that it means very bright, hot colors, such as yellow or red. They seem to be on fire. (Check point: Do all the children understand the word *blaze*? If they haven't seen a fire; they might not!)

   c. How can early seem late? That doesn't make sense, does it? Answers: Talk about the concept of time change in grades 2-3. In younger grades, keep the discussion focused on how it seems dark at a time when you are just getting ready for supper. How is that different than summer?

Creative Arts

1. Mix a tablespoon of cinnamon or ginger into red, orange and brown tempera paints and use the spicy mixture to dip autumn leaves into, then press onto thick paper. The autumn spices spur creativity. (Note: Check out the Teaching & Learning Company book, *Beyond Hands-On: Techniques for Using Color, Scent, Taste, Touch and Sound to Enhance Learning* by Dr. Linda Karges-Bone, for more sensory learning ideas.)

2. Gather acorns, nuts and hard "burrs" from the ground around the school. If you live in the city, bring in bags of nuts and small pinecones donated from a grocer or florist shop. Use these materials to create sound makers by placing them between two metal pie plates and sealing the sides with craft glue. Practice making original rhythms with the shakers.

3. Use rhythm instruments to beat time to the poem as you read it aloud. Turn the experience into a chant. Can you think of hand movements to accompany the poem?

4. Use the poem as a choral reading. Assign small groups of children to illustrate "panels" of scenery made of segmented computer paper, to "unroll" as the poem is recited. You could have a different scene for each of the four lines of verse.

Science and Mathematics

1. Tape adding machine paper at the children's eye level. As the poem is read, invite children to use orange or red markers to write the numbers in order, on the tape. (Hint: Try scented markers for added intensity.)

2. Cut out construction paper leaves in a variety of autumn colors. Use the leaves as manipulatives on an autumn storyboard made of a bare-branched tree. (See page 12 for leaf and storyboard patterns.) Create simple word problems for the children to solve by placing the leaves on the tree.
Example: Tia and James were walking in the park. Each of them found three leaves. Place the right number of leaves on your tree.

3. Give each child a small bag to collect autumn leaves. Bring the leaves back and display them. Investigate the following questions:

   a. Why do leaves fall to the ground? Introduce the concept of gravity.

   b. Why do leaves turn colors? Introduce the concepts of changes in nature as well as the roles of sun, light, heat and chlorophyll on living things.

4. Sort the leaves by color or shape. Count the leaves in each category. Create a graph to represent the number of leaves in each category. Practice "reading" the graph. Introduce the term *data collection*.

Geography and Social Science

1. Introduce the concept of climate. Discuss differences in seasonal weather around your state or region. For example: Do you have mountains in your state? How would autumn be different in that area?

2. Use the cut-out boy and girl shapes to create suitable clothing for autumn, summer, winter and spring seasons. How do the seasons affect other parts of our lives? Travel? Food? Holidays?

3. Use French, German and Japanese dictionaries to look up the words for *summer, winter, spring and autumn* in other languages. Create a flip book of seasonal words from around the globe.

4. Use the globe to demonstrate the concept of the equator. Explain how autumn would not be very different from summer in a country that is very close to the equator.

Storyboard for Autumn Math Problems

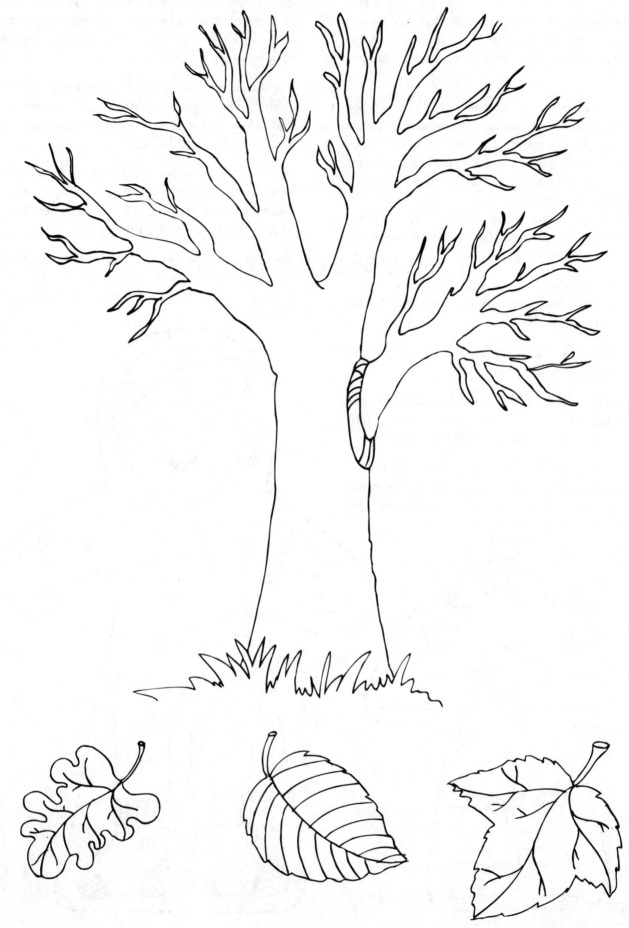

Pancake Day

Quick, grease the griddle! Pancake Day is February 2, if you happen to live in France. In England, Shrove Tuesday is the day for flapjack festivities. In the U.S., there is a whole week during February. Pancake Day in France brings opportunities for a year's worth of good luck. Grown-ups challenge themselves to toss pancakes in the air and catch them in a pan, while holding a coin in the other hand. Children gain good luck by finding a thread baked into a pancake. Festivities in England include pancake races and pancake-eating contests.

Chances are that you would not choose to have pancakes flying and skillets waving in your classroom, nor would you wish to send your students home with stomachaches, but Pancake Day can still be fun. Try these activities for a fun-filled Pancake Day.

by Gloria Trabacca

Pancake Mix Measuring

- complete pancake mix (just add water)
- zippered plastic bags
- measuring cups and spoons
- 1 penny for each child
- large bowl

Pour the pancake mix into a large bowl and provide measuring cups for children to use to fill their own bags. Tell them how many cups of mix to place in their bags.

For older children, make this activity more challenging by removing the one-cup measure and replacing it with assorted sizes of measuring cups and spoons. Provide them with measurement equivalents, such as 3 tsp. = 1 T. and 16 T. = 1 cup.

Tape a penny to the Good Luck card (directions provided on the following page), attach the card to the bag of pancake mix and have children take them home and share the story of Pancake Day with their families.

Pancake Catch

- smallest size plastic cups
- 18" lengths of string (one per child)
- quarter-size tagboard "pancakes"
- tape

Have students cut out a tagboard pancake. Tape the pancake to one end of a length of string. Tape the other end of the string to the inside bottom of the paper cup. Have fun trying to flip the pancake into the paper cup "pan."

176

Pancake Good Luck Cards

Make copies of the card pattern below. Provide tan crayons and brightly colored yarn. Punch holes where marked around the edges of the cover page, and at the top of the inside page. Students may first color their cards, and then lace yarn around the cover page. Have students begin and end the lacing at the top of the pancake. The final few stitches should pass through both pieces of paper to attach the front and back of the card. Or cards may be stapled at the top. In this case, omit holes from the second page of the card. Send Good Luck cards home with a pancake mix gift.

In France, today is Pancake Day,
with food to eat and games to play.
They flip a pancake in the air
and catch it if they may.
If they catch it, then good luck
will be theirs all year through.
So, I'm bringing you this card,
and you can try for good luck, too!

Books to Read

Pancakes for Breakfast by Tomie de Paola. Harcourt Brace Jovanovich, 1978.

The Pancake by Anita Lobel. Greenwillow Books, 1978.

It's Groundhog Day

The Groundhog

The groundhog comes out of the ground.
> (With thumb and forefinger of left hand, make a circle.
> Stick forefinger of right hand through it.)

First he looks up; then he looks down.
> (Stick finger way up, then bring it down.)

If he sees his shadow, he runs back inside
> (Quickly bring finger out.)

For six more weeks, where he stays and hides.
> (Put finger behind back.)

by Judy Wolfman

There are many vital statistics about the groundhog that can be quite interesting for you and your class to know and discuss.

Common Name: groundhog or woodchuck

Family: They are members of the rodent family and the largest species of the squirrel family. They are also related to gophers, which are also called prairie dogs and beavers.

Average Weight: Around 10-15 pounds

Average Length: 1 to 1½ feet long

Coloration: Brownish-black with yellow highlights

Life Span: About six years in the wild and between 10-15 years in captivity

Range: The types we see live in the eastern United States and in southern and eastern Canada.

Population: There is a large amount of these animals. There's as many woodchucks as there are raccoons and opossums, mostly in the rural areas rather than the city.

"To see or not to see its shadow" is the question of the day on February 2. It's officially Groundhog Day when this small creature predicts the upcoming seasonal weather. The legend states that if the groundhog comes out of his burrow and sees his shadow, we're in for six more weeks of winter. If no shadow is seen, spring is on its way.

Many years ago in England, Scotland and Germany, the folk belief was that hibernating animals would awaken in mid-winter to check the weather and decide whether to go back to sleep or stay up for spring. February 2 seemed to be the day of choice. This custom was brought to the United States by German immigrants in the late 1800s. They settled in an area of Pennsylvania called Punxsutawney, which is 100 miles northeast of Pittsburgh.

Punxsutawney Phil is the world's most famous groundhog. He is the one that television networks and national publications arrange to see and film. Phil lives the life of the rich and famous as he resides in a custom-designed den at the Punxsutawney, Pennsylvania, library. He is a tourist attraction, and once a year he treks up to Gobbler's Knob for the shadow ritual, which has been a tradition since 1886. If you need more information about famous Phil, use the following sources to find out what you want to know.

The Punxsutawney Chamber of Commerce 1-800-752-PHIL

Phil's Fan Club ($7.50 a year)
Punxsutawney Groundhog Club
Chamber of Commerce
124 W. Mahoning Street
Punxsutawney, PA 15767

A gift catalog of custom souvenirs is also available through the Chamber of Commerce.

Computer Web Site:
http.//www.groundhog.org

Phil's Fan Club

by Tania K. Cowling

173

Exploring Autumn

It's autumn and the outdoors is brimming with vibrant colors, falling leaves, earthy scents and creatures readying themselves for winter. The air is crisp, the biting insects are at bay—there's no better time for an educational hike! Use nature's classroom and your outdoor Kid Space to make the most of the season's educational opportunities.

Leaf Rubbings

Put those falling leaves to good use for an interesting art project.

You Need (for each child):
- sturdy leaves
- stack of old newspapers
- crayons or markers
- tissue or tracing paper
- masking tape
- construction paper

What to Do:
1. Collect a variety of leaves with interesting shapes.
2. Put the stack of newspapers on a flat work surface.
3. Arrange the leaves in a nice pattern on top of the stack of newspapers.
4. Put the tracing or tissue paper gently on top of the arrangement and fasten it in place using masking tape.
5. Peel the paper from a crayon and rub it back and forth on its side on a piece of scrap paper until it has one flat surface.
6. Rub the flat surface of the crayon very gently over the tissue paper, taking care not to rearrange the leaves.
7. Remove the tissue paper and admire your rubbings.

- Paste the tracing paper rubbing onto a piece of tagboard. When the glue is dry you can cut out the shape and the backing. Cut each leaf individually and hang on a mobile.
- Outline each leaf in black felt tip marker and tape the tissue paper compositions to the classroom window—allowing the sunlight to filter through and light the forms.

by Robynne Eagan

Take a City Hike

If you live in an urban area and your Kid Space is a city environment, take heart! Lace up those hiking boots and slap on a backpack—there's much to explore in the urban outdoors.

Plan a hike around your city with stops at some of the more interesting spots. Where can you find nature in your city? Advise children to wear comfortable clothing and especially appropriate footwear.

City Birds

Take a look up and all around. What birds do you see? Are there any bird feeders in people's yards?

Pigeons are common city-dwelling birds. These birds hang around and add atmosphere. Starlings were originally brought to North America from England and now thrive in the United States and Canada. It is estimated that there are hundreds of millions of them now in these areas. What dangers are involved with importing creatures from another place? What other birds do you see? What do your students know about them?

Plants are Everywhere!

As you walk along the concrete, take a closer look.

- Can children find signs of plants struggling to break through the concrete? Are there any cracks in the concrete? How did they get there?
- Can you find dandelions? Pigweed? Knotweeds or flowers? These plants are very hardy and are able to grow with limited soil, light, water and clean air.
- Look for different types of grasses. Why are some lawns greener than others? What do you think about people adding pesticides, herbicides and fertilizers to their lawns? Where do these chemicals go? Find a sewer drain and think about where the water and waste go.

City Critters

The squirrel is probably one of the most common city creatures you are likely to see. Squirrels are relatively harmless creatures who have adapted well to city life. They are intelligent. Can you find places where the squirrels have been storing their nuts? Did you know that squirrels sometimes work together to gather their nuts? One squirrel will knock nuts from a tree while other squirrels gather the nuts for all to share. Cities are also home to mice, rats, raccoons and skunks. Are you aware of the existence of any of these creatures in your neighborhood? What signs might indicate that they exist? These creatures favor attics, garages, culverts, backyards, alleys, ponds, ditches and trees.

Map Your Kid Space

Learn some valuable map-making skills! What is a map? It's a tool people use to help them find their way around. Maps are like views of an area taken from the sky. They show the permanent features in an area.

You Need (for each child):
- string
- stakes
- measuring tape
- pencil
- large drawing paper
  (graph paper works well)
- clipboard
- directional compass

What to Do:
1. Divide children into groups of four and have each group choose a small area that they would like to map out.
2. Hammer one stake into the ground to form one corner of your mapping plot.
3. Using your compass, measure 10 feet (3 m) directly N, S, E or W of the original stake.
4. Repeat this process until you have a north, south, east and west stake.
5. Now using your ruler, draw this square on your paper. Your map should be made to scale so make each side should be equal and to scale; for example, 10" long (where the scale is 1" = 1') or 40 cm (where 10 cm = 1 m).

Maps are small representations of the area they show, so most include a scale bar that makes it easier for map readers to determine distances between one place and another. A scale indicates the actual distance as it is represented on the map. You can stretch a string from one point on the map to another to determine distance "as the crow flies" or you can wind your string through streets and around paths to determine a route. The measured string can then be held up to the scale bar to determine the distance between the two places. Your Kid Space map might look something like this:

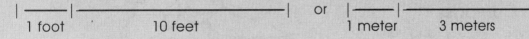

| —— | ———————— | or | —— | ———————— |
| 1 foot | 10 feet | | 1 meter | 3 meters |

6. Using your compass, draw a direction finder on your map. North is always up! If you start at N and go clockwise, this little rhyme will help you remember where to put the letters: Never Eat Shredded Wheat!
7. Maps usually use symbols. Look at several kinds of maps and the symbols they use. Make up your own symbols to sketch on your map showing the location of various features of your plot of land. Include the location of various plants, flowers, stones and grass types. Note the distances between various items so you can map the distances correctly.

Which Way to the Beach?

Long ago people used landmarks, the sun, stars and the wind to help them determine direction and find their way. The invention of the compass gave pathfinders a very reliable directional tool.

What Is a Compass?

A compass is a navigational tool that has been used for thousands of years to help people find their way.

The Earth acts like a gigantic magnet. Compass needles are magnetic and always line up with the Earth's magnetic field, allowing people to use the north magnetic pole to find their way.

On the face of a compass is a diagram know as the "compass rose." It contains letters that represent the four cardinal, or main, directions: north, south, east and west. Compasses designed for specific direction finding also have numbers dividing the compass face into 360 equal sections or degrees. The compass needle turns and points to different letters to help us determine direction.

N stands for North, *E* for East, *S* for South and *W* for West.

Find East

The direction the sun rises in is east and the direction the sun sets in is west. Stand outside. Can you tell from which direction the sun rose? If so, you can point to the east. Point your left hand in the opposite direction and you are pointing west.

How to Use a Compass

- Hold the compass faceup and very still until the needle stops moving.
- When you stop, the red end of the needle will be pointing north.
- Turn your compass so the N is directly under the pointing red end of the needle.
- Draw an imaginary line from the center point of the compass to the W (for West) and point in that direction. You will be pointing west. You can do the same for east and south to find your way.

Fall Leaves

Across the Curriculum

Fall (also called autumn) officially arrives in September. In various parts of our nation, the temperatures are getting colder, and we see leaves in hues of red, yellow and orange on trees falling to the ground. In other parts where temperatures are warmer, we can only imagine the fall colors.

Color changes in leaves are the result of a combination of occurrences: loss of chlorophyll due to the shorter days and chemical changes triggered by cooler weather. Deciduous trees (trees that shed leaves) need a lot of light to produce chlorophyll, giving the leaves their green color. As fall comes, the days get shorter leaving the trees with fewer hours of sunlight to produce chlorophyll. Without this chlorophyll, the green fades and colors of red, orange, yellow and brown begin to appear. These colors have always been present in the leaf, but they have been covered by the chlorophyll.

Art

Fall Tree

Draw a tree trunk on white construction paper. Color the trunk brown with crayons. With a hole punch, make dots of red, orange, yellow and brown paper. Glue these on the tree limbs and all around the base of the tree. There are several variations you can use on this tree:

- Sponge-paint leaves.

- Glue on small squares in fall colors.

- Glue on crumpled wads of colored tissue paper.

Leaf Prints Using Paint

With a brush, paint red, orange and yellow tempera paint onto the front sides of leaves. Press the painted side onto paper. For a variation, place the paint on the back side of the leaf and press down—you might see more distinct markings on this print.

Leaves in Plastic

Place your leaves on the sticky side of clear self-adhesive plastic. Cover with another sheet of plastic and press. Cut around the leaves, punch holes in them and thread yarn or ribbon for a leaf hanging. Or cut a single leaf and use it as a bookmark.

by Tania Kourempis-Cowling

Science

Watercolors

Experiment with water and food colors to discuss the colors that are seen in the fall. Place water in two bowls or clear cups. Start with two primary colors, red and yellow. Then mix colors by adding yellow to the red bowl to make orange and adding blue to the yellow bowl to make green.

Talk about how some leaves change from green to yellow, orange and red.

Leaf Observations

Collect different kinds of fall leaves and place them on your science table. Provide several magnifying glasses for the children to observe the leaf; its color, texture, shape and veins.

Literature

Look for these books in your library and share them with the children. These choices were listed in the Fourth Edition of *Best Books for Children,* preschool through grade 6 by John T. Gillespie and Corinne J. Naden (1990).

McNaughton, Colin. *Autumn.* (1984) A picture book illustrated by the author showing the characteristics of this season.

Barklen, Jill. *Autumn Story.* (1980) A fictional story about mice celebrating the season; illustrated by the author.

Dutton, Sandra. *The Cinnamon Hen's Autumn Day.* (1988) A fictional story about how Mr. Rabbit cleans up Cinnamon Hen's yard and how she missed the crunch of the leaves.

Brandt, Keith. *Wonders of the Seasons.* (1982) An introduction to the seasons and their characteristics.

Lambert, David. *The Seasons.* A simple introduction to the "whys" of the changing seasons.

Kirkpatrick, Rena K. *Look at Leaves.* (1978) Text and illustrations about the subject.

Lerner, Sharon. *I Found a Leaf.* (1978) The story of leaves through the seasons.

Johnson, Sylvia. *How Leaves Change.* (1986)
How and why leaves change color in the fall.

Creative Movement

Blowing in the Wind

Tell the children to pretend they are leaves on a tree blowing in the wind, swaying back and forth. With a strong gust, the leaves break off and fall to the ground. See how many ways the children can act out the falling—floating, swaying, bouncing, spinning, etc.

When the leaves have fallen, have fun in a pretend pile; rolling, sliding, scattering and tossing leaves at each other.

Note: Adding colorful streamers to the child's arms make this activity colorful and authentic.

Shout

Play this game in a pile of autumn leaves on the playground, or if you're not lucky to have the "real thing," make a pile of construction paper leaves. Have the children form a circle around the pile. The teacher says, "If you find a red leaf, shout 'yes' and nod your head up and down." The kids race to pick up a red leaf. If they do not find a leaf of that color, they can wait for the next round. Continue with these commands:

Yellow–Shout "yes" and shake hands with the person next to you.

Orange–Shout "yes" and jump up to the sky.

Brown–Shout "yes" and touch the ground.

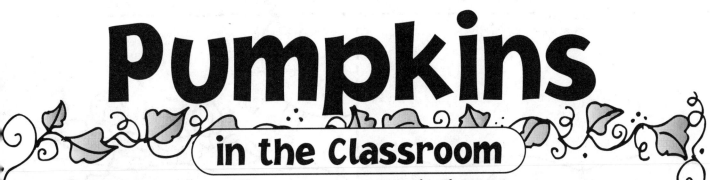

Pumpkins
in the Classroom

Getting Started

Big pumpkins grow from tiny seeds. In spring, they are planted in the ground. Sun and rain help the plant grow. Soon the plant develops into a green vine on which flowers bloom and produce a vegetable called pumpkins. Children are excited about how pumpkins grow to become pies or jack-o'-lanterns for Halloween. For these reasons, pumpkins offer an introduction to science as well as a symbol of the fall season.

Changing as We Grow

Use this opportunity to talk about how change affects pumpkins and other living things. Make a class scrapbook with the title "Changing as We Grow." Design each page to show a living plant, animal or person changing and growing. Help children draw or find magazine pictures such as: baby/child/adult; egg/baby chick/hen or rooster; apple seed/tree/apples; pumpkin seed/vine and flowers/ pumpkin/jack-o'-lantern or pie. Punch holes in each page and secure with metal rings. Place this book in your library center so children can "read" their work. Allow children to check out the book overnight. This will help youngsters understand library rules.

Pumpkin Picture

Show children a picture of a pumpkin with the vine, leaves and flowers. Draw on students' prior knowledge as you begin studying this fall vegetable. Ask the following: Has anyone seen a pumpkin patch? Have you helped with planting or harvesting pumpkins? After this pumpkin is fully ripened, what can we make from it? Does someone in your family make pumpkin pies? Who? Tell about a jack-o'-lantern you made with your family.

From Seeds to Jack-o'-Lanterns

Cut out and paste the pictures on page 20 on index cards. Copy the appropriate sentence on the back of each card. Use this as a sequence activity. You can omit some of the sentences for younger students.

1. A tiny pumpkin seed is planted in the soil.
2. Sun and rain help produce small leaves.
3. Vines with green leaves appear on the plant.
4. Flowers blossom on the vine.
5. After the flower dies, a small green pumpkin appears.
6. The pumpkin grows bigger. It turns orange.
7. The pumpkin is ready to cut from the vine.
8. Now you can make a pumpkin pie or a jack-o'-lantern.

by Carolyn Ross Tomlin

Literature Connection

Read the story *The Berenstain Bears and the Prize Pumpkin* or another book about pumpkins or Halloween. Talk about the differences between making a pumpkin into a pie or a jack-o'-lantern. Ask children to help in creating a chart about these two activities.

Pies:
* made from a pumpkin
* baked in a pan
* contain spices and sugar
* cut in wedges or triangles
* a dessert at Thanksgiving

Jack-o'-Lanterns:
* made from a pumpkin
* carved with a knife
* has a mouth, nose and eyes
* used indoors or outside
* has a light or candle inside

Pumpkin Hopscotch

Make an indoor game for a rainy day. Allow children to practice gross motor development and number recognition by playing Pumpkin Hopscotch. Use 10 pieces of heavy cardboard. Number the cards 1 to 10, drawing one to 10 pumpkins on the cards. Arrange in the traditional hopscotch pattern. Tape cards to the floor. Allow each child two or three turns.

Where Is Pumpkin?

(To the tune of "Where Is Thumbkin?")

Where is pumpkin?
Where is pumpkin?
Here I am; here I am.
How are you this evening?
How are you this evening?
Run and hide, run and hide.

Continue using other words associated with Halloween, such as *black cat, jack-o'-lantern, white ghost, full moon* and other words the children think of.

Pumpkin Puppet Play

Use the pattern on page 87 for puppets. Each student will need five pumpkins. Have them glue the pumpkins onto craft sticks to create puppets. Repeat each line and ask the children to say it after you.

Five Little Pumpkins

Five little pumpkins sitting on a gate,
  (Hold up five fingers.)
"Hurry" called the black cat—"or you'll be late!"
  (Five fingers pretend to run away.)
Four little pumpkins sitting on the floor,
  (Hold up four fingers.)
"Who-o-o" screeched the hoot owl, flying through the door.
  (Four fingers run away.)
Three little pumpkins looking at the moon,
  (Hold up three fingers.)
"Away . . ." called the witch on her broom.
  (Three fingers run away.)
Two little pumpkins looking at the fire,
  (Hold up two fingers.)
It's getting late; we're beginning to tire.
  (Two fingers run away.)
One little pumpkin, lonely as can be,
  (Hold up one finger.)
"Hello!" yelled the other four, "we're back, you see!"
  (Hold up all five fingers.)

Repeat and listen for words that rhyme. Say: Listen and raise your hand when you hear a word that sounds like another. These are called rhyming words. Can you name the rhyming words in each line?

A Pumpkin Patch

Pumpkins are usually grown in a field which is sometimes called a pumpkin patch. First, help the farmer find his pumpkins. Then circle all the words that rhyme with *patch*. How many rhyming words did you find? _____

latch

catch

pig

field

batch

match

hatch

garden

My Little
Pumpkin Patch

In my little pumpkin patch, there are pumpkins big and round.
My scarecrow stands and watches them, and never makes a sound.
He's there to scare the crows away, but it doesn't work at all.
They land on his head in summer and stay on through the fall!
Can you chase the crows away?

Materials:

- patterns
- straw
- 10" bamboo skewer stick
- 8 oz. whipped topping container
- scissors
- crayons
- glue

Directions:

1. Color and cut out the pattern pieces on pages 24 and 25, making sure to color the reverse side of the wings on pieces H and I as well.

2. Glue A and B together carefully, with straw placed securely in between. (Do not glue the top of the head shut. The opening of the straw should be exposed.) Trim edges as needed.

3. With the top of a bamboo skewer in between, glue the body of H and I together. Fold down wings. Place skewer in the straw opening on top of the scarecrow's head.

4. Position pieces E, F and G as desired, separately or together.

5. Invert an 8 oz. whipped topping container and glue pieces C and D to the sides.

6. If desired, cut a 4" circle from green construction paper. Glue to top of container.

7. In top center of the container, poke a hole large enough for the straw to fit through loosely. Once inserted, tap or rotate skewer stick with crow attached to make him fly away. Diagrams and illustrations follow.

Note: Skewer sticks are easily obtainable at any grocery store.

by Barbara Casper

23

My Little Pumpkin Patch

B

A

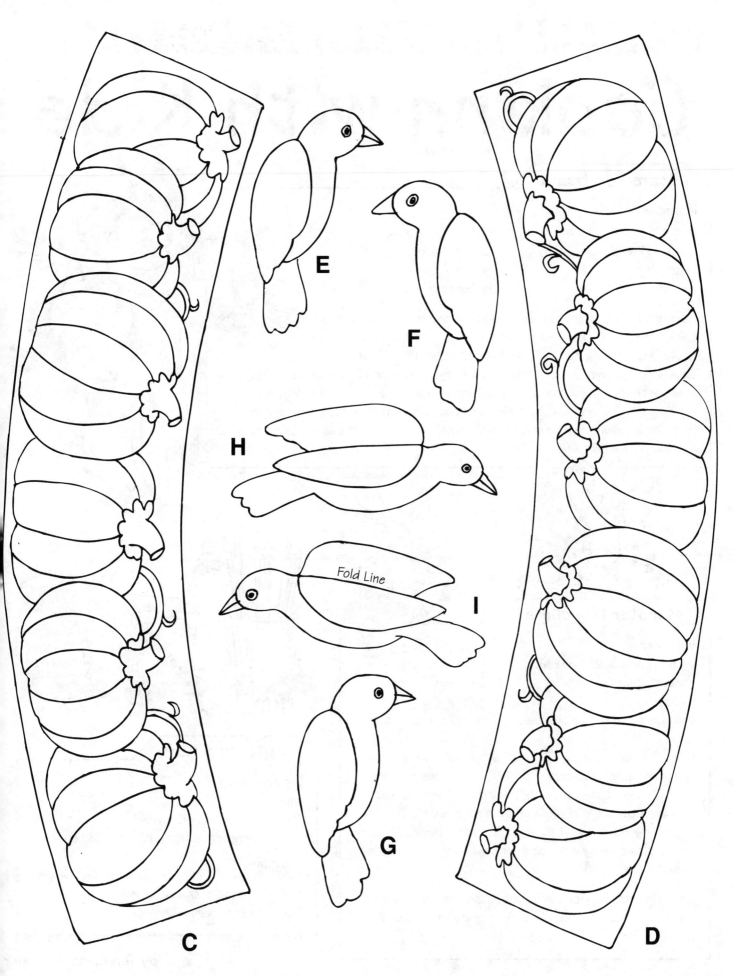

E

F

H

G

Fold Line

I

C

D

Cooking with Kids

Scarecrow Salad

Ingredients:

peaches ($1/2$ peach each)

lettuce (1 whole leaf each)

celery sticks

raisins

pears ($1/2$ pear each)

carrot sticks

grapes

paper towels (2 each)

Have students wash lettuce and place one leaf on a double thick paper towel. Put one peach half on top of the lettuce; this is the scarecrow's head. Place one pear half just below the peach, small end up; this is the scarecrow's body. Using carrot and/or celery sticks, arrange them around the pear body for the scarecrow's arms and legs. Cut one big grape in half and place it below the celery/carrot legs for the scarecrow's feet. Place raisins at the end of the carrot/celery arms; these are the scarecrow's fingers. Eat and enjoy!

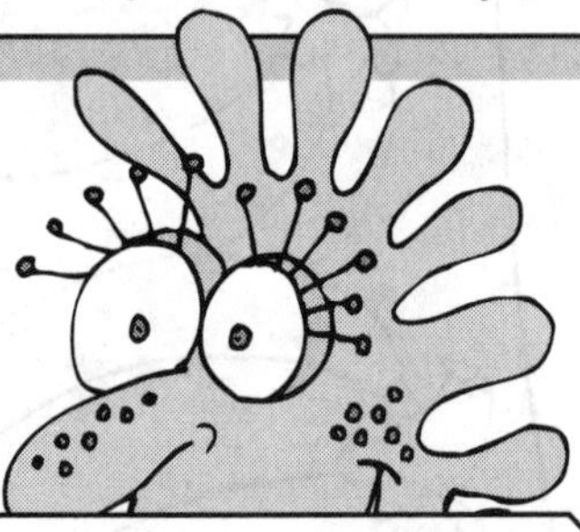

Monster Munchers

Ingredients:

bread (whole wheat or white)

cheese spread

raisins

shredded carrots or cheese

peanut butter

bananas

celery

round cookie cutter

Using the cookie cutter (a glass upside down or knife could be used), cut out a circle from a slice of bread. Spread peanut butter or cheese spread over the entire surface. Cut two slices of bananas for eyes. Place a few raisins for a nose and mouth. Cut celery pieces to use for eyebrows and ears. Use shredded carrots or cheese curls for hair.

With this activity, children can be as creative as they want. You can also use peanuts in place of raisins. Now eat and enjoy!

Ants on a Raft

Ingredients:

raisins

Triscuits®/saltine crackers

cheese spread/peanut butter/cream cheese

Spread cream cheese, peanut butter or cheese spread over a square-shaped cracker. Place several raisins on top.

by Teresa E. Culpeper

Pumpkin Parfait

Ingredients:

orange sherbet

chocolate wafer fingers

Smarties™ or Reese's Pieces™
 (broken into little bits)

chocolate/butterscotch chips

bowls (dessert size)

whipping cream

ice cream scoop

Have each student spoon a large, rounded scoop of orange sherbet into a dessert dish. Gently push the end of a chocolate wafer cookie into the top of the ice cream, far enough to secure it from falling over; this is the pumpkin's stem. Push chocolate or butterscotch chips into the front of the ice cream for the pumpkin's eyes. (If you put the pointed end into the ice cream, they stick easily.) Add more chips for the mouth. Spoon some whipping cream all around the pumpkin. Sprinkle crushed bits of Smarties™ or Reese's Pieces™ on top of the cream. Smile and enjoy!

Spiders

Ingredients:

chocolate chips

chow mein noodles

miniature marshmallows

butterscotch chips

peanuts (optional)

cookie sheet/waxed paper

Melt chocolate and butterscotch chips in a double boiler on top of the stove. Add chow mein noodles (you may want to break them if they're too long). Add marshmallows and peanuts; stir until well covered. Drop on cookie sheet covered with waxed paper. Refrigerate until cool. Scrumpdelicious! Hint: Add ingredients slowly to melted chips making sure there is enough chocolate to cover.

Ants on a Log

Ingredients:

celery sticks

raisins

cheese spread/peanut butter/cream cheese

Wash celery; cut into 4" to 5" sticks. Spread cheese, peanut butter or cream cheese over celery stick. Place several raisins on top.

Marshmallow Sandwich

Ingredients:
round crackers
cream cheese
food coloring (red, green, yellow, orange)
miniature marshmallows

Add a couple of drops of food coloring to cream cheese; mix with a spoon until blended. Spread the cheese over a round cracker. Put several mini marshmallows on top. Spread some cheese on a second cracker. Place on top of marshmallows, cheese side down, to complete your sandwich. Bite down and enjoy!

Chocolate Leaves

Ingredients:
semisweet chocolate baking squares
waxed paper
fresh leaves (assorted)
double boiler

Put a leaf between two sheets of waxed paper and place on a cookie sheet. In a double boiler, melt the chocolate. Pour over leaf. Refrigerate for several hours. Peel off waxed paper from cooled chocolate. You should have a fine imprint of your leaf. Have your leaf and eat it, too.

Fall Fantasy

Ingredients:
gelatin powder (orange, green, red, yellow)
Styrofoam™ cups or clear plastic cups
spearmint leaf-shaped jelly candies (optional)
extra large bowl
mint leaves (fresh)
mixing spoon

Have the children make the gelatin, one flavor at a time, using an extra large bowl. Mix each new flavor into the previous one and stir. Once all four colors are mixed, pour into individual clear, plastic glasses or Styrofoam™ cups. Refrigerate until set. Just before serving, add a fresh mint leaf or spearmint leaf jelly candy to each cup.

I like to use the clear plastic cups so the children can see their mixed fall colors. They love the different tastes.

A variation is to make a Rainbow Fantasy. Make one color each day, pouring it into the clear glasses, then refrigerating. The next day add a second color, and so on, until you have a rainbow. The reactions are worth the time.

Weather WISE

Weather is a constant source of intelligent questions from curious kids. This ever-changing weather provides kids with a hands-on science lab—right on the school doorstep! Weather WISE activities are designed to help kids learn about weather through active investigation, using the natural environment and kids' natural curiosity. Simple procedures and the use of everyday materials make the projects simple for children and educators. Children are encouraged to formulate questions, investigate, make discoveries and become weather wise!

Weather themes can be incorporated into all areas of the curriculum.

Fall Fascination

What better time to watch the weather than fall? Fall begins on the autumn equinox (September 22 or 23), a special day when there are 12 equal hours of daylight and darkness. The power of the sun weakens as we approach the autumn equinox, and there are many changes in the temperature, precipitation and hours of daylight to be observed. The decrease in hours of daylight triggers many changes in plant and animal life, particularly in the temperate regions with four definite seasons.

Name That Season

In North America, the word *fall* is thought to have come from Native people who called this time of year "the fall of the leaf." Talk about other changes in the environment brought on by the weather at this time of year. Can you think of a better name for *fall*?

by Robynne Eagan

Weather Center

You Need:
- window
- table and chairs
- paper or notebook for weather diary
- weather symbols sheet (page 32)
- cloud charts
- weather books
- barometer
- thermometer
- binoculars, sunglasses, camera (optional)
- glue, markers, scissors, pencil, paper

What to Do:

1. Set up a table and chairs by a window.

2. Provide various materials listed above to assist children in directing their own investigations of the weather beyond the window.

3. Encourage "weather watchers" to record their observations and weather reports in a Weather Watch Diary.

4. At the close of the school day, review today's weather reports and summarize on a Weather Watch Calendar.

Try This:

- Decorate the surrounding area with magazine pictures, photographs or drawings of various kinds of weather to stimulate weather observation.

- Provide weather words and symbols to assist children in recording their observations.

- Encourage observations with questions such as "How does the sky look today?" "Which way are the clouds moving?" "Can you see across the school yard today?"

- Add and rotate materials at the center on a regular basis. Add a real barometer, a "tornado maker" (available at hobby and science shops) and newspaper weather reports.

- Invite a local weather observer as a guest to get children excited about the weather as you launch your Weather Reporting Center and Weather Center.

Report Fall's Changing Weather

Is it rainy or cold? Are you having an Indian summer? Is it good kite flying weather? Do you need your warm fall sweater?

A weather report is a statement of the weather conditions at a particular place and time. These reports are prepared by weather observers and collected at forecast offices, where they form the basis of forecasts made by meteorologists. These reports are printed in newspapers, reported on radio and television, cited on computer networks and recorded on telephone call-in lines.

Almost everyone needs to know the weather because it affects each one of us. For various reasons, we might need to know what weather to expect today, tomorrow or at the end of the week. Industries such as agriculture, aviation, building, fishing and tourism depend greatly upon weather reports to help with their success. These industries can benefit economically from accurate weather reports.

Warnings of adverse weather conditions or calls for good weather can be of great importance to many people. From farmers planning the planting or harvesting of crops to children planning sports events or the day's activities, weather reports are most helpful.

- As part of a language arts program, ask students to research and give the weather reports. Add humor, technical information or weather maps.
- Choose a Weather Forecaster to report on the immediate and long-range forecast.
- Take some video footage of your weather forecasters to enrich communication skills.
- Listen to the weather casts and check newspapers for up-to-the-hour weather information.

Weather Walk

From the windy, cool days of autumn to the wildest, harsh storms of winter, weather is a fascinating, ever-changing part of our world. We see and feel the weather as wind that blows our hair, as heat that warms our bodies, as cold that nips our nose and toes and as rain that soaks our skin. We see the weather in billowy clouds, blue skies and sunshine, frost on the ground, swirling snow and foggy days.

Experience the autumn weather using all of your senses in nature's classroom! Take a pad outside or follow up with an indoor activity. Ask children to think about how the weather feels, sounds and looks. List children's responses on large pages shaped to represent the main feature of the day's weather: a sun, a cloud, a snowflake, a raindrop or a gust of wind.

You Need:

- outdoors
- cassette recorder (optional)
- weather-appropriate attire
- blindfolds (optional)

Process:

1. Take students into an outdoor location in various kinds of weather.

2. Encourage children to observe the weather by looking at it up close and from a distance. Discuss what they see. Did they observe anything they had not seen before? Explain that we often miss important details. Explain that careful observation is the most important part of any scientific study.

3. Encourage children to listen to the weather by closing their eyes or wearing blindfolds. Have they taken the time to listen to the weather before?

4. Encourage children to feel the weather by lying on the ground, or touching with their hands. How does the pavement or grass feel? How does their skin feel?

5. Ask children to smell the weather. Do they notice any smells? What are they? From which direction is the wind blowing?

Try This:

- Assign different groups to feel, see or hear the weather and report back to the class.

- Use a cassette, camera or video camera to record the weather for later use. Compile a "Weather Wise" recording including weather reports, facts, songs and sounds.

- Collect leaves, nuts, seeds or other signs of fall.

Weather Watch Symbols

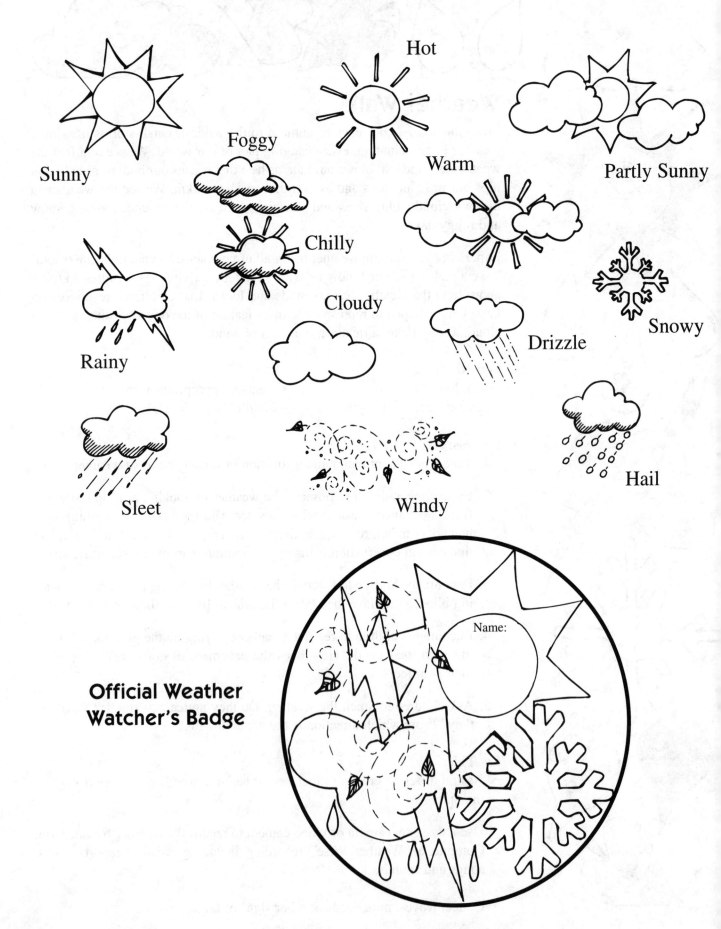

Sunny

Hot

Warm

Partly Sunny

Foggy

Chilly

Cloudy

Drizzle

Snowy

Rainy

Sleet

Windy

Hail

Official Weather Watcher's Badge

Name:

You Are the Weather Reporter!

Dear Parent(s):

_____ has been selected to be the Weather

Reporter for our class on _____. Please help your child

find out the expected weather by observing the sky, listening to the radio, reading the

newspaper or watching the news.

Please take this opportunity to discover what your child has learned about weather. You

can assist your child in completing the attached "Junior Weather Report" and in lending

an ear as your child prepares to predict the weather. Creative reporting and weather

props are welcome!

Thank you for assisting with this project.

The Junior Weather Report by _____

Today, _____, we can expect no precipitation/

precipitation in the form of _____.

The expected high temperature will reach _____, and the

expected low temperature will be _____.

There will be _____ skies and no winds/ _____ winds.

The sun rose at _____ and will set at _____. Enjoy the day!

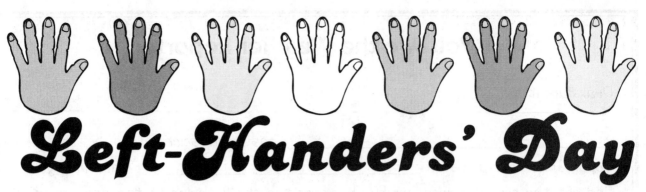

International Left-Handers' Day

"Pooh looked at his two paws. He knew that one of them was the right, and he knew that when you had decided which one of them was right, then the other was the left, but he never could remember how to begin."

A.A. Milne, *The House at Pooh Corner*

August 13

International Left-Handers' Day was created in 1976 to develop an awareness of left-handedness. During periods of human history, being left-handed was considered strange. In Ireland some believed that left-handed people were friends of the leprechauns and fairies of the Irish legends. Some people believed that left-handers brought bad luck or that it was wrong to write with the left hand. Lefties make up about 15 percent of the population and are thought by some scientists to be more creative than right-handers.

Are You Right-Handed or Left?

Young children often have difficulty differentiating between their own hands. Ask parents and children who do know the difference to share their tips and secrets. Ask children to hold their hands out in front of them, fingers together and thumbs facing one another. The left hand will form a capital *L*—which is a nice clue for young students who can remember exactly what this letter looks like!

The Right and Left Board

This is a nice device for teaching right and left. Hot-glue or nail two mittens to a board. Print *right* under the right mitten and *left* under the left. Young children will enjoy slipping their hands into the mittens and reading *right* and *left*.

by Robynne Eagan

Tips for Teachers of Left-Handers

Place your students so that left-handers' hands won't nudge right-handers when students are writing or eating.

Be aware that some ink smears as lefties write and drag their hand across their work.

Allow lefties to make their letters and figures in a left-handed fashion, let the children find their own ways to approach tasks that will afford the best results for them.

Provide left-handed scissors, art tools and sports equipment when possible.

Encourage children to talk about problems a particular task might give them and work together to find a left-handed solution.

Keep in mind that it is believed that some children take a while to establish handedness and should be provided with opportunities to do so.

Be aware that handedness can vary from task to task.

Incidents of mirror writing may be more common in lefties.

Instructions in reading and writing, tying shoes, doing arts and crafts and learning sports skills can be difficult when taught by "someone of the opposite hand." Request the assistance of a left-hander or educational resource if needed.

Celebrate Left-Handed Day

Our Right-Handed World

Have students look around their classroom and their homes for signs of a right-handed world. Did they consider scissors, knives, pencil sharpeners, can openers, the location of doorknobs and watch stems?

Simple Tasks?

Have students try the following "simple tasks" using their left hand:

- Draw a straight line that is 4" (10 cm) long using a rule and a pencil.

- Try sharpening your pencil with your left hand.

- Try opening the classroom door with your left hand.

- Write your name with a smudgy-ink pen.

- Cut with a pair of left-handed scissors.

Discuss the difficulties that students may have encountered. Consider that many objects are carefully designed to be most convenient for the majority of the population.

Switch Hands for a Day

Have all children go through the day trying to do everything with their opposite hand. Some people think that this will stimulate the other side of your brain. If you are ambidextrous, this day will cause you no difficulty at all!

Hand Craft

Have children trace or make a print of their hand and then cut it out. On one side of the hand have the children print their name and information about their handedness. On the other side of the hand have children make up a nickname or a slogan for those who share their handedness.

Lefties are the only people in their right mind.

Charlie

Hand Graph

Make a giant bar graph, large enough for hand-prints to be traced onto. Have children trace their hand and write their name in either the right-handed, left-handed or ambidextrous bar. Invite parents and people within the school community to contribute to your graph.

Designing for Lefties

A wonderful project for your design and technology program! Designing for lefties isn't a new idea. The lefty scissors have been around for quite some time and as early as the fifteenth century, the Scots-Irish Kerr family designed for their predominantly left-handed family. (Kerr comes from the Gaelic word for *left*!) In 1470 the Kerrs built a special spiral staircase in their castle that ran contrary to the right-handed model. The Kerr staircase let you walk up clockwise on the way and counterclockwise on the way down so the left-handed swordsman could best defend the upper floors as they had ample room to swing their swords.

Talk about some left-handed articles already in use. The lefty iron, lefty scissors, lefty opening refrigerators.

Design your own original articles for lefties. How are cars specifically designed for right-handers? What about appliances?

Trivia Collection

Have one chalkboard or bulletin board for students to collect information about famous lefties, lefty facts and fiction and magazine articles, books and items designed especially for lefties. Decorate it with left-handed gloves. *(In early drafts of the Mona Lisa painting, her left hand rests over her right hand, but this was changed for the final painting!)*

How Right or Left-Handed Are You?

Ask students to record their handedness on various activities: handwriting, ball throwing and catching, playing hockey, basketball and other sports, holding the telephone, carrying a school bag and so on. There are various degrees of left and right-handedness.

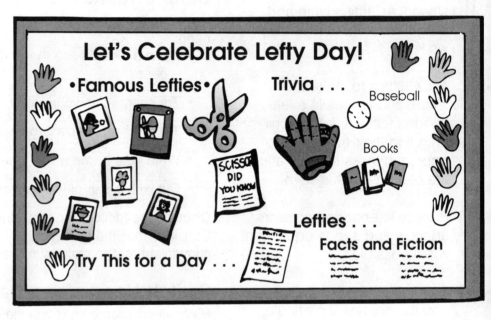

Host a Lefties Baseball Game

Host a baseball game where all players bat like a lefty. If you can round up enough gloves, catch like lefties, too!

Baseball really is a lefty's sport, in fact, the term *southpaw*, originated on the baseball field. Early diamonds situated home plate in the west corner which meant the pitcher's left arm faced the south. A pitcher who used this arm to pitch came to be known as a *southpaw*—a term which is now used to refer to all left-handers. Almost half the batters in the baseball Hall of Fame are lefties or switch hitters. Any ideas why this might be? Lefty batters stand to the right of home plate and have a shorter distance to run to first base when they hit the ball! Southpaw pitchers are very common on the field as well, maybe because they don't have to turn their backs to the first base when they windup for a pitch, making it easier for them to keep a runner on first from stealing second.

Transitions for the
Beginning of School

When you begin the year with children, it is important to get them off to a good start. The interest inventory on pages 38 and 39 can provide you with important information to help you in planning for the year's class. Choose from any of the ideas below.

_____ Send the Interest Inventory home to students in August.

_____ Send the Interest Inventory home with students as homework for the first week.

_____ Have children complete the inventory in class as part of the first day's experiences.

_____ Use the topics for journal writing and picture drawing the first weeks to get to know your students better.

_____ Graph the results to each question for your own information.

_____ Graph the results of each question as part of spare time activities that first week.

_____ Let children graph their own responses on class graphs using name cards.

_____ Have children illustrate responses. Compile into a class book, one for each topic. Write simple sentences at the bottom such as "Chien likes red balloons."

_____ Have children find classmates with three like answers and see how many match.

_____ Have a child sit next to a student who has one answer on the front that matches his.

_____ Have children pair up to get in line by matching one answer on the back with another student.

_____ Read information from the sheet to identify a mystery person as a wait-time activity. "This person likes orange. A favorite story is *Pocahontas*." Keep going until the identity of the child is guessed.

_____ Fill out the Interest Inventory in September, January and June. See what items have changed and what items have remained the same.

_____ Use the songs children know as fillers throughout the day as you move from one time or place to another. Post the titles of the songs on a song chart.

_____ Read stories that are familiar to the children the first week. They will enjoy knowing that you like the stories, too.

by Dr. Jeri Carroll

Interest Inventory

Welcome to our school. I hope you and your child are as excited as I am about beginning a new school year. To make school an even more exciting place to be, we would like some information from your child. Please help him/her fill out this survey as completely as possible. This is designed to help me get to know your child and his/her family better in order to develop a curriculum to meet your child's abilities, needs and interests. We can plan fun and exciting centers which will be sure to interest your child. Thank you.

Child's Name: _____

Nickname: _____

1. What is your favorite thing to do at home when you are inside?

2. What is your favorite thing to do at home when you are outside?

3. What toy is the most fun to play with?

4. Tell me about your friends.

5. If you could choose a balloon, what color would it be? Draw it here.

6. What is your favorite TV show?

7. What book(s) do you like to read again and again?

8. Where do you like to go in the car?

9. What songs do you know?

10. What do you do to help at home?

11. If you could choose a pet, what would you choose?

12. What things do you (would you) like to learn about or read about?

13. What would you like to tell me about yourself?

14. What is your favorite meal?

for

Home & School

Back-to-School
Hands Around the Classroom

In the center of white construction paper, trace or use paint to create a handprint for students. Students may also put their fingerprints at the tip of each finger.

On each finger, students will write an important thing aboutthemselves. The teacher can help students who cannot write yet.

Students can color, paint or use glitter to decorate their handprints.

Discuss the pictures and hang them around the classroom.

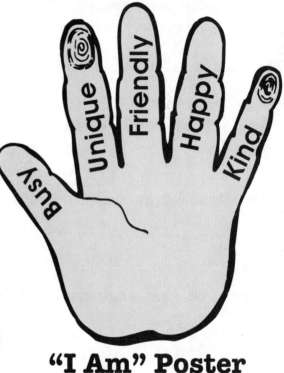

"I Am" Poster

Use this "getting to know you" activity at the beginning of the school year. Have students bring in a picture of themselves from home. Using poster board, have them place the picture in the center.

Using crayons or colored pencils, students will draw six special things about themselves surrounding their photo. For instance, they may draw a person playing a piano if they take piano lessons.

Students can label each picture with a sentence and decorate it.

by Donna L. Clovis

Back-to-School
Room
Decorations

First-Day Photo

Cut a large apple shape out of red poster board and print your class name at the top. On the first day of school, take a group photo of your class. If possible, enlarge it to 8" x 10" Center the photo on the apple and have students sign their names around the border. Hang the class portrait on your "welcome back" bulletin board or on the classroom door.

Class Collage

A class collage makes a great year-long wall display for your classroom. On the first day of school, give each student an 8$\frac{1}{2}$" x 11" sheet of white paper and ask him or her to draw and color a self-portrait (head only).

Encourage even the youngest students to make the portrait as life-like as possible by depicting personal characteristics such as hair color and style, freckles, glasses, braces, etc., as realistically as possible.

Cut around the outline of each completed face and glue collage-style on a large piece of poster board that has your class name printed at the top. Have every student sign his or her name somewhere on the poster.

You might repeat the activity during the last month of school and make a second collage. Hang the two self-portrait collages together in your classroom to show how students have changed during the year.

by Pamela Amick Klawitter, Ed. D.

Grandparents' Day

Grandparents' Day is celebrated the second Sunday in September and is considered a fairly new holiday in the United States. Honoring older members of the family is customary in countries such as Korea, Japan and Asian nations. In most of the western world, families live a distance from each other and sometimes grandparents do not have the opportunity to be closely knit into the family unit. Therefore, it is important to have a day to honor our loved ones and celebrate with small gifts of gratitude to such a loving extended family.

Here is a collection of activities to make and do, celebrating grandparents near and far.

by Tania Kourempis-Cowling

Family Quilt Board

Cover a bulletin board with different-colored squares of construction paper. Ask the children to bring in pictures of themselves with their grandparents. Invite the students to talk about their photos and mount them on the board. Add the children's dictated comments to each square.

Invite a Visitor

Invite the children's grandparents to class. They can read stories, share songs and traditions, and even show a cherished family heirloom. This is a good time to talk about what grandparents are—they are actually the child's parents' parents. Ask the question, "What do you do with your grandparents?" Create an experience chart of the children's responses.

Making a Map

Draw a map showing how to get from your house to your grandparents' house. If you're lucky to have grandparents that live close by, you can draw an easy map on a sheet of construction paper. Include landmarks between the two houses. If grandparents live far away, change your style of drawing to a map of the states. Color the city with crayons and markers. Matchbox™ cars can be used to drive along the roads on your map.

My Grandmother's Trunk

This is a traditional and fun game to play in the classroom, possibly during circle time. Have the children sit in a circle on the floor. Start by stating this phrase, "My grandmother went on a trip, and in her trunk she packed a green apple." Have the child on the right repeat to the next child, "My grandmother went on a trip, and in her trunk she packed a green apple and a _____." Use a color and an item. See how long the chain of items can be remembered and repeated.

Favorite Games

Have children's grandmas or grandpas tell of their favorite childhood games and play some of these in the classroom. Encourage grandparents or parents to write the instructions for the games and send to class.

Picture Frame

Here is a gift idea for your grandparents. Glue four wooden craft sticks together to form a square frame. Attach a picture or photo with glue to the back and let it dry thoroughly. Tie a piece of yarn to the top and use this as a hanger.

Cards

It is customary to send greeting cards to relatives to celebrate holidays. Making such cards offers the children an opportunity to do something thoughtful for others, plan, organize, complete a piece of work and exercise creative self-expression.

Use some of these techniques for making cards:
- finger painting
- splatter painting
- collage
- string painting
- block printing
- crayon resist
- rubs
- chalk on wet paper

For the greeting or message inside, children might dictate their thoughts to the teacher if they cannot print themselves.

Hand Bookmarks

Grandparents like to see how much their grandchildren have grown. This bookmark can be used and treasured throughout the years. Trace around each child's hand and forearm on a piece of construction paper. Cut these shapes out and decorate as desired. Write the child's name and date on the shape. Cover the bookmark with clear self-adhesive paper.

Fingerplay (traditional)

Here are Grandma's glasses,
(Circle fingers around eyes to make glasses.)
Here is Grandma's cap.
(Make big circle with fingers and thumbs and hold on head for cap.)
This is the way she folds her hands
(Fold hands and put in lap.)
And lays them in her lap.
(Repeat this verse substituting Grandpa's glasses.)

Rice Cake Faces

Create faces and unique tastes using rice cakes and various kitchen ingredients. Give the child a choice of a spreadable topping—either peanut butter or cream cheese. Discuss the facial features needed to make Grandma's or Grandpa's face: eyes, nose, mouth, cheeks, ears, hair and even glasses. Think about using these ingredients: shredded coconut, bananas, shredded and rounds of carrots, raisins, sprouts, apples, cereals, etc. Have fun making these faces. Be creative, show creations, eat and enjoy!

Books to Read

Hoguet, Susan Ramsay. *I Unpacked My Grandmother's Trunk: A Picture Book Game.*
Stevenson, James. *"Could Be Worse!"*
Borack, Barbara. *Grandpa.*
Henkes, Kevin. *Grandpa and Bo.*
Raynor, Dora. *Grandparents Around the World.*

Get PUZZLED with
Hands-On Math!
Celebrate the jigsaw puzzle with exciting hands-on mathematics activities!

On September 23, 1985, the world's largest jigsaw puzzle was completed in Keene, New Hampshire, by the Monadnock United Way. Over a three-month period, dedicated volunteers joined together 15,520 puzzle pieces. Celebrate this prize-winning puzzle with these exciting mathematics activities using jigsaw puzzles and puzzle pieces.

Wait! Don't discard jigsaw puzzles simply because several pieces are missing. Save the puzzle pieces in a large plastic container. Purchase low-cost jigsaw puzzles at yard sales. Invite parents and colleagues to donate unwanted puzzles. Mix the puzzle pieces together in a container. Now, let the learning begin!

Sorting Puzzle Pieces

Provide each pair of children with a cup of 20 to 30 puzzle pieces. You may choose to increase or decrease the number of puzzle pieces depending on the age and ability of your students. Invite the children to spread the puzzle pieces on their desks, observing their size, shape and color. Challenge the children to sort their pieces into two or more different groups based on one of these characteristics. When the sorting is completed, ask each pair to share how they chose to sort their pieces. List the categories on the chalkboard. Invite the children to identify the number of pieces in their largest group. The children will be eager to sort their puzzle pieces again. After the pieces have been sorted another time, invite the children to circulate about the classroom, trying to identify the categories that their classmates have divided their pieces into.

Venn Diagrams with Puzzle Pieces

Create a two-circle Venn diagram on your classroom floor using colorful pieces of yarn. Label the first circle *Edge Pieces* and the second circle *Pieces That Contain the Color Blue*. Provide each child with one puzzle piece. Ask each child to step forward and place his/her puzzle piece in the correct circle. Puzzle pieces that do not belong in either category may be placed along the outer edge of the yarn circles. Later, ask the children to identify the number of puzzle pieces that are in each circle, as well in the overlapping section. Challenge the children to make observations about the puzzle pieces based on the number of pieces in each circle. Their observations may range from "Five of our puzzle pieces are edge pieces" to "More puzzle pieces contain the color blue than are edge pieces."

by Nancy Silva

Use the puzzle pieces to create additional Venn diagrams. Use these categories to label the circles. Be sure to select categories that complement each other so that it is possible for one or more puzzle pieces to share both characteristics.

Possible Venn Diagram Labels:
   Pieces Containing Words or Letters
   Pieces Containing All or Part of a Face
   Solid Color Puzzle Pieces
   Two-Color Puzzle Pieces
   Pieces That Contain the Color White
   Puzzle Pieces with More Than Three Colors
   Edge Pieces
   Pieces Containing Sky or Clouds
   Pieces with an Even/Odd Number of "Ins"
   Pieces with an Even/Odd Number of "Outs"
   Pieces with More "Ins" Than "Outs"
   Pieces with More "Outs" Than "Ins"
   Pieces with an Equal Number of "Ins" and "Outs"

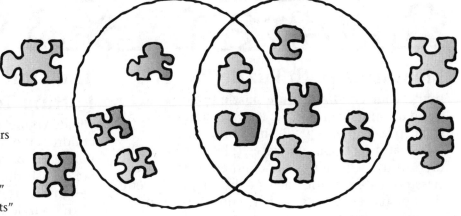

Graphing: The "Ins" and "Outs" of Puzzle Pieces

Create an exciting puzzle piece graph on your classroom floor! On a 4" x 18" strip of paper, write the title of the graph: *The "Ins" of Puzzle Pieces.* Place the strip on the floor. Below the title, arrange four paper strips labeled with the following categories: *One "In," Two "Ins," Three "Ins," Four or More "Ins."* Display examples of each type of puzzle piece for the children to examine. Next, distribute three puzzle pieces to each child. After they have had an opportunity to study their puzzle pieces and count the number of "Ins," invite the children to step forward and place each piece beside the correct paper strip. When the graph is completed, invite the children to count the number of puzzle pieces in each category. Discuss: Which category has the most puzzle pieces? Which category has the fewest puzzle pieces?, etc. Challenge the children to make true statements about the graph, such as "Five of the puzzle pieces with one "In" are edge pieces."

Your class will be anxious to create a floor graph called *The "Outs" of Puzzle Pieces.* You may choose to use the same puzzle pieces with which the children created the original graph, or randomly select an equal number of new pieces. When the "Out" graph has been completed, discuss the results.

The Great Puzzle Piece Grab

Fill a bowl with large puzzle pieces. Invite your class to estimate the number of puzzle pieces that they will be able to grab with their right hand. Record their estimates on a chart. Together, discuss their estimates. Identify: the five greatest estimates, the five smallest estimates, three odd estimates, three even estimates, the number of estimates less than 8, the number of estimates greater than 12, any estimates that are the same.

Now, it's time to put their estimates to the test! Invite each child to take a turn reaching into the bowl and grabbing as many puzzle pieces as possible. Ask the children to count their pieces. List the number of pieces grabbed on the chart, beside each child's estimate. Compare the estimates with the actual number of pieces grabbed.

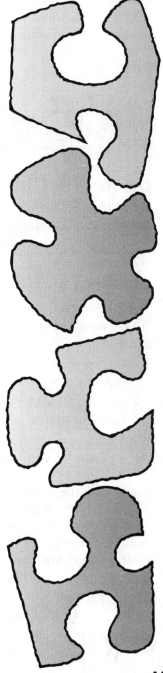

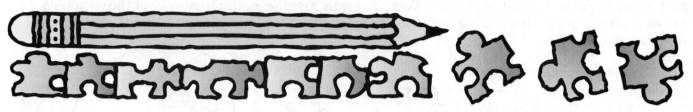

Measuring with Puzzle Pieces

Invite your children to use puzzle pieces as non-standard units of measure. Provide large bowls of small puzzle pieces (SPP), medium puzzle pieces (MPP) and large puzzle pieces (LPP) for the children to use. Challenge the children to measure a classroom item using each of the three different sizes of pieces. Create a chart showing the measurements. Invite the children to read the chart and make statements to describe their observations. Their statements may range from: "Both scissors and a black magic marker were 4 MPP long" to "The ruler was 8 SPP longer than the paintbrush."

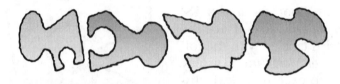

Invite the Children to . . .

Stand if your estimate was greater than the number of pieces grabbed.

Clap your hands if your estimate was less than your grab.

Kneel if your grab was greater than 14.

Jump if an even number of pieces were grabbed.

Touch your knees if an odd number of pieces were grabbed.

Turn around if your grab was one of the three greatest grabs.

Touch your shoulders if your grab was one of the five smallest grabs.

Whistle if your grab was the same as the grab of one or more of your classmates.

Challenge the children to come up with some commands of their own. Together, compare the number of children responding positively to each. Which command, or commands, received the greatest response?

The Time Challenge— Putting Together a Puzzle

Divide your class into small groups of three to five children. Provide each small group with a different puzzle of 25 pieces. Before opening the puzzle boxes, ask the children to look at the picture or design that they will be creating. Discuss the areas of the puzzle that may be challenging and which sections appear to be less complicated. Identify problem-solving strategies that may be applied to puzzle-making.

Ask your class to silently watch the clock as you show the measurement of one minute. Then invite each group to estimate the number of minutes that it will take them to create the puzzle. Record their estimates on a piece of chart paper. Now, it's time for the puzzle-making to begin. Ready! Set! Go!

Circulate around the classroom, keeping your eye on your watch or the clock. You may wish to let the children know each time a minute has passed. As each group finishes its puzzle, record the time on the chart beside their estimate. When all of the puzzles have been completed and admired, focus the children's attention on the chart. Discuss: Which puzzle took the longest to complete? Which puzzle was completed in the least amount of time? How many estimates were too short? Too long? Very close? Challenge the children to identify why some puzzles take longer than others to create.

You may wish to invite the groups to trade puzzles and complete the above activity, or allow each group to improve their time as they make the same puzzle again. As your class repeats this puzzle-making activity, you'll see cooperation increase, estimating skills strengthened and problem-solving strategies put into practice.

Learning About
Citizenship

September 17

traveling in an automobile

in sports

in school

on the playground

at home

at a friend's house

Citizenship—what does it mean? If you can define the term, how can you teach it in a way so that students may learn? Reading books about important citizens, comparing positive and negative aspects and discussing how boys and girls may contribute to their community are only a few ideas. However, teaching students to be good citizens is best taught by role modeling.

The definition of *citizen* is someone who is an inhabitant of a city or town, or a person who owes allegiance to a government and is entitled to protection by it.

Use these ideas to show ways in which students can be good citizens and to learn the importance of taking citizenship seriously.

Recognize others for achievement.

Giving recognition to others is an important aspect of being a good citizen. Design a bulletin board honoring those who work in your school. Use the caption "Good Citizens of (school)." Make individual or group pictures of staff members such as the principal, teachers, custodians, cafeteria workers and secretaries. Mat on bright colored construction paper.

Good citizens dispose of litter properly.

Stress the importance of each person doing their share to keep our world free of litter.

- Litter, litter everywhere! Ask your principal to schedule one day when your students can throw all paper on the floor instead of the trash can. Pick it all up before the final bell. Ask students: Would you like to work in a room filled with litter all day? How would you feel if visitors had come to our room today and were not aware of our plan?

- Personal litter bags. Purchase heavy-duty gallon-size plastic bags with zipper closings. Give two bags to each student. Have students use permanent markers to design a logo that encourages others to keep litter in its place. Place one bag in the family car, the other in or near their desk.

Encourage each other.

Students should encourage others to be serious about being a good citizen. Design a door banner that reads "Our Room Promotes Citizenship."

Identify characteristics of a good citizen.

Get students involved through a brainstorming session. Quickly list the characteristics on a chart or chalkboard as boys and girls call them out. Begin by saying, "A good citizen is someone who is . . . ."

- respectful of others
- honest
- dependable
- responsible
- trustworthy

How do you become a citizen?

Invite a person in your area who has applied for or been granted Untied States citizenship. What was the procedure? How long did it take to become a citizen of the U.S.? From what country did they formerly hold citizenship? Were they born in that country or had they applied for citizenship there? Encourage students to make a list of questions for your visitor.

Make a red, white and blue dessert.

Prepare a 9" x 13" cake and allow students to decorate it like an American flag. Frost with white icing, place strawberries across for stripes and use blueberries for the stars. Cut into serving pieces to celebrate citizenship in the U.S. and your classroom. If your classroom is in a different country, decorate a cake portraying your own symbol of citizenship.

Play a citizenship game.

After your study of citizenship, help students review by playing the game on the following page. Use in a center with two or three students. Make a gameboard from the pattern on page 48 and laminate it. Attach the pointer with a brad. Spin and take turns telling how boys and girls can show good citizenship.

by Carolyn Tomlin

How can we show
good citizenship . . .

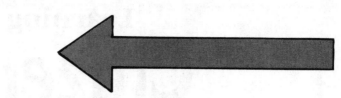

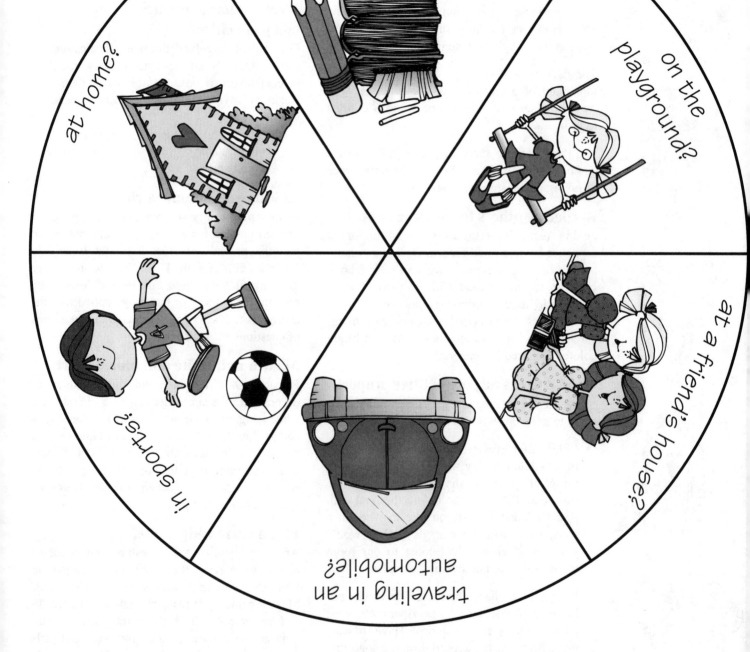

in school?

on the
playground?

at home?

at a friend's house?

in sports?

traveling in an
automobile?

Election Day

A good citizen feels a responsibility to vote in local, state and national elections. A vote carries a message. Teach your students about this important freedom in the United States.

The first Tuesday in November has been traditionally set aside as Election Day. Decorate your classroom using red, white and blue balloons. Hang the balloons from the ceiling or group them in a display. Display the American flag. Discuss the candidates and the major issues. Make a bulletin board displaying magazine and newspaper clippings relating to the election. Mat each clipping on red, white and blue construction paper.

Check with a craft supply house for inexpensive white straw hats for the students to wear as election hats. Use ribbon, markers, etc., to decorate the hats. Ask each student to bring a white T-shirt that can be decorated several days before and worn on Election Day.

Ask students to bring newspaper clippings and magazine articles about a past election. Discuss the candidates and the major issues. Display material on the bulletin board until election day. Ask students to encourage parents and family to save recent magazine and newspaper clippings supporting each candidate. Mat each clipping on red, white or blue construction paper.

Make a list of local elections in which citizens can voice their opinion through voting. Invite a candidate to visit your class. Have students participate in a question and answer period concerning the issues.

Plan an election in your class to elect a teacher or staff member who displays good citizenship. Use a sheet to partition off a voting booth. Insert ballots in a box and tally the results. Invite the winner to your class for a celebration party.

Plan a mock election with the candidates for president and vice president. Set up an election booth and ballot box in the room. Help students realize the importance of voting. Encourage students to ask their parents to vote.

Sponsor an essay contest about why the candidate of their choice will be the best president. Limit the essays to 200 words. The winning essay can be read over the intercom system and published in the school newspaper.

Invite local media to visit your school. Promote student involvement for Election Day.

Work with your cafeteria to provide a red, white and blue lunch on Election Day.
- Election Day hamburgers (top with small paper American flags)
- crisp lettuce and tomato cups
- oven-baked potatoes
- blue grapes
- red cherry cobbler
- white milk

by Carolyn Tomlin

A Cultural Calendar Collection

for the

Classroom

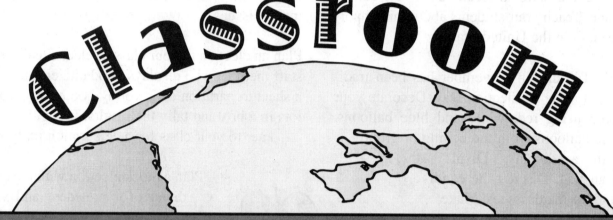

Notable fall dates that are often overlooked can introduce and launch multicultural studies for the year. Juan Rodriguez Cabrillo, Leif Ericson and Casimir Pulaski are as diverse as their achievements. Students can discover this diversity while learning to appreciate the uniqueness of individuals.

Cabrillo Day—September

Cabrillo Day is celebrated in September each year. It is a six-day festival observed in California honoring Juan Rodriguez Cabrillo, Portuguese navigator who discovered California in 1542.

Serving in the military in Spain as a young man, Cabrillo is best known for his extensive explorations of the west coast of the United States. He arrived in Mexico in 1520 and participated in many battles with Spanish forces to try to conquer the country.

Fighting bravely for his native Spain, he was also interested in exploring new lands. He explored the Pacific coast of lower California, continuing northward to what is now San Diego Bay, Santa Catalina Island, San Pedro and Santa Monica Bays. He was very excited by the new lands he had found and claimed it all for Spain.

Cabrillo died on January 3, 1543, near the Santa Barbara channel. He earned many honors for his accomplishments and opened the way for a host of other Spanish and Portuguese explorers. Because of his explorations, Cabrillo Day is almost a week-long celebration. There are fiestas (parties), singing and dancing, special foods are served native to Spain, and there are many retellings of the story of Cabrillo.

The rich heritage left to us by Juan Rodriguez Cabrillo and other Hispanic explorers has influenced many aspects of American life. We all enjoy their cultural influences even today as we see examples of architectural styles, special foods and customs. These have become an important part of our American culture.

Cabrillo Day—Student Activities

1. Explain to the children that before this country was known to the rest of the world, many people from different countries in Europe came here to discover new territories for their own monarchs. Our modern explorers today are venturing out into space. Ask students if they can think of some ways that our astronauts today and explorers long ago are alike. What traits do they have in common? What might astronauts of the future be like when we start to explore other planets? Will they need the same traits? Different ones?

2. Cabrillo Day is celebrated for six days. Ask students to plan a special activity for each day related to Cabrillo Day. They might eat corn chips one day, make shakers from milk cartons filled with dried beans, learn a song in Spanish, count to 10 in Spanish, invite someone of Hispanic origin to speak to the class, draw the flag of Spain, identify Hispanic countries on a map, etc.

Leif Ericson Day—October

Leif Ericson Day is a Norwegian and Icelandic holiday that commemorates the landing of Norsemen in Vinland, New England, about A.D. 1000.

Thousands of years ago, daring seamen known as Vikings lived in the most northern part of Europe that now includes Norway, Denmark and Sweden. They built long, narrow, wooden ships with high, carved prows decorated with colorful, striped sails.

Vikings were skilled sailors who explored places many ships of the time had never ventured. About the year 1000, the Vikings sailed westward across the great ocean called the Sea of Darkness, which today is called the Atlantic Ocean.

Eric the Red was a bold and powerful leader who sailed with his crew to Iceland and Greenland. Here Eric and many of his men built homes and settled the land. Eric's middle son Leif, pronounced Lâve, had sailed with his father many times. When he became a young man, he made several voyages on the Sea of Darkness and discovered a new land mass which he called Vinland, or "Wineland," because of the plentiful amount of grapes he found growing there. The land Leif discovered was part of the eastern coast of North America! When he returned home, he told many stories of his great adventures in the new land. This was over 600 years before Columbus or anyone else sailed to America!

Leif Ericson Day—Student Activities

1. Explain to students that the Sea of Darkness held many fears for the Vikings. Some believed dragons and huge sea serpents inhabited the waters. Others thought that once you sailed into the great sea you would never return home. Try to experience this great unknown. Have students put chairs under desks and pick up everything on the floor, making sure there are no obstacles in the way. Ask them to get into one group, cover their eyes and sit in the middle of the floor. Shut off all lights and cover any windows. Tell them to stand up, turn around two or three times, then stop. Keeping their eyes covered, ask if they can find their own seat. After five minutes, turn on the lights and have everyone "see" where they ended up. Did any find their own seats? How did they "navigate" to get there? Did they use anything special to guide them? How did it feel to be in the dark and not be sure of where they were going? Tell students that their feelings were a lot like those of the early Vikings. Can they relate to these feelings in other ways—doing something different for the first time; how other early explorers might have felt; how it might feel to come to this country for the first time when you don't know your way around, speak the language or know the customs. What children in class have had this happen to them or other family members? Allow time for students to share experiences.

2. Just as fishermen of today depend on the sea as a source of food or commerce, the Vikings had the same need. Set up a time to visit the library and have students find pictures showing Viking life and illustrations of their ships. Have them draw or make paper models of these sturdy ships.

3. The Norse people have many fables and myths that have become part of our cultural heritage. A favorite is "The Three Billy Goats Gruff" and their adventures with a mean old troll. The troll is a symbol of something fearful or something bringing good luck in Norse literature. A reading of this old favorite would be appropriate and children can dramatize the story afterwards.

by Teddy Meister

Pulaski Memorial Day—October

Pulaski Memorial Day commemorates the death of General Casimir Pulaski, a hero of the American Revolution.

Casimir Pulaski was born in Winiary, Mazovia, on March 4, 1747. He was one of the originators of the Confederation of Bar in Poland, a democratic type of constitution that was an attempt to unite all the areas of Poland into one country. Many were opposed to the idea. He fought for what he believed in and was involved in many battles when Poland was at war. Because of this, he became a widely known and famous Polish hero, recognized all over Europe.

In Paris, December 1776, Puaski was introduced to Benjamin Franklin, who was visiting and seeking supporters for the American Revolution and General George Washington. Franklin liked and admired this brave man and asked Pulaski if he would go to America and help with the war effort. Pulaski agreed, sailed to America and joined Washington at the battle of Brandywine. He was made general and chief of the cavalry by a special act of Congress. Pulaski later fought at Germantown and was involved in the terrible winter campaign of 1777-1778. In 1778, as a brigadier, he formed a corps known as the Pulaski Legion. As head of this group, he used his past experiences of guerrilla warfare. In May 1779, he was asked to head the battle of Charleston. He was mortally wounded during the fighting of Savannah and died several days later on October 11, 1779.

Pulaski Day—Student Activities

1. Explain to students that this Polish general was one of several military leaders from Europe that helped the United States win its independence. Pulaski was a brave leader and a great hero. What traits do students think people of this kind have in common? List these on the chalkboard. What people do they know today who might also have some of these traits? List the names beside the traits list. Ask if any students think they have some of these same traits. Does who you are or what you look like have any bearing on whether you have these traits? A culmination of this discussion might be a "Heroes" bulletin board. Students can draw and write about other heroes past and present from all ethnic groups. These can be displayed on the bulletin board.

2. A well-known bridge is named for General Pulaski— the Pulaski Skyway Bridge in New York. It is a reminder for all of us to remember his brave deeds. What other bridges are named for great people? Show pictures of different types of bridges. You might want to embark on a bridge building project. Divide the class into small groups. Give each group a box of wooden toothpicks and some glue. Ask them to construct a bridge that they can name after a hero of their choice.

3. "The Jolly Tailor Who Became King" is a delightful Polish folktale, lively and full of humor. It tells of impossible happenings that seem very logical and satisfactory. The story can be read to students over a period of two or three days, depending on the age and maturity of your students. Folktales provide an excellent vehicle for helping students understand and appreciate the race or nation depicted in the tale. It can open new doors of communication between ethnic groups in your classroom. Perhaps there are family members of your students who can share stories from their native countries. You might want to have an International Story Day and invite these people to school. If they have native costumes, they might be willing to wear them!

Mid-Autumn Festival

A Thanksgiving type of festival is held in China when the crops have been harvested and the farmers can rest from their labors. It is held at a time when the full moon is in its brightest stage sometime during September or October. On the night of the full moon the people gather in the country, in the mountains or by the seashore—anywhere they can get a clear view of the moon.

The Chinese Moon Festival, as it is also known, is a national holiday in China honoring the moon goddess or Moon Lady. There is much folklore about the origin of this celebration. One version says that it is the birthday of a magical rabbit that resides on the moon with the Moon Lady.

Another translation says this day marks the overthrow of the Mongol lords in ancient China. Whatever the origin, this Moon Festival is a time when families gather to feast together, have dances, have parades, sing and just have fun.

Tradition calls for the making of "moon cakes," a crusty cookie made with sweet fillings. There are parades with music, dragons, firecrackers and lanterns. This festival is also celebrated throughout the Far East and in Asian communities all around the world.

Below are a few activities to use in the classroom while discussing the fall holiday of the Chinese Mid-Autumn Festival.

MOON PRINT ART

Collect jar lids or any circular objects in different sizes. Prepare a container of yellow tempera paint. Dip the circular objects into the paint and print onto blue construction paper. This will create an abundant amount of full moon shapes. Children might add gold adhesive stars to the picture.

MOLDING MOON CAKES

Plan an activity where the children can make moon cakes from playdough. Use purchased playdough or make your own homemade variety. Use cookie cutters or jar lids for a round cutting utensil, or flatten out rolled balls of dough. For a permanent variation, prepare a homemade baker's clay, make the moon cakes, bake them, then paint and decorate them.

by Tania Kourempis-Cowling

DRAGON DISGUISE

In class, discuss that the dragon is a Chinese symbol of strength and goodness. Give each child a large grocery bag. Draw the face of the dragon on the sack and add color with crayons, markers or paint. Cut out holes for the eyes. Attach crepe paper streamers with glue or tape over the entire head. Decorate a piece of fabric or sheet to look like the dragon's body and drape it over the child's shoulders.

COOKIE CAKES

This is a cookie recipe that will resemble a moon cake when shaped and baked.

3½ cups flour	2 eggs
1 teaspoon salt	1 teaspoon vanilla
1 cup shortening	jam
²/₃ cup sugar	

Sift the flour and salt together in a bowl or onto waxed paper. In another bowl, cream shortening and sugar until light and fluffy. Add the eggs, beating well. Add the vanilla. Stir in the flour little by little. Roll the dough to a thickness of $1/8$" on a floured board. Cut into circles using a round cookie cutter or the open end of a glass. Lay some of the circles on ungreased cookie sheets. Top each with a teaspoon of your favorite jam. Lay the rest of the circles on top of the jam filling. Seal the edges with the tines of a fork and prick the top a few times. Bake the cookies for about 10 minutes in a 350⁰ oven. Cool and enjoy!

PAPER LANTERNS

Fold a piece of construction paper in half lengthwise. At inch intervals, cut into the fold to within 1" of the opposite side. Open the paper and tape the ends together. Attach a strip of paper as the handle at the top of the lantern.

MOON CAKE LUNCH

Cut round slices of white bread with a cookie cutter. Let the children spread one slice with peanut butter and the other with jelly. Put the moon cake together for a yummy peanut butter sandwich.

PARADE

Some of the students can wear their dragon masks while others carry paper lanterns and parade around the room. Beat homemade drums or play authentic Chinese music.

Fire Safety

During the month of October, set aside time to discuss the theme of FIRE SAFETY. It is educational and fun to focus on some very important community helpers—the firefighters. Theme goals would include learning about the firefighter's job, his protective clothing, the vehicles and equipment used and how to deal with an emergency.

You could use circle time each day to teach necessary concepts that deal with this theme. Start by discussing fire safety precautions such as the dangers of playing with matches, why children shouldn't play near stoves and ovens, and not being afraid of fire alarms and firefighters—they are our friends! Next, teach the children what to do if their clothes catch on fire. Have children practice STOP, DROP AND ROLL by stopping in their tracks, dropping to the ground and rolling over and over to put out the flames. Consider transforming an area in the classroom to make a fire station. Supply props such as plastic fire hats, a telephone, a bell, a hose, boots, a coat (like a yellow raincoat) and lots of picture books about firefighters. Another day, discuss the escape route for your classroom and practice a fire drill with the children.

A field trip to your local fire station would be the ultimate learning tool for this theme. Observe the clothing worn, the building, the tools and the vehicles. If this trip is not possible, contact your local station and ask if a firefighter could bring a fire truck and visit your class. He could point out all the special features such as the hoses, siren, ladders, lights and special clothing kept on the truck.

An important activity for children to practice in the classroom is learning to dial an emergency number on the phone and give their name and address. Practice on toy phones until all the children are familiar with this lifesaving procedure.

by Tania Kourempis-Cowling

Firefighter Mask

To make the basic mask, cut out the center circle from a large paper plate. Staple or glue a tongue depressor to the bottom. Use red construction paper to form the top portion of the firefighter's helmet. Glue this onto the top of the paper plate mask. Don't forget to make a yellow badge to attach in the center of the helmet's front. As the child looks through his mask, he is wearing a firefighter's helmet and can pretend he is playing that role.

Glue badge here.

CHIEF

Sing-Along Song

(To the tune of "I'm a Little Teapot")

I'm a firefighter in a big, red truck,
I bring out the hoses and put the ladders up.
I put out the fires and help keep people safe.
I am a firefighter—won't you be my friend!

Firefighters' Jackets

Construct firefighter jackets out of large paper bags. Begin by cutting a large hole in the bottom of the bag for the child's head. Next, cut armholes on each side and slit the front of the bag to make it like a vest. Paint the jackets red or yellow and draw badges and designs to incorporate your town's credentials.

Firefighter's Workout

The firefighter must stay in good physical shape to do his job efficiently. Lead the children in these exercises: jumping jacks, knee bends, leg lifts, arm rolls and running in place.

Fire Truck

Make a class fire truck for the children to climb into and enjoy. Use a cardboard refrigerator box painted red or yellow. Cut out the middle so the children can climb inside. Attach paper wheels, steering wheel, equipment, ladders, etc. Glue these details on.

Let's Read About Firefighters

Here is a list of fiction and nonfiction books about firefighters that can be shared with your students and enjoyed by young children. Read the stories and share the pictures. Leave the copies in your library corner for the children to review on their own.

I Can Be a Fire Fighter by Rebecca Hankin (Children's Press, 1985)
Both men and women are shown as community helpers. This book has colorful pictures and is a good career guide for the primary grades.

The Little Fireman by Margaret Wise Brown (HarperCollins, 1993)
This book was first published in 1938. It tells about a big firefighter who lives in a big firehouse and a little firefighter in a small firehouse; however, when the alarm bell rings, they both put out the fires, big and small.

Curious George at the Fire Station by Margaret and H.A. Rey (Houghton Mifflin, 1985)
Curious George visits a firehouse and creates all kinds of trouble.

Fire Fighters by Robert Maass (Scholastic, 1989)
Colorful photos show how firefighters are trained for their job, how they fight fires and the various duties they share at the fire station.

Fire Engines by Anne Rockwell (E.P. Dutton, 1986)
An illustrated book telling about the different fire trucks and vehicles—ladder trucks, pumper trucks, fire engine boats, fire chief's car and ambulances.

The Fire Station Book by Nancy Bundt
Great photographs and text explaining the fire station.

Oktoberfest

A famous autumn festival held in Munich, Germany, originated in 1810 and is still celebrated today. It occurs in October and lasts for 16 days. Tents are built in the middle of the city during this carnival celebration. The festivities include feasting, singing, dancing, shows and music played by Bavarian brass bands. People dress in colorful, historical German costumes and dance the *polka,* which is the traditional folk dance that the people enjoy both performing and watching. Oktoberfest is known for its foods such as sausage, sauerkraut and the drinking of beers made in Germany. Cultural dress is *dirndl* dresses for the women and *lederhosen* and *suspenders* for the men. Even outside of Germany, the people of German descent practice these rituals. Listed are a few ideas to bring the Oktoberfest to your classroom:

- Teach your students German phrases such as "hello" (guten tag), "good-bye" (aufwiedersehen) and "thank you" (danke).

- Teach your students a German folk dance such as the polka.

- In the 1800s, the Grimm brothers wrote a collection of fairy tales. Many of these are still very popular today. Read stories to your class such as "Hansel and Gretel," "Snow White" and "Sleeping Beauty." Have the children illustrate these stories. Act out the fairy tales.

- Serve an Oktoberfest feast in class. Serve frankfurters (or sausage links), sauerkraut, pretzels and root beer.

- Create pretzel sculptures using stick pretzels and a molding dough. To make the dough, mix together equal amounts of peanut butter and nonfat dry milk. Add a little honey to taste. Roll the dough into balls and stick the pretzels into the dough to create unique sculptures and designs.

- Make a pretzel wreath for a class decoration. Use eleven large, hard pretzels. On a table, place six pretzels in a circle. Lay five other pretzels on top and in between the first ones. Use glue and adhere all the pretzels together where they touch. After this has dried, weave ribbons through the holes and tie them into a bow. Add a ribbon or wire at the top to hang the wreath.

by Tania Kourempis-Cowling

58

Germany's Oktoberfest

German Travel Kit

Guten Tag! (This means "hello" in German.) Here is a special travel kit just for you! Use your pencils, colors and scissors and follow the directions.

Fantastic Flag

The German flag has three stripes: black, red and gold. Color and cut out the German flag (top stripe: black, middle stripe: red, bottom stripe: gold). Glue your flag to a craft stick.

My German Map

Color the map of Germany. Draw a star to locate Berlin, the capital city.

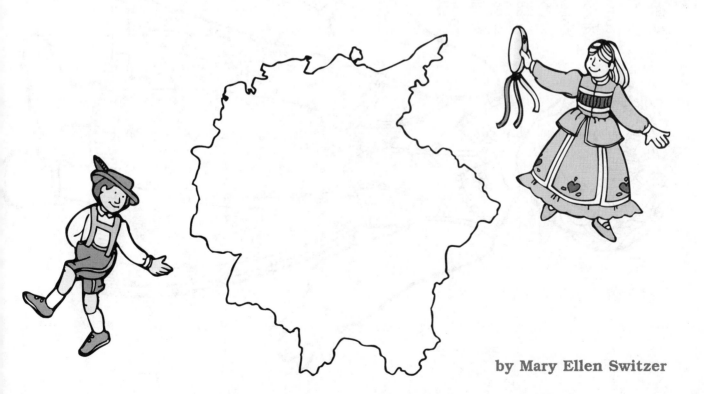

by Mary Ellen Switzer

My German Pals

These paper dolls are dressed in traditional German costumes. The girl is wearing a dress with a full gathered skirt called a dirndl. The boy is wearing leather shorts called lederhosen. Color and cut out these paper dolls. A craft stick could be glued to the bottom of each to create stick puppets.

Dot-to-Dot

Many tourists who travel to Germany visit beautiful castles there. Connect the dots to create your own castle and color the picture.   Bonus: Write a fairy tale about your castle.

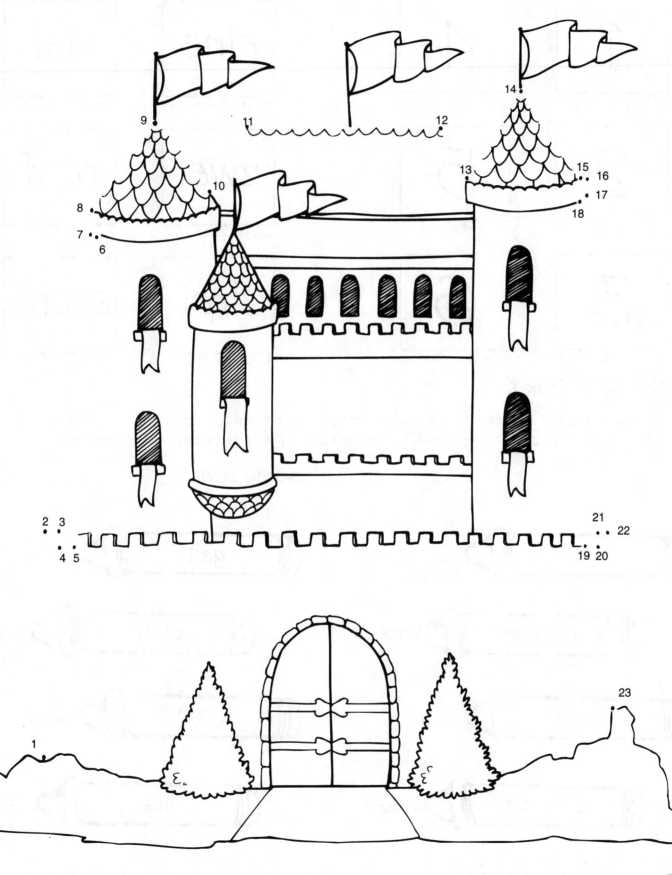

Ready, Set, Let's Count!

Can you count to six (sechs) in German? Cut out the number cards below. Use them for counting or matching.

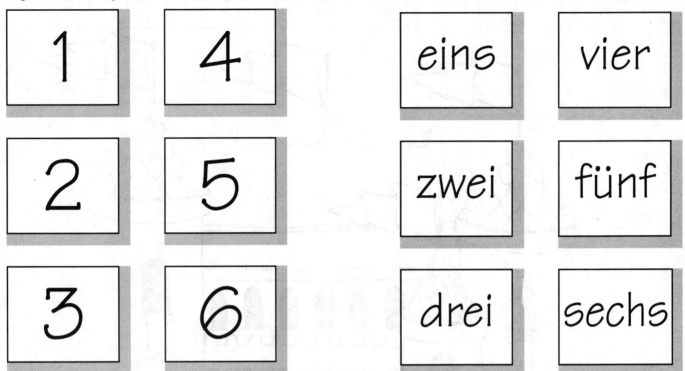

The Color Box

If you were a child in Germany, the crayons in your color box would be labeled with the names listed below. Color all of the crayons. Write the name of your favorite color in German.

My favorite color is _____

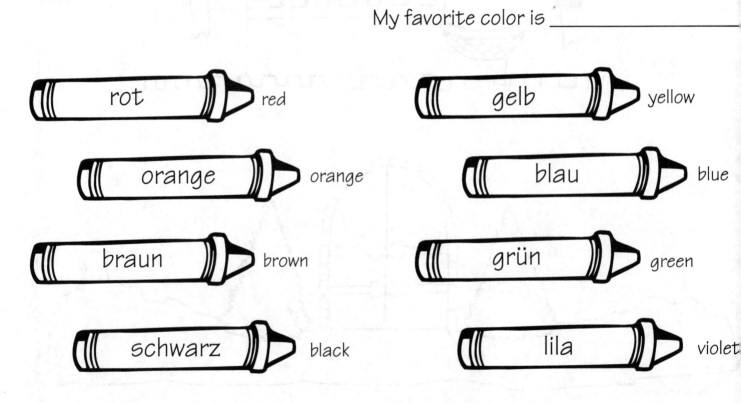

Columbus Day

Columbus Day, sometimes called Discovery Day, honors the discovery of America by Christopher Columbus in 1492. Columbus was an Italian explorer who left Spain on August 3, 1492, to reach India by sailing west. He sailed three ships given to him by the King and Queen of Spain: the *Nina,* the *Pinta* and the *Santa Maria.* He sailed for 72 days and touched land at San Salvador on October 12, 1492. Columbus thought he had reached the East Indies, but instead he had discovered two entirely new continents, North America and South America.

Throughout the years, people have remembered Christopher Columbus as a courageous explorer with vision, imagination and determination. Even though the traditional celebration is October 12, the federal legal holiday is held on the second Monday in October. In 1992, the 500th birthday of the discovery of the Americas by Christopher Columbus was celebrated. This is a great historic holiday to decorate the classroom and get involved in a few activities.

by Tania Kourempis-Cowling

The Ocean Blue

Have the children feel the rhythm of the ocean as they make a finger painting of the sea that Christopher Columbus sailed. Provide blue finger paint and paper; then encourage the kids to make lots of wavy lines.

Ship in a Bottle Art

Cut a sheet of white construction paper into a bottle shape. Have the children draw Columbus' ships sailing the ocean blue. Draw some sea life in the water and a view of land in the distance. Make the drawings colorful with bright crayons or markers. When finished, cover the entire drawing with clear cellophane wrap. Use tape to secure the plastic. This gives the illusion of the boats in a bottle.

Columbus Day Garland

Children can use construction paper to draw and cut out pictures of boats, flags, telescopes and maps. Attach these to crepe paper streamers and use as garlands to decorate doors, windows and to drape along the ceiling.

Walnut Ship

Use half of a walnut shell for the ship. Place playdough in the bottom of the ship. Glue a triangular-shaped sail made of construction paper or fabric to a toothpick. Stick the toothpick into the playdough. Sail the ship in a pan of water, navigating it by blowing on the sail. What happens if there is no wind? Too much wind?

I See Something New

Columbus and his sailors were on their ships for many days with nothing to see but open waters. They were constantly looking for something new, especially land. Have the children sit in a circle and take a few minutes to observe each other, what they are wearing, the order where they're sitting and how they're sitting. Now instruct the kids to hide their head in their laps and close their eyes. The teacher changes something in the circle. Have students open their eyes and try to determine what is different.

Three Ships Mural

Draw three large ships on a sheet of mural paper. Let the children cooperatively color the ships brown. Have each child draw their own mast on one of the ships—a unique drawing of their own. At circle time, have each student show their individual mast and discuss their drawing and its meaning.

This is also a good time to sing songs such as "Row, Row, Row Your Boat"; "Merrily We Roll Along" and "Blow the Man Down," just to name a few.

Egg Boats

For lunch or snack, make these cute egg boats. Cut a hard-boiled egg in half. Make a sail from a slice of cheese and thread this onto a toothpick. Insert the toothpick into the egg boat. Add a few olives as the sailors. Bon appetite!

Help Columbus Find the New World

Name _____

Help Christopher Columbus

Match the number words to the numbers on his ship's masts. Cut out squares and glue them on the matching mast.

two | four | one | six

Trick-or-Treat for UNICEF

by Tania K. Cowling

Pledge a Book: Set up a reading center with storybooks about countries around the world. Have the students get a monetary pledge from parents, relatives or friends for each book they complete.

Chores for Coins: Ask the children to do a chore each day at home. Send a letter to the parents explaining how the kids are helping kids in other nations by working for a coin a day. The students then deposit their coins in the collection box each morning. Small contributions add up, and the containers can be filled in a short time.

Halloween Carnival: Plan a Halloween carnival at school. Ask parents and friends to donate refreshments, plan a haunted house, costume contest, games, pumpkin carving contest and any other events that add to holiday fun. Charge a small admission per person, placing the money directly in the UNICEF containers.

Art Auction: Have the children work on an art project during the week. Display the work around the room. Hold an old-fashioned auction one evening, having the parents bid on the artwork of their choice (probably on their own child's masterpiece). Place all the money in the collection cartons.

United Nations Day is celebrated on October 24th, and 1996 marked its 50th anniversary. Through the UN, the United Nations Children's Fund (UNICEF) was founded in 1946 to help the needs of children in the war-torn countries of Europe and China.

In the 1950s, UNICEF expanded its mission to help save millions of children from diseases such as malaria, leprosy, tuberculosis and trachoma. For its deep concern and help, UNICEF was awarded the Nobel Prize for Peace in 1965.

Now in the 1990s, representatives from over 150 countries attended a World Summit for Children and promised to achieve health and developmental goals for the children of the world. Children's lives are being saved by these efforts.

Peace, kindness and much-needed help is why we celebrate Trick-or-Treat for UNICEF on Halloween each year. Here are a few ways to integrate fund-raising ideas with your students in the classroom. If everyone will help just a bit, UNICEF's mission will succeed.

This October, introduce your students to cultural diversity around the world and the fact that these children are not as fortunate as we. Order the famous orange collection boxes and display these in the classroom. They are free from UNICEF along with a teacher's guide. Call 1-800-252-KIDS.

Peace: Peace in all nations would be the ultimate goal in providing a better life for all the children in the world. Each day teach your students the word *peace* in another foreign language. Here are a few to try:

Greek—**eip'nvn** (i-RAY-nay)
Swedish—**fred** (frehd)
Vietnamese—**hou-binh** (hwah-beeng)

French—**paix** (peh)
German—**friede** (FREE-duh)

Spanish—**paz** (pahs)
Swahili—**amani** (ah-MAH-nee)

If you have students from other countries, have them teach the word *peace* in their native tongue to the class.

Halloween Book Nook

Celebrate the Halloween season with our selection of fall book favorites.

Delight your class by reading *The Thirteen Hours of Halloween* by Dian Curtis (Illinois: Albert Whitman & Company, 1993). This lively adaptation of "The Twelve Days of Christmas" features all sorts of spooky "gifts" and creatures. While reading the book, ask your students to illustrate some of the gifts the little girl receives.

Spark your students' enthusiasm for the fall season with *When Autumn Comes* by Robert Maass (New York: Henry Holt and Company, 1990). The large, bright photographs in the book give this season a hearty, warm welcome. Have your youngsters create a "Hooray for Fall" picture book illustrating it with autumn pictures.

Cook up a batch of tasty holiday treats with your class, using the recipes in *Holiday Treats* by Esther Hautzig (New York: Macmillan Publishing Company, 1983). Some of the recipes for fall include Be-witch-ing Dessert and Easy Pumpkin Pie. Have a yummy holiday season!

Lionel in the Fall

Krensky, Stephen. Illustrated by Susanna Natti. New York: Dial Books for Young Readers, 1987.

Come along and join Lionel as he gets ready for the fall season. Follow him on his first day back to school as he meets his new teacher. See how he tackles the job of raking a yard full of leaves and "chases" a dragon on Halloween night.

- Fall favorites! What do you like best about fall? Fold a blank sheet of paper into four equal parts. Draw four pictures of what you enjoy doing in the fall.

- Be an inventor! Fall is here and that means colorful leaves everywhere! Invent a new Supersonic Rake that would make the job of raking leaves easier. Draw a picture of your new invention and label the parts.

- It pays to advertise! Design a billboard ad telling about your new invention.

Porkchop's Halloween

Pearson, Susan. Illustrated by Rick Brown. New York: Simon & Schuster for Young Readers, 1988.

Meet Rosie's lively orange Halloween cat named Porkchop in this charming holiday story. Porkchop falls in love with the family's big Halloween jack-o'-lantern and moves right in. The perky cat even helps liven up Rosie's chicken pox Halloween party by bobbing for apples. Don't miss this Halloween feline delight!

- At the party, Porkchop climbed into Rosie's paper bag robot mask. Draw a picture of what the cat looked like.

- Would you like to have a pet cat like Porkchop? Why?

- Pretend that Rosie took Porkchop to school for show and tell. Write a funny story telling what happened.

by Mary Ellen Switzer

Huff and Puff on Halloween

Warren, Jean. Illustrated by Molly Piper. Washington: Warren Publishing House, 1993.

Meet two adorable clouds, Huff and Puff, who decide to play a trick on Halloween. The two mischievous clouds hide the moon that night, so everything will become dark below. When the young trick-or-treaters become scared, Huff and Puff turn their trick into a real treat for everyone—they create a fluffy, white jack-o'-lantern in the sky.

- As an added treat, there is a "Halloween Fun" section in the back with seasonal activities and songs. Have fun with your class making Jiffy Jack-o'-Lanterns or Gluey Ghosts. Why not have a special party with tasty Halloween Brew or Orange-Pumpkin Pudding?

- Huff and Puff created a giant, fluffy, white jack-o'-lantern as a treat for the children who were trick-or-treating. Draw a picture of what the children saw.

- Create your very own "Amazing Clouds" book. Write a fact about clouds on each page and draw a picture to illustrate it.

The Old Witch and Her Magic Basket

DeLage, Ida. Illustrated by Ellen Sloan. Champaign, Illinois: Garrard Publishing Co., 1978.

Poor Polly! It's Halloween and she won't be able to trick-or-treat this year because she is sick. An old witch comes to the rescue and gives Polly a Halloween that she will never forget.

- Design a Halloween get-well card for Polly.

- The old witch had lots of surprises in her magic basket. Draw a picture of one of them.

Pumpkin Light

Ray, David. New York: Philomel Books, 1993.

Welcome the pumpkin season with this endearing Halloween tale about a boy named Angus who loves pumpkins more than anything else. One Halloween, Angus gets into trouble with an angry scarecrow when he sneaks away from home with a fresh pumpkin pie. The beautiful illustrations enhance this wonderful seasonal story!

- Draw a picture of your favorite pumpkin treat.

- Congratulations! You have just won the prize for the World's Scariest Jack-o'-Lantern. Draw a picture of what your pumpkin would look like.

- It's game time! Make a list of all the words you can think of using the letters in *pumpkin light.*

Oliver and Amanda's Halloween

Van Leeuwen, Jean. Illustrated by Ann Schweninger. New York: Dial Books for Young Readers, 1992.

Celebrate Halloween with two adorable pigs, Oliver and Amanda. The brother and sister pigs select just the right costumes from the dress-up box and help their father carve the "perfect" jack-o'-lantern. Join the two "pigs from another planet" as they encounter monsters while trick-or-treating.

- Write directions on how to carve the scariest Halloween jack-o'-lantern. Draw a picture of how it would look.

- Oliver and Amanda dressed up as "two pigs from another planet." Design two costumes they might have worn.

- Be a pig detective. Look in an encyclopedia and find out all about pigs. Write three facts that you have learned.

PAPER PLATE SKELETONS

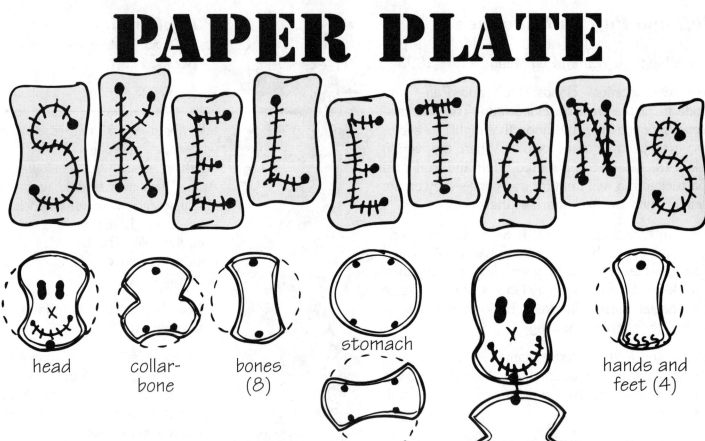

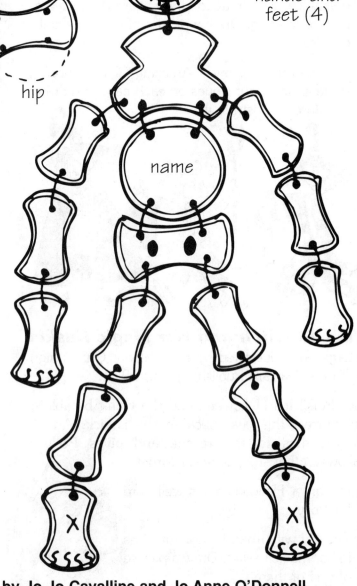

head

collar-
bone

bones
(8)

stomach

hip

hands and
feet (4)

name

Materials:
- paper plates (inexpensive flimsy kind)
- white yarn
- black marker
- scissors
- hole punch

Each student is given 16 paper plates. One is left whole for the stomach. Follow the patterns for cutting the plates into bones. Outline each bone with black crayon. Punch a hole or holes in the bones according to the pattern and attach with yarn. Begin with the head and work down to the feet. When your students have finished, an attractive display can be created in a hall or on a bulletin board. Hang the skeletons by taping them to the wall in different positions. Title your display with one of these captions: "She Is Working Us to the Bone; We're Fat Free This Halloween; No Bones About It, Have a Happy Halloween." In white chalk write the letters of the title on $8^1/_2$" x 11" black paper. Make the letters look skeletal by drawing lines through them.

by Jo Jo Cavalline and Jo Anne O'Donnell

TLC10100 Copyright © Teaching & Learning Company, Carthage, IL 62321-00

Who-o-o-o Are You?

3-D Haunted House

Using the patterns provided on page 72, copy one ghost for each child. Print each child's name, address and telephone number on their ghost.

Help students review names, addresses and phone numbers with the help of this "spooky" haunted house. Cover a rectangular box (approx. 36" high) with brown, grocery bag paper.

Using a permanent black marker, draw doors, windows, trees and bushes around the sides.

Don't worry if doors and windows come out crooked, it only adds to the spooky atmosphere. Glue a black construction paper roof to the top.

This is a high impact visual effect for your classroom and a terrific Halloween decoration. Plus, you can pack it away and use it year after year!

Door Decoration
Use this same concept as a door decoration in your classroom. Cover your door with brown paper. Draw a roof, windows, doors, etc. Tape the ghosts to the door.

Finally, ask each student, "Who-o-o are yo-o-u?" If they answer correctly, staple their ghost to the haunted house.

by Ann E. Scheiblin

I know my

Name _____

Address _____

_____

Phone _____

I know my

Name _____

Address _____

_____

Phone _____

I know my

Name _____

Address _____

_____

Phone _____

I know my

Name _____

Address _____

_____

Phone _____

Native American
ARTS AND CRAFTS

November is the perfect month to discuss and experience Native American art. As early as 1621, during the first Thanksgiving, Native Americans taught the early colonists about nature and natural art. To the Native American, art is an important component of everyday living; the blues in the sky, the greens of grasses, plants and trees. Nature is part of the "visual vocabulary" of the tribes.

Nature's ingredients are used as paints. Berries are crushed for reds, blues and purple. The earth is mixed with water to form a rich array of browns. These paints are used for decorations on tepees, totem poles and pottery, as well as face and body painting. Stones and shells are polished and strung as necklaces and sewn on clothing as decorations. Many tribes weave colorful yarns to use for blankets, clothing, mats and basket weaving. There are numerous tribes throughout the United States with many beautiful works of natural art to appreciate. If possible, arrange a visit to a local museum or historical society in your area. In the meantime, obtain informative books about Native American arts and crafts in your library or bookstores. Study their artifacts. These artifacts, both ancient and present day, tell stories about these people's culture. They deserve admiration and aesthetic appreciation.

On these pages you will find several craft ideas for young children. They are simplified Native American ideas that can be made, studied and displayed during this month and holiday season.

Totem Poles

A totem pole is a Native American artifact. Symbols representing a legend or tribe's history were carved and painted on large logs. Make a mini totem pole in the classroom using nuts (whole in the shell). Glue several different nuts onto a wooden tongue depressor. Paint faces and masks onto the nut shells. For preservation, lightly spray varnish onto the finished totem poles.

by Tania Kourempis-Cowling

Indian Potato Printing

To prepare the potatoes, have an adult cut them in half and carve out a Native American pictograph shown on this page. Carve the excess potato around the design so that at least $1/8$" of the pictograph is raised. Make several different designs. The children can now dip these potatoes into tempera paint and print their own Indian pictographs onto paper.

Dream Catcher

Many Native Americans believe that good and bad dreams float around in the night. A dream catcher is a web that captures the bad dreams. As the sun comes up the negative dreams disappear. Good dreams float through the web and down the feather to the peron sleeping below. To make classroom dream catchers, you will need paper plates. Cut out the center of each plate for each child. Punch out 16 holes around the rim of each plate. Take a length of yarn (wrap masking tape around the end to make a good tip) and begin creating a web by crisscrossing the yarn between all the holes. Leave the center of the web open. Tape the end of the yarn securely to the back. Then tie an 8" piece of yarn into the bottom hole of the dream catcher. Add several plastic or wooden beads onto this yarn and knot the end. A synthetic feather can slip into the beads and hang down at the bottom. Tell the children to hang their dream catchers above their beds at home.

Kachina Doll

[I]n the Hopi and Zuni tribes, kachinas are sacred spirits representing vari-[o]us aspects of nature. They are named according to what they represent [o]r help, animals, crops or human attributes. Each tribe has their own ver-[si]on and style of kachinas. The kachina dolls are not realistic human [f]orms, their masks and bodies are colorful with lots of symbols. In the [cl]assroom, make a simple kachina doll by decorating a toilet tissue tube. [C]ut out shapes (squares, triangles, circles, etc.) from colorful construction [p]aper. Glue these shapes onto the tube doll.

Clay Pottery

Make pottery from uncolored baking clay. Mix two cups of flour, one cup of salt and water to form a clay-like consistency. Mold little pots or roll coils to make pottery. Place these on a shallow baking pan and bake in the oven at 300°F for 20 to 30 minutes or until fully dry. Paint and decorate with Native American symbols.

Rock Painting

[M]any desert tribes painted murals [o]n cliffs and canyon walls. The [st]udents might enjoy drawing and [p]ainting Native American symbols [o]n smooth rocks, such as river [r]ocks. Collecting the rocks on a [n]ature walk is just as much fun as [p]ainting the finished product.

Thanksgiving Book Treasures

Welcome Thanksgiving Day with our seasonal collection of holiday book favorites:

The Dragon Thanksgiving Feast, Things to Make and Do by Loreen Leedy (New York: Holiday House, 1990) is the perfect book to liven up this holiday season. Join some lovable blue dragons as they celebrate Thanksgiving with some wonderful craft and holiday decorations. Using the book's handy simple-to-follow directions, have your students design a "Thanks Collage," create a bird feeder and make an edible necklace. The book also features Thanksgiving recipes and games, such as I Sailed on the *Mayflower* and Count the Popcorn.

Delight your class with some delicious "munchies" using the recipes in *Holiday Treats* by Esther Hautzig (New York: Macmillan Publishing Company, 1983). Some of the tasty Thanksgiving recipes include Easy Pumpkin Pie, Pilgrim Pumpkin Cookies and Cranberry-Apple Crisp. Bon appetite!

Riddles, Please! Here's a Thanksgiving book that will tickle everyone's funny bone! *The Purple Turkey and Other Thanksgiving Riddles* by David A. Adler (New York: Holiday House, 1986) is a collection of riddles perfect for the season. Find out: "How can you get a turkey to fly?" and "Which side is the left side of a pumpkin pie?" After sharing some of the riddles with your class, ask your students to write and illustrate their own Thanksgiving riddles. Compile their work into a class booklet.

'Twas the Night Before Thanksgiving

Pilkey, Dav. New York: Orchard Books, 1990

Celebrate the Thanksgiving season with this delightful read-aloud favorite. Join eight school children and their teacher on a hilarious visit to Farmer Mack Nuggett's turkey farm. Find out how the clever children manage to rescue their feathery friends from being someone's Thanksgiving feast. This lively poem, based upon *'Twas the Night Before Christmas,* will surely brighten any holiday season!

- Fantastic Field Trip! Where would you like to go on a field trip with your class? Tell why. Draw a picture of the place.
- Create your own tall tale about how you rescued a turkey on Thanksgiving morning.
- The best thing about Thanksgiving is . . . . (Finish the sentence.)

Thanksgiving Treat

Stock, Catherine. New York: Bradbury Press, 1990

It's a busy Thanksgiving morning, and a little boy wants to help his family prepare for the big holiday feast. There's a problem though—everyone thinks he's too little to help. Finally, his grandfather takes him to gather a special Thanksgiving surprise for everyone.

- Think about it. How could you help your family prepare for a Thanksgiving meal?
- Draw a picture of a Thanksgiving treat you would like to make for your family.
- Create a picture book called *How I Spent a Perfect Thanksgiving.*
- Congratulations! You just snapped off the biggest piece of your turkey's wishbone. What wish would you make? Draw a picture of your wish.

by Mary Ellen Switzer

Friendship's First Thanksgiving

Accorsi, William. New York: Holiday House, 1992

This entertaining book tells the Pilgrim's story from a dog called Friendship's point of view. Friendship leads quite an exciting life in the New World, especially his encounter with a pack of wolves. And best of all, he enjoys the first Thanksgiving feast with his new friend—Caniscoot, a Native American dog.

- Friendship gave Caniscoot a bone that he brought over from England. What did Caniscoot give Friendship?
- Blast off! Write an adventure story about the first dog who travels to the moon.
- Design a special space suit for the dog to wear on the moon. Draw a picture of the space suit.

Squanto and the First Thanksgiving

Kessel, Joyce K. Illustrated by Lisa Donze Minneapolis: Carolrhoda Books, 1983

Read all about the very first Thanksgiving celebration and the friendly Native American Squanto who made it all possible. Squanto, a Native American who could speak English became friends with the Pilgrim settlers and taught them how to hunt animals and plant crops. Thanks to this helpful Native American, the Pilgrims produced a bountiful crop and were able to celebrate their first Thanksgiving feast.

- What a feast! Draw a picture showing some of the food the Pilgrims and Indians enjoyed on their first Thanksgiving celebration.
- What games and activities did the Pilgrims and Indians participate in during their first Thanksgiving?
- Your parents let you plan the Thanksgiving dinner this year. Design a menu telling what food you would serve.

Three Young Pilgrims

Harness, Cheryl. New York: Bradbury Press, 1992

Get an interesting history lesson about the Pilgrim's journey aboard the *Mayflower* and their busy year after landing at Plymouth! This beautifully illustrated book tells the Pilgrims' story from the eyes of three young children—Mary, Bartholomew and Remember. Enjoy the detailed illustrations of a cutaway of the *Mayflower*, a map showing the Pilgrims' journey and pictures of the passengers aboard the ship.

- The best thing about being a Pilgrim was . . . . Finish the sentence.)
- Write a Dear Diary entry that one of the young children might have written telling about a day aboard the *Mayflower*.

Thanksgiving at Obaachan's

Brown, Janet Mitsui. Chicago, Illinois: Polychrome Publishing Corp., 1994

Join a Japanese American girl as she celebrates Thanksgiving dinner at her grandmother's (obaachan's) house. Get a firsthand look as the family blends traditional Japanese customs with new ones to enjoy this festive holiday.

- Think about it. Compare the little girl's Thanksgiving at her grandmother's house to your Thanksgiving dinner.
- Draw a picture to illustrate these Japanese words used in the story: *obaachan, grandmother; gohan, rice; ohashi, chopsticks; sakana, fish.*

Poems, Please!

Share with your students the beautifully illustrated poems in *Celebrating Thanksgiving* by Shelly Nielsen (Abdo & Daughters, 1992). Some of the selections include "Sail Away, Mayflower"; "Finally—Dinnertime"; "Pretend Turkey" and "Eating . . . Again?" After sharing the book, have your students create their own holiday poems. Create a class booklet of all the poems entitled *Our Thanksgiving Poems*.

"Tales" of Thankfulness

Share "tales" of thankfulness with your class during the month of November. Use the slogan "Tales" of Thankfulness as your bulletin board header. Beneath it, in the center of your bulletin board, place a cut-out pattern of a large tailless turkey. Have each student trace a big feather pattern on a piece of construction paper. Vary the colors so that you have many beautiful, bright feathers. On each tail feather, have the students write something they are thankful for. Have each child place a cut-out school photo of themselves at the top of the feather to identify the proud author. Their smiling faces and wonderful "tales" will brighten everyone's Thanksgiving Day!

by Ann Scheiblin

Thanksgiving
PAST AND PRESENT

The Pilgrims came looking for religious freedom. Through the years more people followed them. Many came searching for work so they could better support their families. Some people's homes were destroyed and lives upset because of war. They wanted a chance to make a fresh start in a new land. People still come from many places and for many different reasons. They bring their customs and learn new ways of doing things. Those who are lucky will find people to help them learn about their new home. They, too, will have something to be thankful for in a new country. Note: Refer to the books listed at the end of the unit. They may be used to review the story of the Pilgrims' arrival at Plymouth and the events that led to their Thanksgiving celebration. The illustrations in *The Pilgrims of Plymouth* and *N.C. Wyeth's Pilgrims* may be shown to younger students as a simplified version of the events is related.

THE FIRST THANKSGIVING

Long ago people came across the ocean to a new land. They were called Pilgrims. The Pilgrims were newcomers to America. They came to a new country so they could practice their beliefs freely. The Pilgrims set up a colony and named it Plymouth. The winter was cold and wet. Many people died.

There were plants they had never seen before. They didn't know if they were good to eat or if they were harmful. Unfamiliar animals roamed about in the forest. They wondered if they were dangerous.

Indians who lived nearby helped them. They knew all about the land and what grew there. They knew how to plant and care for corn. The Pilgrims had never seen corn before. The Indians knew the best way to catch fish in the rivers and along the coast. They knew how to hunt the wild turkeys that lived in the woods. They showed the Pilgrims many new ways of doing things.

Everyone in the colony worked hard. Men, women and children had special jobs to do. There were crops to plant and care for. Food had to be gathered and meals had to be prepared.

When the time came to harvest the crops, everyone was smiling. There would be plenty of food to last through the coming winter. There would be seeds to plant in spring. They were rewarded for their hard work. Governor Bradford decided to have a party to give thanks for the fine harvest and to thank their friends, the Indians, who had helped them so much.

The celebration lasted three days. There were prayers to say, food to eat and games to play. This was the first Thanksgiving feast in Plymouth Colony. Ships continued to bring more people to test their strength and courage in America.

by Patricia O'Brien

A DAY IN THE LIFE

Select one of the activities below. Imagine what it would have been like to grow up long ago.

1. Write about your experiences as a member of Plymouth Colony. What does it feel like to live in a new place? How do you spend your time? What do you enjoy doing? What do you dislike the most?

2. Pretend you are a member of a Native tribe. How has the arrival of the colonists changed your life? Write to explain what you think of the Pilgrims. What surprised you most about them? What do you think is important for them to understand?

THANKSGIVING TODAY

People coming from other countries have different ways of celebrating. They bring their own customs and ways of doing things.

Poll the students to discover how they plan to celebrate Thanksgiving. Discuss special ways their families give thanks.

THE PLYMOUTH TIMES

Reporters have been assigned to write news articles about the Thanksgiving celebration. Pretend you are one of those reporters. Gather information to answer the following questions:

a. Why was the celebration held?

b. What events took place?

c. Who was there? What did they have to say?

Think of additional questions that may be asked. Write articles to answer the questions. Add eye-catching headlines. Compile the articles to create a newspaper that might have been published in Plymouth.

THEN AND NOW

Use the following questions to compare Thanksgiving celebrations:

1. What were the Pilgrims thankful for at the first feast at Plymouth? What do you give thanks for at Thanksgiving?

2. The Pilgrims appreciated the assistance given by the Indians. What were some ways they helped?

Think of some people who have helped you. Who are they and how did they help? How can you thank them?

ADDITIONAL ACTIVITIES

1. Brainstorm to make a class list of things for which you are thankful. Use the list as an idea starter.

   a. Write an acrostic poem using the letters in *Thanksgiving* or *Thank You* to start each line. Use words, phrases or sentences to complete the poem.

   b. Make a Thanksgiving booklet. On each page feature something or someone for which you are thankful. Write a few lines explaining your choices.

   c. Create a class Thanksgiving ABC Book. Each student is responsible for one letter of the alphabet. They may draw or use magazine pictures to show things and people they are thankful for that begin with that letter.

   d. Assemble a bulletin board quilt. Each student will need a square of paper. On the square, they should draw a picture of something they are thankful for or ways they celebrate the holiday. Strips of colored paper separating the squares will give the quilt a finished appearance.

2. Fold a sheet of paper in half. On one half, draw a picture to show the Pilgrims' Thanksgiving, and on the other half, draw a picture to show how the holiday is celebrated today.

3. Think of a new way to prepare cranberries, corn, squash or turkey. Write a recipe for a special Thanksgiving treat. Include a list of ingredients and the directions for making it.

References
Anderson, Joan. *The First Thanksgiving Feast*. New York: Clarion Books, 1984.
Gibbons, Gail. *Thanksgiving Day*. New York: Holiday House, 1983.
Jupo, Frank. *The Thanksgiving Book*. New York: Dodd, Mead & Company, 1980.
San Souci, Robert. *N.C. Wyeth's Pilgrims*. San Francisco: Chronicle Books, 1991.
Sewall, Marcia. *The Pilgrims of Plymoth*. New York: Atheneum, 1986.

Feeding Turkeys

Materials: crayons, glue, unpopped corn kernels. Color the turkeys. Feed each turkey the correct number of corn kernels by placing the kernels on the numbers. Glue in place.

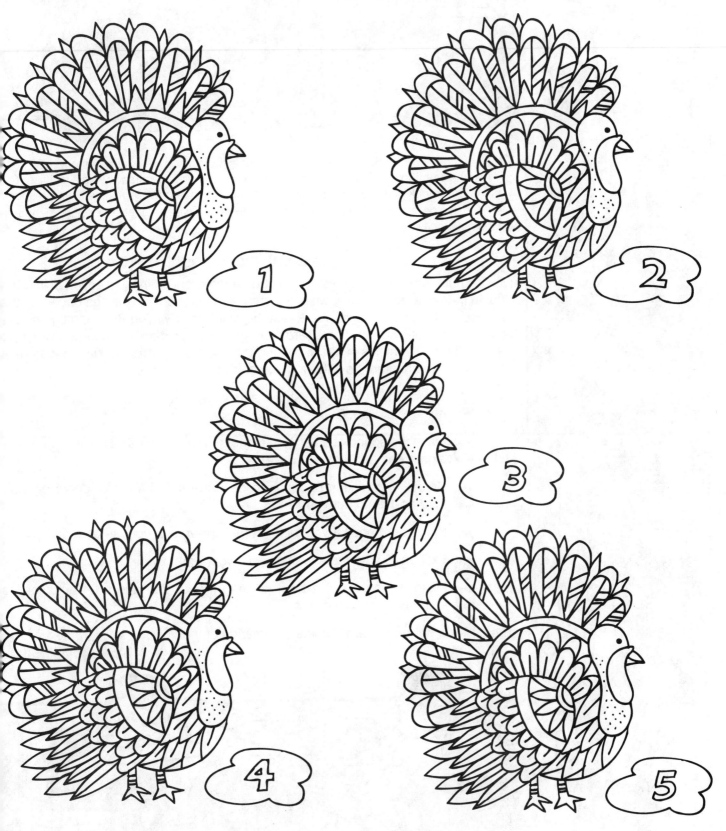

by Marie Cecchini

Start Your Engines!

Hands-On Mathematic Activities

On November 28, 1895, the first U.S. auto race took place in Illinois. Although 80 cars entered the 54-mile challenge from Chicago to Evanston, only six cars were able to finish. The winning driver took close to eight hours to complete the race, traveling at the average speed of 7 1/2 miles per hour. Celebrate the birth of auto racing with a variety of exciting hands-on mathematic activities!

Ordinal Numbers

Divide your class into small groups. Provide each group with a collection of 10 cars and 10 index cards. You may wish to increase the amount of vehicles based on the age and ability of your students. Assist the children in writing the ordinal numbers first through tenth on the index cards using crayon or marker. Ask each group to arrange their 10 vehicles in a row, placing the appropriate ordinal number in front of each. Give the children the following commands:

- Stand up if your first vehicle and your seventh vehicle have an equal number of wheels.

- Make the sound of an engine starting if your sixth car is heavier than your eighth car.

- Create an addition equation to describe the number of doors on your third and tenth automobiles.

- Clap your hands if your ninth car is longer than your second car.

- Exchange your fourth vehicle with your eighth vehicle.

- Make the sound of a horn honking if your fifth and sixth automobiles share two or more colors.

The children will be eager to create commands of their own.

by Nancy A. Silva

Calling All Cars!

Invite your class to bring their favorite toy cars to school! From Matchbox™ cars to Barbie's dune buggy, all are welcome! You may wish to send a note home to parents informing them of the upcoming celebration and letting them know the number of days that the cars will remain at school. To avoid any confusion, ask parents to include their child's name on a piece of masking tape attached to the bottom of each car.

Sorting

Your class will be delighted with the wide variety of automobiles parked in the front of the classroom! Invite the children to identify ways that the cars may be sorted into groups. Their suggestions will amaze you! Record their clever ideas on a piece of chart paper. Here are a few that you're sure to hear:

Color: one color, two colors, three colors, four or more colors

Color: mostly red, mostly black, mostly blue, mostly white, other

Doors: two doors, four doors

Material: metal, plastic, wood, other

Size: small, medium, large

Type: convertible, sedan, jeep, other

Function: police, fire, military, recreational, other

Wheels: four wheels or less, greater than four wheels

When the list of categories is complete, work together to sort the vehicles in one of the ways suggested. After the cars have been sorted, ask the children to identify the number of vehicles in each group. Compare the amounts. Challenge the children to create addition equations to describe the arrangement. Identify the number of vehicles in each group as odd or even. The children will be eager to try each of the categories on their list.

Creating Car Patterns

Invite the children to work in small groups to create patterns using the toy cars. The patterns may be simple A-B-A-B patterns such as large car, small car, large car, small car; or facing front, facing back, facing front and so on. Older children will welcome the challenge of creating more complex car patterns incorporating a variety of characteristics.

Parking Problems

Provide small groups of children with 24 toy cars. Explain that they are the new managers of a popular parking lot. The boss has left just one requirement: Each day, the cars must be parked in even rows. Invite the new managers to arrange their 24 cars to discover the variety of ways that they may be parked. You're sure to hear enthusiastic shouts as the children park the cars in: two rows of 12, three rows of eight, four rows of six, six rows of four, eight rows of three and 12 rows of two. Invite the children to create parking lot diagrams. You may present repeated addition, multiplication and division equations to describe each arrangement. Be sure to discuss the divisions that did not meet the boss's rule: rows of five, seven, nine, 10 and so on. Repeat this activity with smaller (12, 16 or 20) or larger (36, 42 or 50) groups of cars.

Children, Start Your Engines

The highlight of your celebration is sure to be your classroom auto race! Measure a track on a wooden or tile floor. Mark the starting line and finish line with pieces of colorful plastic tape. Along the side of the track, attach a measuring tape so that the children with cars that don't reach the finish line may identify how far their car traveled before it stopped. Invite each child to enter one toy car. Assign a number to each toy car or invite the children to create unusual names for their automobiles. Divide the children into groups of five and let the race begin! The winning car from each round may be entered into the final championship race. Create a chart listing the race results. Beside each car name and/or number, list the distance that each car traveled. Together, review the data. Identify: the car that traveled the shortest distance, the car that traveled the greatest distance, two or more cars that traveled equal distances, the number of cars that reached the finish line. Award a prize to the fastest car finishing the race.

Busy Little Fingers

TRAFFIC LIGHT

The red at the top
Tells us to STOP!
(Extend arm with palm out as a traffic
cop.)
The green below
Tells us to GO!
(Sweep arm across body as a traffic
cop would do.)
The yellow in the middle
Tells us to WAIT!
(Extend both arms out.)
Please don't worry—
You won't be late!

BE SAFE

Play safe. Walk safe.
Always look around.
(Look around in all directions.)
Never talk to strangers.
(Put finger to lips and shake head
back and forth.)
Listen for traffic sounds.
(Cup hand around ear.)

Cross streets only at the corner,
And watch the traffic light.
(Pretend to look at a light.)
Look for cars all around—
In front, the left and right.
(Look in those directions.)

Be careful on the playground,
Though it's a lot of fun.
(Walk around carefully.)
Accidents can happen,
Especially when you run!
(Run in place, then fall down and
pretend to be hurt.)

LABOR DAY

We work so hard all year
(Do various types of work.)
And do our very best,
(Stick thumbs under arm to show pride.)
Now Labor Day is here
So everyone can rest!

FIVE LITTLE FIREFIGHTERS

Five little firefighters
(Show five fingers.)
Sleeping in a row.
(Rest cheek on hands, close eyes.)
Ring goes the bell—
Down the pole they go.
(Pretend to slide down pole.)
They jump on the engine
(Jump up.)
And put out the fire.
(Pretend to squirt out the fire.)
Now they're back home—
My, but they're tired.
(Stretch and yawn.)

by Judy Wolfman

Busy Little Fingers

ROSH HASHANAH WILL SOON BE HERE

Rosh Hashanah will soon be here.
It's the beginning of the year.
At the temple, the shofar sounds.
(Cup hand to ear.)
We eat bread—its shape is round
(Use both hands to show a large circle.)
Apples are dipped in honey sweet.
(Pretend to dip apples.)
They taste so good—what a treat!
(Lick lips, rub tummy.)
New Year's cards are sent to friends.
Before you know it—the holiday ends.

TALKING LEAVES

All the leaves are falling down
(Flutter fingers downward.)
Orange, green, red and brown.
(Flutter fingers.)
If you listen, you'll hear them say,
(Cup hands to ears.)
"Wintertime is on its way."
(Whisper these words.)

SQUIRRELS

(Point to each finger in turn.)
This little squirrel said, "I want to play."
This little squirrel said, "Let's find nuts today."
This little squirrel said, "Yes, nuts are good."
This little squirrel said, "They're my favorite food."
This little squirrel said, "Let's climb this tree
(Hold forearm up, run fingers of other hand up arm.)
And crack our nuts—one, two, three."
(Clap hands three times.)

OCTOBER TIME

October time is pumpkin time,
The nicest time of the year.
When all the pumpkins light their eyes
(Encircle eyes.)
And grin from ear to ear
(Big grin.)
Because they know at Halloween
They'll have a lot of fun
Peeking through the windowpanes
(Put hands over eyes and look.)
Watching children run!

GRANDMA AND GRANDPA

My grandpa always laughs out loud.
(Laugh heartily.)
Grandma smiles with crinkly eyes.
(Smile and let eyes crinkle.)
And when they come to visit me
They always bring a big surprise!
Once they brought a kitty,
(Pretend to stroke kitty.)
Once they brought warm gloves,
(Spread hands out to show gloves.)
But every single time they come,
They bring me lots of love!
(Hug self and smile.)

by Judy Wolfman

Clip Art for Fall

Clip Art for Thanksgiving

Creative Ideas
for Clip Art

Mobile

Here are two suggestions for you to make a mobile using the clip art on pages 89-91.

Use a sturdy paper plate and punch holes around the outer edge of the plate. Use string or yarn to attach the clip art. You may want to enlarge or reduce art depending on what you need. Cut out the patterns and color them. (Note: You may want to laminate them for longer use.)

Another suggestion is to use sturdy tagboard. Cut a rectangle shape approximately 3" x 20" and write a message on it lengthwise. (Or use 3" x 32" and staple the ends together to form a circle.) Punch holes around the outer edge of the plate. Use string or yarn to attach the clip art.

Different Uses for Clip Art

- Bulletin Board Decorations
- Tabletop or Desktop Decorations
- Party Favors
- Take-Homes for Parents
- Refrigerator Magnets
- Ceiling Decorations
- Window/Door Decorations
- Greeting Cards
- Portfolio Pieces on Folders

(Note: You may want to reduce or enlarge the art according to your needs.)

by Kim Rankin

Welcome Back to School

Snowclothes

Today I put my snowclothes on,
But nothing came out right.
The snow pants wound up backwards.
My scarf was much too tight.

The mittens went on crooked.
The jacket wouldn't zip.
My bootlace got all knotted
And my hat began to slip.

But now my clothes are on just right.
I fixed them all quite fast.
I'm warm and ready. Out I go—
In the snow, at last!

by Mary Ryer

Meltdown

I'm worried about Sammy.
He has lost a lot of weight.
His scarf is hanging off him
And he does not look so great.
Just yesterday he stood tall,
His barrel chest puffing out,
As healthy as a grizzly
(But perhaps a little stout).
Although I hate to say it,
There's a dent in Sammy's head.
His hat is sliding forward.
Sam's eyes are becoming spread.
He's standing in a puddle.
I'm afraid that he may drown.
The sun keeps beating on him.
He will soon be falling down.
I have to leave the window,
I can't watch poor Sammy wilt.
He was the greatest snowman
That anyone ever built!

by Timothy Tocher

Melted

My snowman sees me
From inside his glass dome,
While I peek at him,
Inside his wee home.

He's chubby and chunky,
A jolly snow-elf,
As I smile at him
He grins from his shelf.

His nose is a cherry,
His head has a hat
And his belly boasts buttons,
All lumpy and black.

His plump, snowy arm
Is waving at me,
And when I shake, shake him,
A snowstorm I see.

My snowman and I
Were friends from the start,
For this little snowman
Has melted my heart.

by Jeanene Engelhardt

Snow Store

Trash can lids are frosted white
Like sugar cookies overnight.
Popcorn balls cover spruce and pine;
And marshmallow fluff, so pretty and fine
Coats the grass and the sidewalks, too.
See those whipped cream swirls where my
    garden grew?
Last night it snowed—and it's snowing
    some more.
Now my yard is a winter bakery store!

by Jean Conder Soule

Warming Up with Fingerplays

January Snow

All night long the snowflakes fell.
(Wiggle fingers downward.)

They didn't make a sound!
(Put index finger to lips.)

When they came, I cannot tell,
(Shake head back and forth and shrug.)

But they covered all the ground!
(Indicate with arms.)

by Judy Wolfman

A Snowy Day

These are the snowflakes as they fall.
(Flutter fingers downward.)

Here is the snowman, straight and tall.
(Put up index finger on right hand.)

Here is the sun at the end of the day.
(Use thumb and forefinger of left hand and put over the index finger.)

Now the snowman melts away.
(Slowly put down index finger.)

by Judy Wolfman

Let's Warm Up!

We're cold! We're cold! We've been out in a storm!
(Cross arms and shiver.)

Let's run back inside so we can get warm!
(Pretend to run.)

Off come our mittens. Pull your boots—really try!
(Pull off "mittens" and "boots.")

Now take your coat off to hang up and dry.
(Pretend to take off coat.)

The wood in our fireplace goes snap! pop!
and crack!
(Make loud noises.)

First warm your hands, and then warm your back.
(Hold out hands; then turn around.)

Now for some good warm soup, and then—
(Pretend to eat soup.)

Back out to play in the snow again!
(Clap hands.)

by Bonnie Compton Hanson

Frosty Friends

Looking for a way to present one of children's most beloved winter characters? Have them make a "frosty friend." They're fun, easy and edible, too!

Ingredients
- marshmallows (big and small)
- lollipops
- cloves
- LifeSavers™
- gumdrops
- icing
- toothpicks

Directions
Each child receives three large marshmallows. With a dab of icing, join two of the marshmallows together, one on top of the other. Using another dab of icing, put a LifeSaver™ candy on top of the marshmallow. This is the snowman's scarf. With a dab of icing, put the third marshmallow on top of the LifeSaver™. With a dot of icing, put a gumdrop on the top of this third marshmallow. This is your snowman's hat.

by Teresa E. Culpeper

Push a toothpick about half way into each side of the middle marshmallow. Attach a small marshmallow onto the end of each toothpick. These are the snowman's arms. Taking a little bit of icing, attach a lollipop to the small marshmallow on one arm, candy part up. This is your snowman's broom. To finish, push two cloves into the top marshmallow for eyes.

The children now have their "frosty friend" which they may eat or keep as a party decoration or favor.
Follow up this activity by singing the song, watching the movie or going outside and building your own real snowman.
Have fun and enjoy.

Snowmen on Parade

Listen as your teacher reads these directions:

1. Draw a hat on the first snowman.
2. Give the second snowman a happy face.
3. Place a broom to the right of the third snow- man.

4. Draw a wig on the second snowman.
5. Draw a surprised look on the third snowman.
6. Make a funny face on the first snowman.
7. Give each snowman three buttons.
8. Draw a sun over the last snowman.

by Carolyn Ross Tomlin

Have an EARTH-FRIENDLY Winter

Although the official Earth Day isn't until April, children should practice being "Earth friendly" every day of the year. Here are some special winter practices.

Indoors

 Save fuel; instead of turning up the thermostat, put on an extra sweater or sweatshirt.

 Save electricity; turn off TV when not watching, lights when you leave the room.

 Open drapes or blinds during the daytime to let sunlight bring added warmth to rooms.

 Cover windows with shades or drapes at night to keep the daytime heat in and the nighttime cold out.

 Use rugs or rolled newspapers to keep cold drafts from coming in under door spaces.

Outdoors

 Remember that animals are part of Earth's treasures. Shovel paths for pets that go out.

 Be sure not to leave pets outdoors for long on very cold days.

 Fill bird feeders or hang up pinecones coated with peanut butter and rolled in birdseed.

 On icy steps and walks, use kitty litter or sand instead of harmful salt products.

These Three Months Are Full of Holidays with Parties, Gifts and Cards

 Remove gift wrap carefully so it can be reused.

 Wrap your own gifts with newspaper, comic pages or decorated grocery bags.

 If valentines or other cards are to be passed out in school, make "cookie cards" instead. (Be sure to find out if any classmate cannot have sweets before doing this.)

 Use soft washcloths, napkins or shredded tissue instead of plastic "grass" inside baskets.

 Find ways to reuse greeting cards (as gift tags, bookmarks, puzzles, mobiles, magnets).

by Elaine Hansen Cleary

Activities to Use with Earth-Friendly Winter Lessons

Fun Ways to Reuse Greeting Cards

 Cut out circles or squares to use as gift tags.

 Cut strips to use as bookmarks. (Your school librarian will welcome these bookmarks.)

 Make a jigsaw puzzle by cutting the front picture into interlocking parts.

 Make a mobile by cutting out pictures of animals or flowers. Then string them at different lengths to a wire coat hanger or piece of doweling.

Cut and glue a cute picture to a magnetic strip to make a refrigerator magnet.

 Cut off the inside of a French-fold card, using the outside half to make a new card or note paper. Make up a poem or write your own greeting inside.

 Cut large letters apart and see how many other words you can make.

 Glue pictures cut from several cards to a piece of plain paper to make a new picture. You may want to color in the background with crayons or markers.

 Make a picture for your wall by creating a paper frame for the front of a pretty card.

 Build a house of cards by stacking them against and on top of each other.

* Safety Note: When using scissors, have an adult or older child supervise or help!

Earth-Friendly Practices

Grades PreK–1

 Give each child a construction paper circle with a smiling face on one side and a frowning face on the other. (Or have children practice smiling and frowning—this saves paper!) Then read each of the practices listed, rewording some to give them a negative slant. Children evaluate the practice by showing the appropriate facial expression.

 Teacher (or child) names a winter Earth-friendly practice. Have children respond with a designated action according to whether it's an indoor or outdoor activity.

 Teacher names a situation or shows a picture (eg., icy sidewalk). Have children give an Earth-friendly practice to go with it.

 Make a big collage of illustrations, some showing good practices, others showing harmful ones. Let children put green circles around good practices and black Xs over bad ones.

Grades 2-3

Write a list of 15 statements (some Earth-friendly DOs, others harmful DON'Ts). In front of each statement, write two letters, making certain the correct answers under DO or DON'T spell out ALWAYS HELP (or LOVE) EARTH. As children read the list, have them circle the correct letter for each statement. Then write the letters in order below. If correct, they will spell out Always help (or love) Earth.

Make posters to put in classrooms and hallways, as well as at home, showing or listing Earth-friendly winter practices.

Give each student two 3" x 5" index cards. On one, have them write a bad situation (eg., "The sidewalk is icy.") and on the other a good solution (eg., "Sprinkle kitty litter on it."). Mix up the cards, giving each student two that do NOT match and that they did NOT write. Have students take turns reading one card. Whoever has the match answers by reading their card.

Play a circle game similar to Grandmother's Trunk, where one person makes a statement, the next person repeats that statement and adds one of his own, the third person repeats the first two statements and then adds one of his own and so on, until everyone in the circle has had a turn. For this game, make statements about an Earth-friendly practice. (Ex. 1: I made a bird feeder. 2: She made a bird feeder, and I put on a sweatshirt to keep warm. 3: She made a bird feeder, he put on a sweatshirt and I turned off the TV when I left the room.) If you have a large group, try making several smaller circles of five to eight children each.

102

Exploring Winter

The word *winter* comes from an old English word meaning "water and wet"—a good description of the cold, damp winters in Europe.

When That First Flake Falls!—Seize the moment! When the first flake of the season falls from the sky, kids' minds aren't on their seat work. Take advantage of the excitement and interest generated by the first snow. If children are dressed appropriately, take them outside for fun (and learning).

Name the Snow

Begin by staying together as a group and discussing snow:

* Catch snowflakes on your hands. Why do they melt? Are the flakes melting when they hit the ground? Why or why not?

* Breathe in that first snow air! How does it feel? Does it have a distinct smell? Can you describe the feel and smell? Introduce the words: *fresh, crisp, clean, frosty, pure, invigorating, refreshing, brisk, wintry, cool, frigid, icy.*

The Inuit people of the North experience some of the coldest and longest winter conditions on Earth. It's no wonder that these people have about 100 words to describe the different kinds of ice and over 100 words to describe the snow and snowy conditions.

Have your group come up with their own, imaginative names for the different kinds of snow they see. Use these words in haiku poetry, picture book story writing or weather reports.

by Robynne Eagan

Allow the children to explore, experience and use up some of that first snow excitement. Encourage the following activities and observe other creative explorations of the winter wonderland:
* Make footprints and trails.
* Follow the trails of one another.
* Form initials in the snow.
* Make snowballs, castles and figures.
* Make snow angels.
* Stomp out a snow fort with rooms and add shapes on the ground. Invite friends in for hot chocolate.
* Try snow hopscotch, fox and geese or "frozen" tag.
* Play a game of snow baseball. Stomp a small, simple diamond onto the ground. Make a new snowball after very hit. Use your arm for a bat.

Keeping Warm Is for the Birds!

As winter approaches, many birds in North America head south for warmer climates. Ask your students why they think this happens.

Birds that rely on insects, nectar or on bodies of water for their survival must migrate when the insects disappear, the flowers die off, the waters freeze and the temperatures drop. Some birds migrate like the ruby-throated hummingbird that travels one nonstop trip of about 600 miles (970 km)!

Some birds stay right where they are and prepare for the winter ahead. But how do they survive? Birds are fragile-looking creatures. Take a look at their tiny feet and think about the size of their bodies (minus the feathers!). Have you ever thought about how birds keep warm and find food in the winter? Lead a discussion about the ways that people keep warm when the weather turns cold. Did you know that we have learned a lot about staying warm by observing birds?

Winter Bird Math

Materials
- warm clothing
- binoculars (as many pairs as possible)
- clipboard, paper and pencil
- bird feeder and birdseed
- bird field guide

	Day 1	Day 2	Day 3
chickadees			
blue jays			
sparrows			
cardinals			

sample chart

Instructions
1. Prepare for outdoor recess a little early and take children outside to a bird feeder or other place where you know birds congregate.

2. Be very still and quiet and watch the birds for 5-10 minutes.

3. Record the number and type of birds you see in that time frame.

4. Go to the same spot on several separate days and record the results.

5. Prepare a chart or graph to represent your bird-watching observations.

Using the chart, ask children to answer the following questions:
- On what day did we see the most birds?
- How many birds did we see altogether?
- On all of the days put together, how many _____ did we see?
- What type of bird did we see the most of?
- On what day did we see the most _____?
- What type of bird did we see the least of?
- How many more _____ did we see than _____?
- How many more birds did we see on day ___ than on day ___?

Beyond the Feather Coat

Birds need more than just a feather coat to help them through the long, cold winter. Think about other things humans need to keep warm in winter. How about shelter? Birds seek shelter from the wind and blowing snow, just as we do. Chickadees gather in tree holes, starlings roost in protected areas and snow buntings shelter under the snow. Evergreen trees provide excellent shelter for many of the birds who hang around for the winter. Every bird has its own way of finding shelter from the cold.

Take your students outside on a cold, windy day. Ask them to try to find the warmest spot they can. They will quickly discover the importance of finding shelter from the wind!

Huddle for Warmth

On an especially cold and blustery day, take students outside for a group huddle. Begin by having students find their own spot to stand for one minute. How did they feel?

Now have them huddle together. Does it feel any different? What does that tell them?

Birds know the importance of huddling together for warmth. Many of them do it. Watch them on a very cold day, and have students watch for birds in the evening.

Take a Look

Take your students to a bird feeder or popular birding spot. Do the birds look any different than they did in the summer? Can you notice any new plumage? Are the birds plump? Do the birds look fatter or puffier than they did in the warm months? (The gray jay can puff itself up to almost three times its usual size.) Ask your students why this might be.

Fueling Up

Like any living thing, a bird needs fuel to run on—food that is. Birds need more food in the winter to help them keep warm. They require high-energy foods to give them the fuel they need to keep their bodies warm, especially on the coldest of nights.

Provide a well-positioned bird feeder for the birds in your area. Keep it filled with cracked corn, millet, peanuts, fruit and suet or fat, which is especially popular with chickadees. The birds will need this food supply most after fresh snow falls or icy storms have covered any remaining natural food sources. The colder the winter, the more popular your feeder will be.

- If you put your feeder out in the fall, you might entice birds who usually migrate to stay around. Your feeder will become their main source of food energy when their other sources disappear in the winter, so be sure to keep your feeder full.

- Sunflowers make wonderful bird feeders throughout the winter. They provide lots of seeds and don't need to be filled on cold winter days. If you didn't plant some last spring—plan to this spring!

Try Out Some Feathers

Feathers provide protection from the rain and snow and can be fluffed in such a way that they trap a layer of warm air. This air is the bird's insulation against the falling temperature. Most birds also grow some extra feathers to help them keep warm. Some birds can grow an extra 1,000 feathers. The extra feathers and the insulation provided by the trapped air become the winter coat that keeps birds warm in the winter.

- One of the warmest coats people can wear is the down-filled jacket. Down is tiny bird feathers, and it works great at keeping us warm. Ask students to try out a down jacket of their own—perhaps a friend or family member has one they might try.

F.Y.I.

For your information about birds in your area, contact:

National Audubon Society
950 Third Avenue
New York, NY 10022

National Association for Interpretation
P.O. Box 1892
Fort Collins, CO 80522

Canadian Wildlife Service
Environment Canada
Publications Section
Ottawa, ON Canada   K1A 0H3

For more information about birds in your area, try the following resources:

The Audubon Society Pocket Guides; Familiar Birds of North America: Easter Region; Western Region. Chanticleer Press/Knopf.

Everybody's Everywhere Backyard Bird Book by the editors of *Klutz Press,* Klutz Press, Palo Alto, CA 1992.

The Kids Canadian Bird Book. Pamela Hickman, illustrated by Heather Collins, Kids Can Press, Toronto, Ontario, 1995.

The Great Bird Detective. David Elcome, illustrated by John Cox and Spike Gerrell. Chronicle Books, San Francisco, 1995.

It's never too cold to snow!

Snowflakes consist of tiny six-sided ice crystals. The seven basic snow shapes are: columns, capped columns, spatial dendrites, stellar, plates, needles and irregular crystals.

The largest snowflake measured on record was 15 inches (38 cm) across.

If snow sticks to the trees, it probably won't stick around.

The heaviest snowfalls occur when the air temperature is hovering around freezing.

The snowiest part of the world is from a latitude of about 66 to a latitude of about 40 in the Northern Hemisphere. All of the Canadian provinces, the southern parts of the Northwest Territory, the Yukon and about half of the U.S. are within these bounds.

No one has ever found two snowflakes that are exactly the same.

Snow can form in the clouds in the summer, but as it falls it melts and becomes rain.

Big, wet snowflakes are a sign of a short storm. The small, powdery dry flakes are a sign of a long storm.

Winter Tally

In Canada and parts of the United States, the weather we associate with winter blows in long before winter officially arrives. It is sometimes confusing to children who think the arrival of snow signals the arrival of winter! Talk to your students about the quarterly official changes in seasons and the unpredictable arrival of seasonal weather!

In the Northern Hemisphere, winter officially begins on December 21 (and sometimes December 22), with the winter solstices. On this date, we experience the shortest day of the year. Winter may officially arrive on this date, but when does it really appear in your Kid Space? When winter weather arrives, take kids on a winter hike. Take notice of the seasonal clues that tell us winter weather has arrived.

Complete your Winter Tally Sheet to determine if winter has arrived in your Kid Space.

_____ The days are getting shorter and the nights are getting longer.

_____ Summer birds have migrated and can't be found in your area.

_____ The deciduous trees are bare.

_____ The plants and grasses have died off.

_____ The temperature is very cold.

_____ We can see our breath when we breathe outside.

_____ Water freezes and becomes ice.

_____ Snow (or lots of rain) falls from dark clouds.

_____ There is frost on the windows in the morning.

_____ People are wearing warmer clothing, maybe coats, boots, mittens or hats.

_____ Furnaces and wood stoves are needed to keep indoor spaces warm and dry.

Follow-Up

- Take a photograph of your students enjoying the first snowfall. Use it on your next newsletter, for the school yearbook or to decorate your classroom.

- Have students make pictures that show the arrival of winter.

Hiding Hares

Every winter, people bundle up against the cold. Hats, gloves and heavy coats all help keep us warm. Animals have winter coats, also. Their coats help to keep them warm, but with some animals they also help them hide.

Snowshoe hares have winter coats that are a different color than their summer coats. Their summer coats are brown, and their winter coats are white. This helps the rabbits blend in with things around them.

Snowshoe hares are long-legged members of the rabbit family. Their feet are wide and heavily furred so that they can easily run on snow and ice. They can run almost as soon as they are born and can zigzag while jumping, to confuse their enemies. In "Edgar's Winter Coat," a young snowshoe hare discovers the importance of wearing his winter whites.

Related Questions

- Why do you think snowshoe hares got their name?
- How many facts can you find in Edgar's story?
- What parts of the story are make-believe?

Camouflage Sundaes

Ingredients

vanilla ice cream	coconut
marshmallows	chocolate chips
bowls or plates	spoons

Each child gets a scoop of ice cream, one large marshmallow, another marshmallow cut in half (to resemble bunny ears), two chocolate chip eyes and coconut for sprinkling.

Let everyone make their own snowshoe hare, then eat and enjoy!

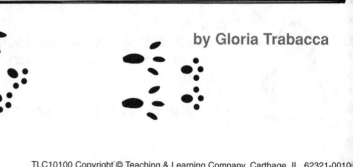

by Gloria Trabacca

Edgar's Winter Coat

Edgar bolted for the front door and ran right into Mama's soft warm fur. "It feels like snow today. Better wear your winter coat!" she said.

Edgar frowned. "Oh, Mama. I hate that old thing! All of my friends wear exactly the same kind of coat every winter. It's boring. I like my beautiful brown summer coat." Mama wasn't listening. She struggled to get his long feet into the winter suit. Edgar tried again. "No one will even notice me in this horrible white coat! I'll blend in with everyone!"

"I hope you do!" Mama exclaimed, pulling the coat up over Edgar's shoulders. "It's dangerous enough with that wolf around. If it snows, and you're wearing that beautiful brown summer coat, you won't be able to hide!"

"He's not so great. I can mmm, ggld, mmmph!" Edgar glared at his mother when his face reappeared in its white, furry mask.

"I'm sorry!" Mama laughed. "I didn't quite understand that last sentence."

"I said, I can run faster than that old wolf any day! Remember, I've got snowshoes!" Edgar dashed out the door.

"I remember," Mama called after him, "but so did that little hare on the other side of the woods, and he wasn't fast enough!"

Edgar was still boasting to himself when he got to school. "A wolf is no problem for me. Sometimes I leap 20 feet at once, and I can always zigzag to confuse him if he gets too close."

Edgar was right. He and his friends had been able to run almost as soon as they had been born, and when the teacher measured the long leap contest, most of them went 15 or 20 feet! Edgar looked around. He had been right about something else, too. Almost everyone was wearing a white winter coat. Only one rabbit was wearing brown, and he was coming over to Edgar's desk.

"Why'd you wear white so soon?" Scamp sneered at Edgar. "Scared of snow or something?"

Edgar's brown eyes blazed. "I'm not scared of snow! I'm not scared of anything! I can outrun wolf— and you—any day!"

"How about today?" Scamp called back over his shoulder as he headed for his seat. "After school I'll race you through the field."

Edgar took out his books and tried to study, but he kept thinking about the race. They would be running through the field; the one that was right beside wolf's house. He couldn't concentrate, so Edgar looked out the window instead. Snow!

Edgar nudged the hare at the next desk. "It's snowing. Hard! Pass it on!" Soon the whole class was watching as the snow covered everything in a blanket of white. Edgar heard the throat-clearing noise that meant his teacher wanted them to listen.

"I am dismissing class early today. Run home quickly, and do not stop to play! Wolf will be out today."

Edgar would have gladly run home, but Scamp blocked his way. "There's the field. Ready, set, go!"

They both ran out into the field. Scamp started out ahead, but Edgar was close behind. Suddenly, someone else was close behind, too. It was Wolf. Edgar could feel his wide, furry feet land on top of the snow with each leap. Wolf's narrower feet would sink. That should slow him down a little, Edgar thought. Faster, feet; faster! Edgar wasn't racing Scamp anymore. He was only thinking about the wolf. He zigged and zagged, and then very quickly darted under a snow-covered bush.

Wolf had not seen him. He sniffed at the snow with his long gray nose, then ran off after Scamp. Edgar waited until it was safe, and then ran all the way home.

"Mama!" he called as he dashed in the door. "Wolf was chasing us and I hid under a snowy bush, but Scamp was wearing his brown summer coat and had no place to hide!"

Mama put her arms around Edgar and held him close. "Hush child. Scamp was lucky enough to run into a skunk in the woods, and Wolf ran away. I saw Scamp get home a short time ago, and although his lovely brown coat smells too bad to be worn again, he is okay. I guess he'll have to wear his white coat after all."

Edgar reached up to kiss his mother. "I'm sorry I complained about wearing my winter coat today, Mama. I'm glad you made me wear it." Edgar's brown eyes twinkled. "I guess blending in isn't so bad after all!"

110

Camouflage Pictures

Supplies Needed
copies of rabbit outline
glue
cotton balls
flour, bleached
white rice
powdered sugar

Have your students each pick two different white items from those presented. First spread glue on all the paper that is around the rabbit's outline. Sprinkle with one of the chosen items, completely covering the glued area.

When this is completed, glue may be spread over the entire rabbit shape. Color, cut and glue one eye onto the face before proceeding. Then sprinkle the second of the chosen items so that the rabbit is covered in white.

You may wish to compare the result to another picture where cinnamon or seed-starting soil has been used to color the hare brown.

Winter Coat Relay

Divide the class into two groups, each child with his own coat. Have each group put their coats in a pile and then form a line on the opposite side of the room. There should now be two piles of coats on one side of the room and two lines of children on the other.

At your signal, the first person in each line hops down to the appropriate pile of coats, finds his own, puts it on and hops back to his original line. When everyone is safely in their winter coat, it's time for winter treats!

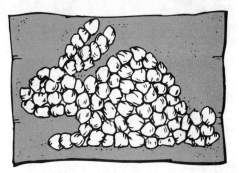

Find the Hare

How many hares are hidden here? Circle or color all that you find.

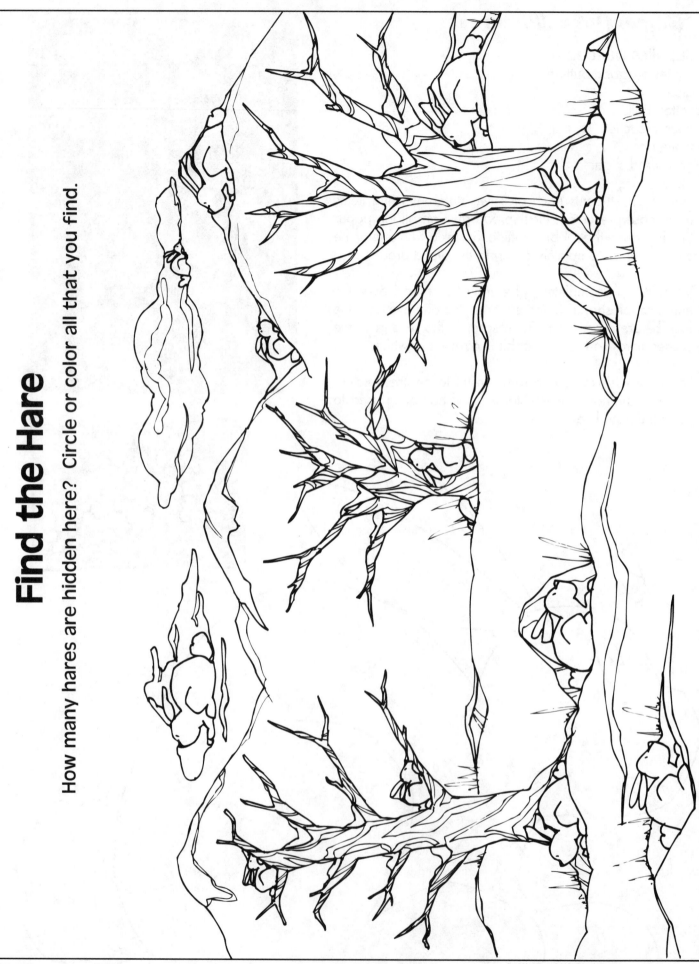

Weather WISE

Report the Winter Weather

A weather report is a statement of the weather conditions at a particular place and time. Have your students observe the weather, study the weather and research the weather to provide the winter weather report.

Weather provides a constant source of intelligent questions from curious kids. The ever-changing weather provides kids with a hands-on science lab—right on the school doorstep! Weather WISE activities are designed to help kids learn about weather through active investigation, using the natural environment and kids' natural curiosity. Simple procedures and the use of every-day materials make the projects simple for children and educators. Encourage young learners to formulate questions, investigate their environment, make discoveries and become weather wise!

Winter weather reports are very important to many people. Warning of adverse weather conditions or calls for good weather are very important during the winter months. Discuss this with your group. Talk about the effects winter weather can have on road conditions; farm animals; travel to and from school, work and special events; and the temperature of homes.

As part of a language arts program, ask students to research and give the weather reports. Young children can merely look out the window and report what they see. It is an important job and can be done on a daily basis along with the calendar.

Students in grades one or above are capable of studying the classroom weather station (if you have one), checking the newspaper or listening to the news to help them prepare their weather reports.

Encourage students to use weather maps, technical information, props and creativity in these reports.

Weather Portfolio

Old calendars and magazines offer wonderful pictures to stimulate discussion about the weather and the seasons. Round up as many as you can and laminate them for display and discussion purposes.

by Robynne Eagan

Winter Weather Walk

Winter weather can have a great effect on almost everyone. Take winter walks on days when you are experiencing different weather conditions.

Ask students to observe and discuss ————— • —————

- How does the sky look? Discuss the types of clouds you see.
- Is anything falling from the sky? What kind of precipitation is falling? Is there more precipitation than usual?
- Describe the rain or snow.
- How does the air feel? Is it damp or dry?
- Discuss the temperature. How does it feel when you take a deep breath? How does your exposed skin feel?
- Is there any wind? How does it feel? Which direction is it blowing? What kind of weather might it be blowing in?
- What conditions are making you feel cold or warm?
- Is there evidence of any animals? How will this weather affect them? How will this weather affect people you know?

Follow-Up ————— • —————— • —————— • —————— • —————— • —————

- Keep a record of your observations. Compare these with observations made on other days.
- Keep your Weather Record from year to year and show students the observations made on the same day last year or the year before.

Why Is It Winter?

To answer this question we need to look at the seasons. Seasons are caused by changes in the position of the Earth in relation to the sun.

The year is divided into four quarters, or seasons, each beginning when the Earth is in a particular position relative to the sun.

Seasonal weather is affected by the Earth's tilt as it goes around the sun. We experience winter because the sun's energy is less direct at the time, and the days are shorter.

The Winter Solstice

Winter begins on the winter solstice which falls on December 21 or sometimes 22. At this time there are about nine hours of daylight and more than 15 hours of darkness in southern Canada and the northern United States. The farther north you go, the longer the night becomes. In Tuktoyaktuk, in northern Canada, it stays dark for a very long time–the sun doesn't rise for the three weeks before and the three weeks after the winter solstice!

114

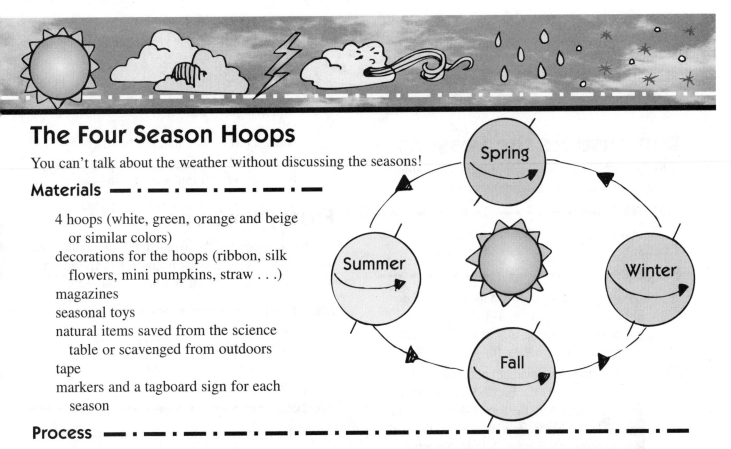

The Four Season Hoops

You can't talk about the weather without discussing the seasons!

Materials

4 hoops (white, green, orange and beige
   or similar colors)
decorations for the hoops (ribbon, silk
   flowers, mini pumpkins, straw . . .)
magazines
seasonal toys
natural items saved from the science
   table or scavenged from outdoors
tape
markers and a tagboard sign for each
   season

Process

1. Talk about seasons. What do your students already know? Do they remember the spring, summer fall? What does winter feel like right now? What do they remember about late winter?

2. Decorate one hoop to represent each of the four seasons. Your students can help! Try decorating the white one with cotton balls for snow; the green one with paper or silk leaves and flowers; the orange one with toy bees, flowers and sunglasses; and the beige one with fall leaves, straw and mini pumpkins.

3. Attach a season sign to each hoop and place the hoops in a safe place.

4. Set up a magazine search-and-cut-center for activity time. Have children cut out pictures of various seasonal activities, scenery and weather and place them in the appropriate hoops.

5. During circle time, pull out a hamper of assorted seasonal wear. Have students, one at a time, take a piece of clothing and place it in the appropriate hoop. During another circle time, provide a box of seasonal toys for children to sort into the appropriate hoops.

6. Mix up the season signs and have children help to get each sign back to the right place.

Giant Mobile

Tie the various items to hang from the inside of the hoops. Hang the hoops from the ceiling for a wonderful display of the seasons.

Bulletin Board Idea

"We're All for the Four Seasons!"—When you have completed the hoop activities, fasten the hoops to a bulletin board (they may overlap) and tack the various seasonal articles inside each hoop. Clothing, toys and other articles make for an interesting bulletin board collage! Elastic and string will make it easier to fasten some objects to the wall.

Demonstrate the Seasons

Allow students a hands-on opportunity to internalize the concept of changing seasons.

Materials

2 toothpicks   orange
flashlight   dark room

Process

1. Divide your class into small groups of no more than four pupils. Darken the room you will be working in. Cover the windows with paper if necessary for greater effect.

2. Hold up the orange and explain that the orange represents the Earth. Have students stick a toothpick in the top of the orange to represent the North Pole and one in the bottom to represent the South Pole. Spin the orange to help them visualize the axis.

3. Shine the flashlight about 2" away from the orange and explain that the flashlight represents the sun. One child in each group holds the flashlight steady 2" away from the orange that is being held by another student. The flashlight's beam should be focused on the "equator" (the middle of the orange).

4. Ask students to hold the orange in a way that will show the position of the sun and the Earth when it is summer in the Northern Hemisphere. The orange should be held so that the beam of light is hitting the middle of the orange. The North Pole should be tilted just a little toward the light. Talk about how most of the light is shining on the top portion of the Earth. This demonstrates the positions of the sun and Earth when it is summer in the Northern Hemisphere.

5. Ask students how they think the positions should change to cause winter in the Northern Hemisphere. After discussion, tilt the North Pole slightly away from the light to demonstrate. What is happening in the Northern Hemisphere at this time? Lead

students to realize that the Northern Hemisphere is receiving less sunlight than the Southern Hemisphere in this case.

Frosty Patterns

Frost often covers the trees and ground in cold weather. But where does it come from? Find out where frost comes from and how it forms!

Materials

1 cotton swab for   glass
  each student   crushed ice
petroleum jelly   salt
spoon

Process

1. Have students dip their swabs into petroleum jelly.

2. Students then "paint" simple figures on the outside of the glass.

3. Fill each glass $3/4$ full with crushed ice.

4. Add the salt and stir it all together.

5. After several minutes children will see crystals form before their eyes on the outside of the glass as water vapor in the air condenses on the cold surface of the glass and freezes to form a thin layer of ice crystals. Where the petroleum is painted the water can condense, and the frost cannot form.

Explain

Air contains invisible water vapor that freezes into a thin layer of crystals when it meets the cold glass or ground. We see this thin layer of crystals as frost.

Try This

Breathe on a window on a cold day. Then observe condensation, or frost designs on the window. (**Caution:** Be very careful when using glass with children.)

National Children's BOOK WEEK

Each November, during the week before Thanksgiving, a celebration called National Children's Book Week is conducted in schools, libraries, bookstores and throughout many communities. It is sponsored by a nonprofit association of children's publishers making up The Children's Book Council Inc.

Back in 1919, a Boy Scout librarian, Franklin K. Matthews started a campaign for the quality of children's literature. He worked with publishers and booksellers to promote a celebration that would honor literacy and the love of good books. This was the birth of Children's Book Week. The Children's Book Council has promoted this event since 1945.

Caught in today's world of technology, Book Week simply encourages everyone to look at books and reading as a fun activity. Teachers are now taking literature across the curriculum; enhancing the stories with art, music, history, sometimes even math and science. Cultural awareness is also important these days, with books using multiculturalism as a learning tool. We can visit other countries and appreciate their cultures through books.

Each year the Children's Book Council sponsors Book Week in November. On these pages, take a ride on a hot-air balloon as you "travel with books." Using the concepts of travel, imagination and pretending, we'll journey with some famous books and proceed through the curriculum with fun activities.

Be aware that the Children's Book Council has many thematic materials (posters, streamers, bookmarks, etc.) that can be sent to you for the asking. Some are free or sold at a minimal fee. The proceeds from these sales help the Council promote their mission of book enjoyment and literacy. For information and a materials list, send a 6" x 9" SASE to:

Children's Book Council
Attn: Materials Brochures
568 Broadway, Suite 404
New York, NY 10012
or call: (212) 966-1990
(800) 999-2160

by Tania Kourempis-Cowling

Make a Bookmark

Cut out balloon shapes from construction paper. Attach a fabric ribbon to the paper with glue or a stapler. Print the Book Week theme and dates on the paper balloon and use this as a fun bookmark as you read.

Bulletin Board

Affix a world map as your background on the board. Cut out small hot-air balloon shapes from construction paper. Print a child's name on each balloon. Let the student pick a place on the map to attach their balloon. Use a cute title such as "Journey Around the World with Books!"

Balloons Everywhere!

Decorate the classroom with helium-filled balloons attached everywhere. Perhaps you can use black permanent marker to place a book title on each balloon. Rouse the child's attention as you discuss the fact: Float in the air—travel with books!

A Basket of Books

Construct a hot-air balloon from construction paper. This colorful balloon is attached with lengths of yarn to the basket below. The basket part should be two pieces glued together. Make a slit at the top edge to insert paper books. Cut out paper books for each book the child has read. Print the title on the front of the faux book. Insert these into the balloon's basket.

118

Enhancing BOOKS

Books can be used as stepping-stones to learning. The stories can be thought of as "bridges" to anywhere and everywhere. Children find books interesting as they discover special stories, colorful pictures and a sense that books open new worlds and ideas for them to explore.

Involvement with books should extend beyond reading. Plan several projects "step by step" and "hands-on" activities to enhance the story across the curriculum. It is our role as the teacher or caregiver to share our love of books and to keep the interest alive.

As we "travel with books" we'll find some that question our minds, spark imaginations, give confidence and experience new cultural awareness. Listed are a few books along with some project enhancements.

Before I Go to Sleep is the story of a young boy with quite a vivid imagination as he tries to settle down to sleep. He envisions animals that he would like to be, all in a unique fashion. After his intense journey of the mind, the boy falls fast asleep. Try a few of these ideas to enhance the story.

Giraffe Wind Sock

Trace around a fully spread hand to make a giraffe shape on yellow construction paper. Cut this out and glue it onto a paper plate. To make the giraffe's spots, dip a finger into brown or black tempera paint and print random spots. Draw in facial features with black marker. Attach lengths of colorful ribbon with a stapler to the bottom edge of the paper plate. Punch a hole at the top of the plate and thread ribbon to use as a hanger. Place this wind sock in a breezy spot and watch the streamers fly!

Cookie Cat

You will need two paper plates (painted if desired). Staple these together to form the head and body of the cat. Draw in cute cat facial features with crayons or markers. Add extra embellishment with felt or construction paper pieces. Punch a hole at the top edge of the head plate, adding ribbon or yarn as a hanger.

Staple a small plastic bag to the bottom body plate. Fill each plastic bag with two or three animal cookies. Before story time, let each child remove a bag of cookies to enjoy as you read the book.

Polar Bear Play

Polar bear, polar bear, turn around.
Polar bear, polar bear, touch the ground.
Polar bear, polar bear, stretch up high.
Polar bear, polar bear, touch the sky.
Polar bear, polar bear, crawl so slow.
Polar bear, polar bear, play in the snow.

Adapted Traditional

Before I Go to Sleep by Thomas Hood. Illustrated by Maryjane Begin-Callanan. G.P. Putnam's Sons. © illustrations 1990.

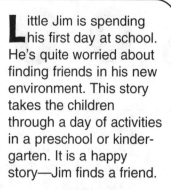

Will I Have a Friend?

Little Jim is spending his first day at school. He's quite worried about finding friends in his new environment. This story takes the children through a day of activities in a preschool or kindergarten. It is a happy story—Jim finds a friend.

Thematic Pictures

Fold a sheet of drawing paper into fourths. Ask the children to draw a scene in each block relating to the school activities in the book. Have each student stand and share his or her picture with the class.

Friendship Collage

Let the students go through old magazines and cut out pictures of children. Glue these in random fashion onto construction paper. Discuss diversity in the classroom. Find some pictures of different ethnic groups to include in the collage.

Song

The more we get together,
    together, together,
The more we get together
    the happier we'll be.
For your friends are my
    friends and my friends
    are your friends.
The more we get
    together the happier
    we'll be.

Traditional
Will I Have a Friend? by Miriam Cohen. Illustrated by Lillian Hoban. Macmillan Publishing, New York © 1967.

The Runaway Bunny

A little bunny wants to run away from home. His mother loves him so much that she will try to find him no matter where he decides to go. It's a loving story.

Bunny Ears

Make a set of bunny ears. Make a strip of paper to fit around the child's head. Staple to size. Cut out bunny ears from construction paper and staple to the headband. Glue pink or white cotton onto the ears.

Game

Wearing these bunny ears, proceed to play this fun game. Follow the commands. Bunny says:

Run in place, to run away.
Swim like a fish in the trout stream.
Pick up your feet up high, like a mountain climber.
Pretend to grow up like a flower
    (Squat down and slowly wiggle up)
Pretend to swing on a trapeze at the circus.
Walk the tightrope at the circus.
Run *(in place)* home and throw a kiss to your mother.

The Runaway Bunny by Margaret Wise Brown. Illustrated by Clement Hurd. Harper © 1972.

This book tells the story of how vegetable soup is made, from the growing process to the delicious finished product. The illustrations are full-page graphics with the use of bright fluorescent colors.

This book shows an airplane ride from the time people board the aircraft until it reaches its destination. It is full of colorful pictures of the plane taxiing down the runway, taking off and flying through the skies.

Flying Pictures

Use a piece of white paper. Using watercolors, paint a blue sky scene. For texture, add white cotton for the clouds. Little airplanes can be made of chenille strips (pipe cleaners) and glued onto the sky picture.

Airport Buildings

Give the students wood blocks and small manipulatives such as Lego™ blocks. Tell the kids to build airport buildings. Add plastic toy airplanes, helicopters, cars and even people. If possible, use a Polaroid™ camera to take pictures of the finished construction. Post these photos on your class bulletin board.

Flying by Donald Crews. Greenwillow Books, New York © 1986.

Creative Dramatics

The creative dramatics area should be equipped with gardening clothes and tools. Hands-on play is conducive to the learning experience. Provide gardening gloves, hats, bandanas, overalls, gardening aprons, small shovels, weed claws, watering cans and pots. Let the children play among these household items and let their pretend skills flourish.

Science

Plant a small vegetable or flower garden on the school grounds. If that is not possible, plant seeds or small germinated seedlings into plastic cups or pots. Let the children examine the seeds, comparing their similarities. Prepare a growth chart to explain the necessary components of gardening—water, sunlight and fertilizer.

Cooking

Bring in vegetables to chop and prepare homemade vegetable soup. If that is too cumbersome, use canned soup pointing out all the different varieties of vegetables in a bowl.

Growing Vegetable Soup written and illustrated by Lois Ehlert. Harcourt Brace Jovanovich, © 1987.

Manipulative Math

for the Winter Season

The manipulation of actual objects allows children to use all of their senses as they reinforce their math skills. Using real things also makes math a lot more fun and the concepts taught easier to remember.

"Count" on having fun as you share the following activities with your class.

Outdoor Fun

Write various numbers on individual paper lunch bags. Distribute one bag to each child, then take the class outside on a leaf hunt. Each child is to collect the number of leaves written on his or her bag.

When the leaves have been collected, empty the bags. Sort the leaves by color, size or type. You may also want to name the varieties and count the points on several kinds.

Work with the children to glue the leaves in a wreath shape on a large piece of cardboard. Add a bow and hang your autumn wreath on the classroom door.

Shell Game

Cut strips of brown paper and glue them into margarine containers to simulate squirrel nests. Provide the children with a container of mixed nuts with shells. Have them pretend to be squirrels and sort the different kinds of nuts.

Popcorn Cupcakes

Write numbers in the bottoms of cupcake papers. Have the children glue the papers to a paper plate. To make the cupcakes, they need to dip popped corn into glue and stick the correct number of puffs into each paper cup.

by Marie E. Cecchini

Playing Santa

Use actual Christmas stockings or paper lunch bags with stockings drawn on them for this counting game.

First, number each stocking. Then provide the children with a container of small toys. Let them take turns filling each stocking with the correct number of toys.

Candy Cane Sort

Use poster board to make candy canes in several colors. Have the children sort them by color and count how many of each color. Have them compare two different colors. Which group has more? Which group has less?

Nut Cup

Fill a measuring cup with nuts (in shells). Ask the children to estimate ("make their best guess") how many nuts it took to fill the cup. Count them together to check. Try a 1 cup measure first, then a 2 cup measure.

Count the Beat

Have the children sit in a circle. Ask one child to hold a drum (either a rhythm instrument or a coffee can with a lid). Have the children listen as you tap a simple beat. Ask the drummer to copy or repeat your beat. Pass the drum around the circle, giving everyone a turn.

Toy Wagon

Draw or glue a rectangle shape on several pieces of paper. Write a different number at the top of each paper.

Distribute the papers to the children. Ask them to add wheels and a handle to the rectangle, making it a wagon. Provide them with catalogs and magazines from which to cut pictures of toys to put into their wagons. Each wagon will only hold the number of toys written at the top of the page.

Presents

Wrap several boxes of different sizes to look like gifts. Have the children arrange them from smallest to largest. Ask them to count how many they can stack before the gift tower tumbles.

Wreath Snack

• bagels, sliced
• small chunks and/or slices of various fruits and vegetables
• cream cheese (softened)
• green food coloring

Use the green food coloring to tint the cream cheese. Spread tinted cream cheese on a bagel half. Make a number chart for the children to read as they decorate the wreaths with the fruit and vegetables. Write numbers down the left side of the chart and glue, tape or staple an actual piece of food beside each number. This way the children will know to use two carrot slices, four raisins or three blueberries, for instance.

Holiday Verses

Happy Hanukkah

Hanukkah has come at last.
Candles in the night.
Another year has now gone past.
How many will we light?
1, 2, 3, 4, 5, 6, 7,
Eight when we are through;
And with each one I'm wishing
Happy Hanukkah to you.

Gingerbread Man

Gingerbread man with your frosting clothes,
Raisins for eyes and a chocolate chip nose;
Would you be happier
Hanging on the tree?
Or is your smile meant
Just for me?

A Special Gift

The clock strikes seven, Christmas morn,
I jump right out of bed.
I do not wake up Mom or Dad
But softly play instead.

This special gift is just from me;
It's sure to bring a smile.
I'll wait to open up my gifts
And let them sleep awhile.

Holidays

Holidays are fun for me.
Lights are all around.
Special songs can fill the air
With a lovely sound.

Yummy foods that Grandma makes,
Snow on every tree;
But having friends and family near
Means "holiday" to me!

Winter Clues

Winter's here!
How can I tell?
There's many ways, you know.

I feel the cold.
I hear the wind,
And I can play in SNOW!

by Gloria Trabacca†

Winter Festivals

Saint Nicholas Day

Saint Nicholas is the patron saint of children. He lived in Myra (now the country Turkey) during the 4th century. He was a bishop and a very generous man. There are many stories about Saint Nicholas throughout Europe and even in the United States. December 6th is his special day. In parts of France, Switzerland and Germany, children still receive their gifts on this day. The children in the Netherlands call him Saint Nikolaus or Sinterklaas, and there he travels from house to house on horseback. The Dutch children set out their wooden shoes with hay for the horses on December 5th. During this eve they dream of their shoes being filled with goodies by morning. Some children in the United States still place hay outside for Saint Nicholas' horse on this patron saint's day. Some old customs have not been forgotten.

In the classroom, introduce various customs involving Saint Nicholas using Christmas books from other countries. Discuss the differences between old customs and how we perceive Santa Claus today on December 25th. During art, draw and decorate stockings and wooden shoes (very popular in Europe). You might want to photocopy an older version of Saint Nicholas. The students can color this and compare it to how Santa Claus looks today.

Las Posadas

Las Posadas is a Mexican custom that commemorates the journey that Mary and Joseph took from Nazareth to Bethlehem. It is held from December 16th-24th, for nine nights before Christmas both in Mexico and Hispanic communities. *Posada* means "lodge or inn." The families take part in processions that represent the Holy Family's search for lodging in Bethlehem long ago. Today, people either dress up to look like Mary and Joseph or carry nativity figurines as they march along the streets going from house to house asking for a place to spend the night. They are always refused until they reach the last home of the procession where they are accepted and a miniature stable is built and the nativity figurines are placed inside. Everyone sings religious carols and a party follows. On the last night of the processions, the people gather at the last house and then they all proceed to midnight mass together.

by Tania Kourempis-Cowling

TLC10100 Copyright © Teaching & Learning Company, Carthage, IL 62321-001

During this season you will see many brilliant piñatas. These colorful, hollow papier-mâché figures are filled with small toys and candies. The children take turns trying to break the piñata open with a stick while blindfolded. The piñata breaks and all the kids scatter picking up the treats. The following activities can be done in the classroom to enhance the study of Las Posadas.

Poinsettia Flower

This famous Christmas flower was discovered in Mexico by Dr. Pointsett. The red and green plant grows wild throughout this country. The old legend says that a poor girl wanted to give a gift to the Virgin Mary. The child had nothing to offer but some wildflowers. Miraculously, they turned into beautiful red and green star-shaped flowering plants. Using all kinds of art materials, cut, glue and create beautiful poinsettia flowers to decorate the classroom. Draw and cut five petal-shaped leaves and place these in a star formation. Attach several green leaves and add yellow seeds in the center.

Farolitos

Paper lanterns with candles are used to light the way during the processions. Today, these farolitos are called luminarias. Candles are placed in these special bags and then can be positioned around the room for shadows to be cast. Adult supervision is necessary with candles. To make the farolitos, use a brown lunch bag. Draw a simple pattern such as a star, bell or evergreen tree. Fold the bag in half. Draw only half the pattern along the fold and proceed to punch out holes along the design. Open the bag and place sand in the bottom. Insert a votive candle in the sand, and you are ready to light the farolito.

Piñatas

Piñatas can be made by the papier-mâché method using newspaper strips and flour paste placed over an inflated balloon. Or an easier piñata can be made using brown grocery bags. Stuff a bag with newspaper, candies and small toys. Tie a string around the open end leaving enough string to hang it from the ceiling. Decorate the bag with tissue paper, scraps of decorative trims and crepe paper streamers. Go on and play the game with your students. Individual piñatas can be made with small lunch bags, decorated, filled and used as treat bags.

St. Lucia's Day

In Sweden, Christmas celebrations start on December 13th, which is St. Lucia's Day. On the morning of this day, young girls in each family dress to represent St. Lucia, Queen of Light. She dresses in a long white robe, red sash and wears an evergreen wreath on her head adorned with candles. Sweden has long winter nights, so St. Lucia's candles represent the taking away of darkness. She serves a breakfast of saffron buns and coffee to her parents. If there are other girls in the family, they dress up also. Brothers are called star boys, wearing long white shirts and a cone-shaped hat decorated with stars.

From this day until Christmas, the homemakers and mothers are busy cooking special foods for this holiday. One of these dishes is called *lutfisk* made from fine fish of the season. Rice porridge *(risgrynsgrot)* has a special almond hidden inside. Whoever finds it is promised good fortune.

Decorating with straw animals is also a tradition. The straw symbolizes grain that represents food and prosperity. The *julgrisar* are yule pigs and the *julbockar* are yule goats.

In the classroom, you can present two projects to celebrate St. Lucia's Day. Have your students make candle crowns for the girls and star boy hats for the boys. Construction paper cut-outs work fine when assembled with glue. Next, make straw decorations in animal shapes. Have the children trace around pre-made stencils of goats and pigs. Color the animals and then glue real straw on top. You can easily find straw at a feed and grain store. Raffia could also be used and is found readily in craft stores. Cut out these shapes, punch a hole at the top and thread with ribbon as a hanger. These can be hung on the child's Christmas tree. If you have a cooking area, make this Swedish Christmas bread together. The recipe is:

Julekaka

1 loaf frozen bread dough (thawed)
1/2 cup candied fruit including raisins
1/4 teaspoon cardamom
1/4 teaspoon cinnamon

Roll out the dough in a big circle about 1/2" thick. Sprinkle on the spices and candied fruit. Roll up the dough and shape into a long roll. Place this on a greased cookie sheet. Let the dough rest and rise in a warm place for at least one hour. Bake the bread at 350°F for 30-40 minutes. Remove the bread and let it cool on a rack.

HANUKKAH

Hanukkah Card

After displaying some Hanukkah symbols such as candles, dreidels, menorahs, etc. Let students create their own greeting cards. Be sure students know the true meaning of Hanukkah so that they can add appropriate verses to the cards.

Star of David

Have students make their own Star of David. Put a variety of materials for this project and encourage the children to be as creative as possible. Some options might be:

> craft sticks, glue and glitter
> toothpicks and marshmallows
> stick pretzels and frosting
> playdough

Spin the Dreidel

If a dreidel is not available, try to find a top with four sides. On one side of the top write HAY, on another write SHIN, on another write GIMMEL and on the final side write NUN. Have students sit in a circle and take turns spinning. Each side of the top can represent a different action (singing, skipping, jumping, etc.) or treat. One person spins and does the action before the next person takes a turn.

Potato Pancakes

2 c. grated potatoes
1 sm. onion, grated
2 eggs
pinch baking powder
pinch salt and pepper

½ c. bread crumbs or
　matzoh meal
vegetable oil
applesauce

Mix all ingredients together except for oil and applesauce.
Heat frying pan with a little oil in bottom of pan. When hot,
spoon mixture into frying pan and make small pancakes.
When golden brown on one side, turn and cook other
side. Drain and eat with applesauce.

Menorah Decoration

Materials

menorah pattern (page 195)
colored construction paper
black construction paper

needle or pushpin
cardboard

Place menorah pattern on sheet of black construction paper. Place both sheets on cardboard. For
younger children, you may need to tape the sheet together. Using a needle or pushpin, poke holes
through the black dots. Tape or glue the black paper on a sheet of colored paper. Poke a hole in
the top and hand in a window or near a light. The light will shine through the holes making a beautiful Hanukkah decoration for your classroom.

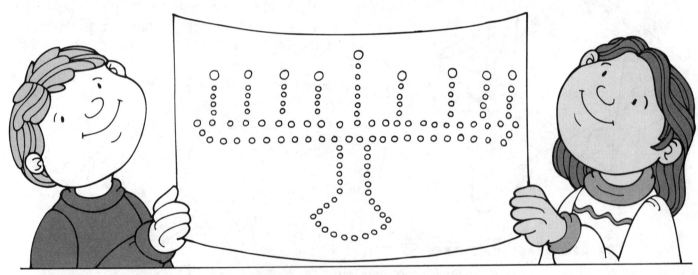

Children's Literature

Cohn, Janice. Illustrated by Bill Fransworth. *The Christmas Menorahs: How a Town Fought Hate*. Albert Witman, 1995.

Drucker, Malka. Illustrated by Eve Chast. *Grandma's Latkes*. Harcourt Brace, 1992.

Jaffe, Nina. Illustrated by Louise August. *In the Month of Kislev*. Viking, 1992; Puffin, 1995.

Kimmel, Eric. Illustrated by Trina Schart Hyman. *Hershel and the Hanukkah Goblins*. Holiday House, 1989.

Kimmel, Eric. Illustrated by Katya Krenina. *The Magic Dreidels*. Holiday House, 1996.

Minelli, Toli Marcus. Illustrated by Stewart Walton. *Chanukah Fun*. Tupelo, 1994.

Modesitt, Jeanne, compiler. Illustrated by Robin Spowart. *Songs of Chanukah*, Little Brown, 1992.

Moorman, Margaret. *Light the Lights*. Scholastic, 1994.

Cabbage for *Christmas*

The wind blew icy slivers of dust into Anna's eyes as she pedaled her rusty, blue bicycle into the courtyard of the teachers' compound. Anna shivered. The cold, harsh Chinese winter was so different from Christmas in Georgia. Back home in December it was often so warm that the roses were still blooming in her grandmother's garden.

Anna thought about last Christmas. She had been helping her grandmother bake rich, buttery pecan sands, her favorite kind of cookies, when Mother burst into the room.

"I got it!" her mother had shouted. "The invitation to teach in China next fall—I was selected. Just think, Anna, a year at the university in China. Won't that be grand!"

Dr. Jayne Smith, Anna's mother, worked as a professor of American literature at the University of Georgia. Sometimes ten-year-old Anna would go to class with her mother. Sitting quietly in the back of the room, she loved to hear her mother talk about American folktales and authors. Anna's favorite character was Tom Sawyer.

"We'll have a real adventure next year, Anna," laughed her mother. "Tom Sawyer may have seen the Mississippi River, but you will be seeing the Yangtze River, far away in China."

Georgia, pecan cookies and even Tom Sawyer seemed very far away as Anna hurried into the cramped, tiny apartment that she shared with her mother. The kettle was whistling on the rickety wood stove. Anna's mother called, "Did you bring the tea, Sweetheart?"

Anna carefully unwrapped the tin of green tea that was nestled in her basket. Hot tea would be good for Mother's cold. It seemed that Mother had been sick ever since they had arrived in China. And now it was Christmas. Anna sighed.

by Dr. Linda Karges-Bone

China was nothing like Anna had imagined. At the China Garden restaurant back home in Atlanta, the food was delicious and there was so much to choose from: egg rolls, fried rice, chow mein. But here in China, food was terribly scarce. Every day after her classes were over, Anna's mother scoured the town for eggs, peanuts, rice, vegetables or perhaps a bit of pork or fish. People stood in lines, patiently waiting for their turn to buy enough for that evening's meal. There were no grocery stores, just simple markets and a few small farms.

When Anna's mother walked up to the line, the townsfolk would stand aside out of respect for her position as a university professor. Still, Anna's mother waited her turn, too. In the larger cities, professors often enjoyed plentiful food and more lavish apartments, but in this distant province, the university was less important, and the food shortages were more difficult to manage.

The cold was hard to get used to. With only a wood stove to warm the small apartment, it was seldom very comfortable. Anna had learned to wear a thick sweater and cap almost all the time.

"This hot tea will taste wonderful, Anna," her mother said, smiling. "Thank you for going to fetch it. My tutoring students will be here shortly, and we must have something to offer them."
In addition to teaching four literature classes each day, Anna's mother and the other professors tutored students until 10 o'clock at night.

"Do you think that Mae Lin will come with her mother tonight?" Anna asked eagerly.

Mae Lin was the daughter of Ms. Smith's best student. She and Anna had become good friends. They attended school together in the compound. Anna loved to braid Mae Lin's shiny black hair into fancy designs. And Mae Lin would bring delicate, hand-painted combs to pull back Anna's red curls. Each girl thought that the other was beautiful, funny and smart. They had a wonderful friendship.

"Tell me about the pine tree that grows in your house," Mae Lin had asked that morning.

"Oh, silly, the tree grows in the woods. We cut it down, put it in a stand in our house and decorate it for Christmas," laughed Anna.

"And how does it smell?" Mae Lin had asked.

"It is just piney—woodsy—like Christmas," Anna said sadly.

"There is no 'piney' in China, and you are most sad," said Mae Lin.

"I guess I am sad today," agreed Anna. "Mother has a cold again, and Christmas is in two days. No cookies, no presents, no vacation from school. It doesn't even seem like Christmas."

"I am sorry," Mae Lin had said. Her almond-shaped black eyes looked troubled.

That evening as Anna and her mother prepared tea and set out books for the tutoring session, there was a knock at the door.

"Mae Lin, you are early!" Anna hugged her friend. Mae Lin's mother stood behind her, holding a covered tray.

"Merry Christmas," Mrs. Lin smiled. She offered the tray to Anna's mother. Lifting the cloth, Anna smelled a delicious, spicy smell.

"It is stuffed cabbage leaves," explained Mae Lin. "Mother mixes ground pork, onions, spices and mushrooms and rolls cooked cabbage leaves around the mixture. It is delicious."

"We have no pecans or pine trees in China," said Mrs. Lin. "Perhaps this will fill your stomachs and make you less lonely for home."

"Thanks you so much," said Ms. Smith. She smiled warmly at Mrs. Lin. "Let's all sit down and eat together." Mrs. Lin and Mae Lin politely said that they could not eat a bite. But Anna's mother insisted.

She knew that this special meal meant that the Lins had made a great sacrifice in their own home. "Please celebrate with us!" she urged. "It would honor our home to have you. Put some Christmas music on, Anna!"

Anna put her favorite cassette tape in the player. It was "Rudolph, the Red-Nosed Reindeer." Mae Lin looked puzzled.

"Do people in Georgia really believe in flying reindeer?" she asked Anna.

"Not really," laughed Anna. "It is just a fun song."

"It is a good song, I think," hummed Mae Lin. "You have cookies with nuts in them, trees growing in your house and flying reindeer in Georgia. I think that is most fun."

"It is fun," agreed Anna. "But whenever I think of Christmas from now on, I will think of cabbage rolls, too!" Anna and Mae Lin smiled and sipped their hot tea. Outside, the bitter Chinese wind blew fiercely. But inside the tiny apartment, it felt warm and cozy.

Fine Arts

1. Mae Lin and Anna enjoyed listening to traditional holiday songs such as "Rudolph, the Red Nosed Reindeer." Mae Lin thought the song might be about a real animal. Discuss familiar holiday songs. Where do they come from? What do they tell us about our traditions and beliefs? Why are songs so important to culture?

2. Create original Christmas cards to send to missionaries or teachers in another country. Ask a church group, a Peace Corps representative or an armed services officer to help you find an appropriate group. Use locally found materials, such as acorns, pressed flowers or old postcards of your town to make the cards distinctive.

3. Scents are an important part of holiday celebrations. Bring in examples of traditional holiday scents: pine, cinnamon, incense (from church rituals). How do scents make us feel? Create a holiday pomander by pressing whole cloves into a small, fresh orange. Each child can make his own scent ball.

4. Using red and green paint, scented with cinnamon or ginger (to promote creativity), and sponges cut into holiday shapes, create a holiday fresco to decorate the door of your classroom.

5. Go to the library or a local Chinese restaurant and borrow some tapes of traditional Chinese music. What kinds of instruments do you hear? What is the rhythm like? Borrow a set of rhythm instruments from the music teacher. Re-create some sounds that you hear in the Chinese music.

6. Check out the book from the Teaching & Learning Company, *Beyond Hands-On: Techniques for Using Color, Scent, Taste, Touch and Sound to Enhance Learning*, for more ideas in the area of creative arts.

Language Arts

1. Create a word list using chart paper, scented green markers (pine) and the children's input (whole group or small cooperative groups). Invite the children to submit words that fit under the category: "Familiar Holiday Things That Make Me Feel Safe and Happy." This is a language fluency activity.

2. Select words from the list generated in the prior activity or age-appropriate words selected from the story "Cabbage for Christmas," and use the words for your weekly spelling challenge.

3. Review the parts of a friendly letter. Then work in cooperative pairs to write a friendly letter to Anna and her mother. The purpose of the letter is to help them feel better about being away in China.

4. Use the CD Rom Encyclopedia to research American literature. Make a list of writers who might be included in that category. How does the character Tom Sawyer fit into this list? (Mark Twain aka Samuel Clemens)

5. Review one-, two- and three-syllable words. Discuss the ways that dividing words into syllables helps us to read and understand words. Make a three-column chart, and problem-solve to fill the chart with words from the story. Here is an example.

   One-Syllable Words: wind, blew
   Two-Syllable Words: Anna, into
   Three-Syllable Words: different, December

6. Parallel this story by reading the short story "Tom Whitewashes the Fence." Why do you think Anna liked the character Tom Sawyer? Why would Chinese students want to know about American literature?

Social Studies

1. Visit a Chinese restaurant to sample egg rolls and tea. This is less expensive than a full lunch. Go early in the morning so that you can make arrangements for the students to watch the chef prepare egg rolls, or even help.

2. Invite a few grandparents to come in and help make pecan sands, a traditional southern holiday treat. Eat some of the cookies for a treat, then pack a coffee can full to take to a local retirement home or nursing facility. In Chinese culture, the elders are treated with great care. How do we treat our elders?

3. Locate China on a map. On what continent is it located? What continent is your country located on? What oceans surround China? What can you tell about the climate of China from the story and from the map? Write your findings in your social studies journal.

4. Mae Lin and her mother spoke some English. We cannot tell from the story if Anna and her mother spoke Chinese. Do you think they did? Why or why not? More importantly, which dialect of Chinese did they speak? Divide students into groups of two or three. Use library resources to find the names of several Chinese dialects and the provinces in which they are spoken.

5. Why is cabbage an important crop in China? Make two lists. First, just think about the question and write your guesses. Then do some research as a group to answer the question. Then make another list. Compare your lists. Why are research and critical questions both important in social studies?

6. Anna and her mother came from the state of Georgia. Find Georgia on a U.S. map. In what region of the U.S. is the state located? Why was Christmas in Georgia so different from China? How does it compare to your state and region?

Values and Character Building

1. Discuss: What are the qualities of a good friend? How did Mae Lin and Anna demonstrate their caring for each other? Make a list of these qualities.

2. The story tells us that there are a lot of differences between Christmas in China and Christmas in Georgia. How can cultural differences teach us to appreciate one another? Make a sentence strip: My culture is special because _____, and the Chinese culture is special because _____.

3. What is the Christmas story? Who are the characters? What is the message? Use the Bible as a reference tool (the book of Luke). How is the celebration of Christmas important to what happens between the two families?

4. How can your class reach out to people who are lonely during the holidays? Create a simple class service project to fulfill this goal.

Holiday Gifts
Fast, Easy and Inexpensive

Children in first, second and third grades will all appreciate these small tokens of holiday greetings. You may wish to make more than one and surprise your students by putting them on their desks throughout the month.

Measure Up

Students can always use a ruler. Make a paper apple and on the front print: *No one measures up 2 U.* On the back print: *Merry Christmas to _____, from your teacher.* Attach the apple to the ruler with ribbon or yarn.

No one measures up 2 U.

Memory Book

Make a memory book for your students. Cut a Christmas tree shape for the cover. Glue school pictures on the tree and write *Merry Christmas to the "Tree" of You.* On the first page write a nice Christmas wish. Mention that you are giving the "gift of good memories." Fill the other pages with funny jokes and incidents that happened in your room. Make it as personal as you can and leave a page blank for students' autographs. Make a copy for each student.

Merry Christmas to the "Tree" of You

Erase Your Mistakes

Primary students never have enough erasers. Make a red and green paper tag. Print on it *May your right answers be many and your mistakes be few. A Christmas wish from your teacher to you!* Attach the tag onto an eraser with a pushpin or staple.

Homework Rock

Make these homework rocks using flat stones of any size. Cut green holly and red berries from felt or paper and glue to each stone. Attach the poem below.

Students can use their stone in place of homework one time whenever they wish during the month of December or January. Students find this gift most appealing and won't forget to use it!

I found this festive stone,
Under my Christmas tree.
I don't remember asking for it,
I wonder what it could be.

Attached was a note from Santa,
Telling me to share it with you.
It forgives you from doing your homework
One time . . . whenever you wish not to!

*by Jo Jo Cavalline and
Jo Anne O'Donnell*

137

Christmas Decorations

from Trash to Treasures

If you're like most teachers, you have numerous ideas for turning discards into room decorations or holiday gifts. Here are several more ideas for turning those resources into simple crafts. Your students will enjoy learning while being creative.

Cookie Cutter Ornaments

Choose cookie cutters with Christmas designs to turn plastic foam produce trays into holiday ornaments. Let children trace around the shape with a marker. Next, cut out the shape. Younger children may need help in handling scissors. Paste a school picture in the center. Punch a hole near the top. Hang on the tree with a Christmas ribbon. Children may take these home to place on their own tree.

Seasonal Note Paper

Cut potatoes into halves. Have an adult carve a star or other seasonal shape into the potato. Dip in red or green tempera paint and press on small sheets of writing paper. When dry, this becomes a collection of Christmas note paper to give a parent or older friend.

Festive Fruit Baskets

Send notes home requesting a piece of fruit or two from each child. Arrange them in a simple wicker basket. Cover with red cellophane paper and a big Christmas bow. Invite your school's custodians to stop by your room for punch and cookies. Ask them to join in singing a few Christmas carols. The children will be delighted to present their own decorated basket to each person.

Pencil Holder

Turn aluminum cans (such as vegetable or fruit cans) into attractive pencil holders for a parent's desk. File down any rough edges before children begin to work. Remove outside paper. Cover the bottom third of the can in school paste. Starting at the bottom, wind yarn or cord around the can. Add more paste and continue until the can is covered in yarn. Allow to dry. Spray with a heavy coating of hair spray.

Leather-Like Vase

No, it really isn't leather—it only looks that way! To make this unique craft, use an empty (clean) dressing bottle, such as French or honey mustard with a narrow neck. Tear 1" pieces of masking tape and cover the entire bottle. Rub brown shoe polish over the container. Rub off any excess. This makes an attractive vase for small dried flowers.

by Carolyn Ross Tomlin

'Twas the Night

'Twas the night before Christmas Eve
An evening quite cool.
Not a teacher was stirring
Throughout the old school.

The lights had been turned off
All books put away.
Everything was ready
For the next busy day.

Mrs. Tailor had straightened
All the books on her shelf.
If only she'd stayed late
She would have seen for herself,

That just after midnight
A bright light from the sky
Came down towards the old school
In the blink of an eye.

Upon further inspection
It would have been clear,
It was jolly old Santa
And his trusty reindeer.

He got into the school,
I don't know just how.
But Santa could do that,
Please listen carefully now.

Because what I'm about to tell you
You may not believe.
But this really happened
On a cold December eve.

Before Christmas Eve

Santa walked through the halls
And although poorly lit,
He happened to find
A place in the library to sit.

He reached for a book,
I don't know which one.
Santa began to read it
And when he was done,

He put it back on the shelf,
Got up on his feet,
Walked towards his sleigh,
And got into his seat.

Santa called to his reindeer
Up in the sky they did float,
And left on the ground
He wrote me this note.

It's a real simple message
The words on it are few.
Now at this time
I'd like to share it with you.

It said, "If you want to receive a gift
That you give to yourself,
Go to the library
And pull a book from the shelf."

by Al Rubeck

Cooking with Kids
Holiday Fun Fare

Veggie Wreath

Ingredients

lettuce, shredded
any variety of fresh vegetables, sliced and/or shredded
   (broccoli, cauliflower, carrots, celery, radishes, beans, cabbage, etc.)
licorice string

Arrange shredded lettuce in a wreath shape on a plate. Decorate with fresh vegetables. Top with a licorice string bow.

by Marie E. Cecchini

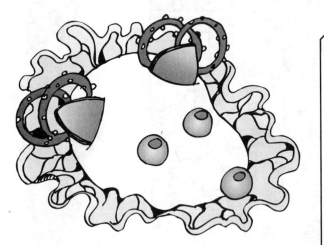

Rudolph Salad

Ingredients

lettuce leaf	cherries
pear half	cranberries, halved
almond slices	"3-ring" pretzels

Set the lettuce leaf on a plate. Lay the pear half on the lettuce leaf, flat side down. Add the cherry to the narrow end of the pear, for a nose. Use two cranberry halves for eyes. Push two almond slices into the pear near the back for ears. Push pretzels into the pear behind the ears for antlers.

Edible Ornament

Ingredients

lettuce, shredded	fruit cocktail, drained
English muffin, toasted	peanut butter
pineapple, sliced	

Cover a plate with shredded lettuce. Spread peanut butter on the toasted muffin. Set the muffin on the lettuce.

Decorate with fruit cocktail. Quarter a pineapple slice and set one of the pieces at the top of the muffin as a ornament hook.

Light Snack

Ingredients

saltine crackers
cream cheese, softened
red and green food coloring
sliced yellow cheese
carrot shavings

Mix cream cheese with individual food colorings. Spread tinted cream cheese on three crackers. Arrange the crackers in a vertical row on a plate, forming a candle. Top with a triangle-shaped piece of yellow cheese as the flame. Set carrot shavings around the bottom to make a candle holder.

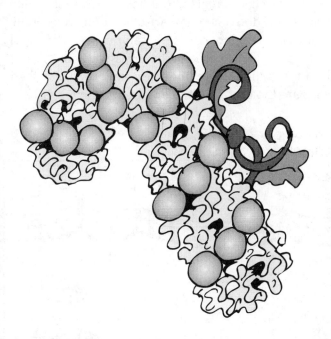

Candy Cane Creation

Ingredients

cottage cheese
cherries or strawberries
carrot shavings
celery leaves
flaked coconut

Spoon cottage cheese onto a plate in the shape of a candy cane. Decorate with cherries or strawberries. Add a carrot shaving bow. Arrange some celery leaves for "holly." Sprinkle with flaked coconut.

Christmas Mouse

Ingredients

lettuce leaf
hard-boiled egg
peanuts
whole cloves (for decorative purposes only)
cinnamon candies
licorice string
cheese, shredded

Set the lettuce leaf on a plate. Slice the egg lengthwise and set it on the lettuce, flat side down. Push two peanut halves into the egg near the narrow end for mouse ears. Push two cloves into the egg for eyes. Push a cinnamon candy into the front for a nose. Set a piece of licorice string at the back for a tail. Sprinkle shredded cheese onto the plate around the mouse.

The Nutcracker

First developed for Metropolitan Ballet of Wichita, December 1995. One of the staples of the holiday season is the production of *The Nutcracker*. From performances by local schools of dance and professional ballet companies to televised productions, motion pictures and video releases, chances are good that children are familiar with at least parts of the story. Your students will enjoy knowing the story, and these lessons will enhance their enjoyment.

Story Sequencing

At a center, provide children with 4$\frac{1}{2}$" x 6" sheets of blank paper. Have them draw their favorite parts of *The Nutcracker*, a different scene on each sheet of paper. Have them put the "snapshots" in order. Staple together and design a cover.

Math

The Kingdom of Sweets is sure to be very popular with children. Expand on this interest by using these activities. Purchase or gather a large supply of candy bars and/or wrapped candy. Use this candy in a number of ways: sorting, weighing, counting, identifying and tasting. Sort the candy according to the manufacturers and post the results. Find the favorite candy of each student and graph those results. List the first three ingredients of each candy bar. Sort by similarities and differences.

With older children talk about how much each candy weighs and do some comparisons. You can also talk about calories and compare calories per ounce of each candy. This can also be done with cost. Chart the most expensive to the least expensive and then compare the cost per ounce of each candy.

by Jeri A. Carroll and Pat Mhate Ngansa

144

Art

In an art center, children can be responsible for re-creating the different backdrops on butcher paper using tempera paint (Party Scene, Dream Scene and Kingdom of Sweets). When a team of children has finished their dancers, they can cut them out and attach them to the backdrops.

Music

Play different selections of *The Nutcracker* music for the students. Have them verbalize what scene of *The Nutcracker* is being played. Provide young children with sets of pictures of the different dancers. As the music is played, ask them to select the picture of the dancer they think is dancing and hold it up for you to check.

Cooking

Make gingerbread cookies with the class and decorate them. Or have some of the parents make the cookies ahead of time and let the children decorate them with tubes of frosting, sprinkles and other candies.

Language Art

As a class discuss *The Nutcracker*. As children tell you their favorite parts, give them a sheet of 9" x 12" storybook paper. Have them illustrate their favorite part and write about it at the bottom. Let each child illustrate a different scene. Ask the children to hold their pictures in front of themselves and try to put themselves in order with no talking. Read the story to them. Correct the sequence. Collect the sheets in order and staple together to make a class book.

Compare and Contrast

Have children bring nutcrackers from home or provide them with a variety of nutcrackers to examine. Usually discount stores carry them in various sizes as nutcrackers, ornaments or as decorations. In addition, get a metal nutcracker, one you might see placed in a bowl of nuts during the holiday season. Let children tell you how they are similar and different. Place the nuts and nutcrackers at a center. Let children try to crack the nuts (probably only using the metal nutcrackers), then eat them.

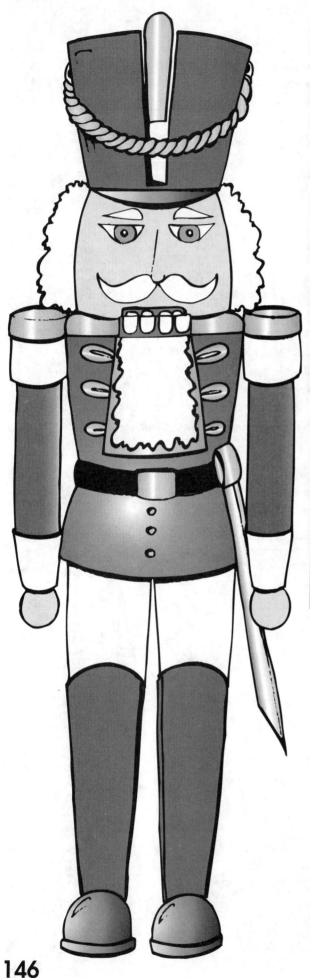

What If?

Directions

Use one of the story starters below. Write a new scene for *The Nutcracker.* Read your new story to a friend using the story of *The Nutcracker* and your addition.

Herr Drosselmeyer gave Fritz a nutcracker. Clara was jealous. She grabbed the nutcracker and threw it to the floor. Herr Drosselmeyer fixed it and give it back to Fritz. Later, Fritz couldn't sleep. Tell the story from this perspective.

How would the story be different if Clara and the Nutcracker Prince went to the Land of Rain in-stead of the Land of Snow?

What types of sweets might Clara and the Nutcracker Prince see in the Kingdom of Sweets? What might they look like? How might each dance?

What if Clara and the Nutcracker Prince visited the real places in your community? How would the story go? Where would they visit? Who would greet them? What gifts would they receive?

Many dancers from differ-ent countries brought gifts. What are some dancers from other countries and what might they bring?

Resources

There are many versions of the story in many different forms. Here are a few suggestions.

The American Ballet Theater and Mikhail Baryshnikov Production of **The Nutcracker**, MGM/UA Home Video.

George Balanchine's **The Nutcracker** *with Macaulay Culkin and the New York City Ballet*, Warner Home Video.

Nutcracker, E.T. Hoffmann. Tr. by Ralph Manheim. Illus. by Maurice Sendak. Crown, 1991.

Nutcracker, E.T. Hoffmann. Illus. by Lisbeth Zwerger. Adapted by Anthea Bell. Picture Book Studio, 1991.

Nutcracker Ballet. Retold by Melissa Hayden. Illus. by Stephen T. Johnson. Andrews & McMeel, 1992.

Nutcracker: A Story & A Ballet. Ellen Switzer. Photos by Costas Cara and Stephen Cara. Atheneum, 1985.

Challenge: Try to find the old 78 rpm recording of *The Nutcracker* by Fred Waring. It is presented as a choral piece with appealing orchestration and clever lyrics. It is a treat.

Party Scene

Illustrate your favorite part of the Party Scene. Draw the characters and color the backdrop.

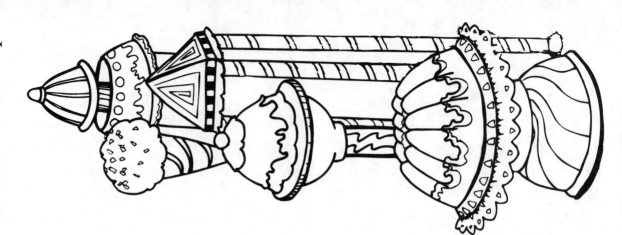

Kingdom of Sweets

Illustrate your favorite part of the Kingdom of Sweets. Draw the characters and color the backdrop.

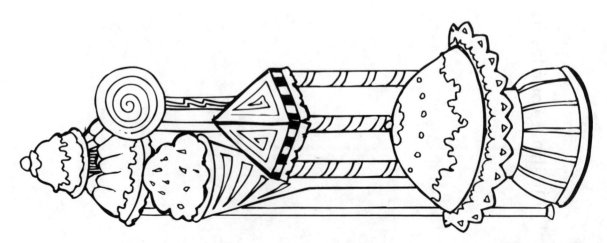

The Little Red Wagon

Words by Leonard Kirby

Music by Don Mitchell and Tom Brooks

1. In a large toy ___ store ___ high up-on a shelf, the
2. The __ day be-fore Christ-mas an old man and a boy, came

lit - tle red wa - gon sat all by him - self._____
in - to the store ____ look - ing for a toy. They

All the oth - er toys____ in the large store, were
looked at toy___ trains and most ev - 'ry - thing else, then the

sold for Christ-mas gifts just two days be - fore._____ On the
boy saw___ the wa - gon high up-on a shelf.____ "Oh___

rest of the shelves there were lots of hap - py toys, who
grand - pa! look up there," the lit - tle boy____ said, Please

knew that they would glad - den the hearts___ of girls and boys.___ The
buy me that wa - gon so bright shi - ny___ and red.___ Some

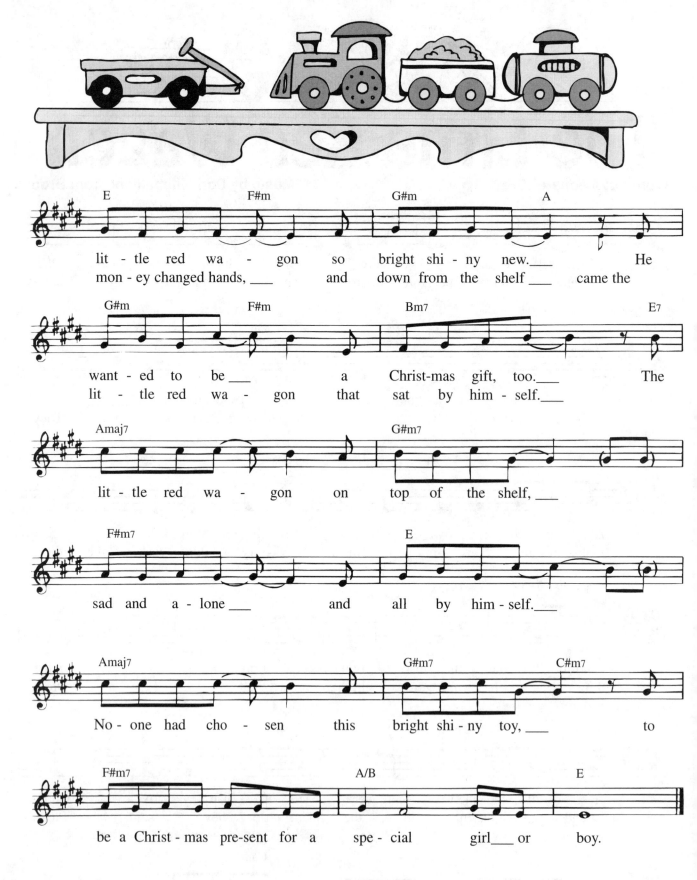

lit - tle red wa - gon so bright shi - ny new.___ He
mon - ey changed hands, ___ and down from the shelf ___ came the

want - ed to be ___ a Christ-mas gift, too.___ The
lit - tle red wa - gon that sat by him - self.___

lit - tle red wa - gon on top of the shelf, ___

sad and a - lone ___ and all by him - self.___

No - one had cho - sen this bright shi - ny toy, ___ to

be a Christ - mas pre-sent for a spe - cial girl___ or boy.

Verse 3

Now the top shelf is empty in this large toy store,
And the little red wagon is lonely no more.
He's loved and adored by a happy little boy
Who has made this little wagon his favorite toy.

Chorus 3

The little red wagon that sat on the shelf,
Isn't sad anymore, he's no longer by himself.
A little boy has chosen this bright shiny toy
To be a Christmas present that will bring him lots of joy.

150

Activities for "The Little Red Wagon"

Put Motions to the Song
Example: Verse 1

large toy store—spread arms way out to sides shoulder height

high upon the shelf—look and point upward

two days before—hold up first one finger, then the second finger

gladden the *hearts*—hand over heart

Let children help decide motions to use with other words such as *happy, sad, down* (Verse 2). Be careful to keep motions simple and don't get too many.

Retell the Story
Use a paper plate with a sad face drawn on one side and a happy one on the other. Retell the story in your own words, changing faces according to the wagon's feelings. Let children take turns, first with the teacher handling the faces, then the children. Children may even want to make their own paper plate faces.

Talk About Words That Describe
Sing or say the song again. What word tells about the wagon? (little, red, shiny, new) Encourage children to talk about their favorite toys (not games). Ask each one to bring a small toy to show the class. Elicit words that describe the toy. Put all the toys on a shelf. Later try remembering which was whose. Harder still: close eyes and try to identify a toy by the shape and feel.

Talk About Feelings
Sing/Say the grandson's words. How did the wagon feel in different situations (examples: high on the shelf after others were sold; when the little boy got him)? Ask children if they ever have those feelings? In what situations? What other feelings do we have? Which are good feelings? Bad ones? What can we do about bad feelings?

Make a Wagon
Paint a shoe or tissue box red (or child's choice of color). Cut four wheels from a tissue or paper towel tube, and glue wheels to the bottom of the box. Thread a 2" string through two holes in the front panel (teacher punched) and tie for handle.

Do a Choral Reading
To read the words instead of singing, divide the class into three groups: A—low voices, B—mixed voices, C—high voices. For reading: Verse 1—Group A, Chorus—Group B, Verse 2—Group C, Chorus—Group B, Verse 3—A and B, Last chorus—all groups.

Adapt the reading for presentation to parents or another student group. Make a large paper Toy Store banner, and use a bookshelf to display toys the students bring in. For the wagon, use a real one or make one from a small cardboard box. Position Group A to one side, Group C to the other side and B in the middle. A girl can act out the shopkeeper and two boys as the boy and his grandfather. As Verse 1 is read (by Group A), members of Group C, one by one, take toys off the shelf. In Verse 2, the boy should say the boy's quoted words.

by Elaine Hansen Cleary

Write a Creative Story

Pretend you are the little red wagon. Write the story of your life. Here are some questions to get you started: Where were you born? How did you get to the toy store? How did you feel when you first got there? Did you make friends there? What did it feel like to be on the top shelf? What was the little boy like? Where did he take you? How did he treat you? Were there any other children in his family? What did you and he do together that you liked best? Did he get another new toy that next Christmas? What happened to you then? Finish the story.

Listen to the Rhyming Words

Songs, like poems, often contain words that rhyme, or have the same ending sound. Some are spelled alike, such as *dew* and *few*. Others that sound alike may be spelled differently, such as *blue* and *few*. As you sing or read the song, listen for words that rhyme with *shoe* in Verse 1 (answers: new, too); with *more* in Verse 1 (store, before); with *bed* in Verse 2 (said, red); with *joy* in Verse 3 (boy, toy); and with *boy* in Verse 3 (toy, joy).

Write a two-line poem using two of those rhyming words or a four-line poem using the rhyming words at the ends of lines 2 and 4.

Follow Directions to Make a Wagon

Give each child an 8½ x 11" sheet of paper (red, if preferred) on which the teacher has drawn dotted lines 2" in from the edge on all four sides. Make the short lines at each end solid, and mark each corner square with an *X*.

Instruct students to listen (or read) carefully and follow these directions:
1. Fold along the two long dotted lines.
2. Fold along the two short dotted lines.
3. Cut along the four short solid lines.
4. Fold in the corner squares marked *X* at each end, forming a box.
5. Glue these squares to the end pieces they touch.
Hand out small squares of paper on which four circles are drawn. Cut out all four circles. Glue two circles on each side of the wagon for wheels.

Give each child a drinking straw that has a pencil mark 2" from one end. Bend the straw where you see the pencil mark. Flatten the short piece from the bend to the end of the straw. Glue that piece to the front of the wagon for a handle.

Multicultural Holiday Banners
Reusing Last Year's Christmas Cards

Materials
- thin dowel rod (about 10" long)
- piece of felt about 6" x 8"
- fabric pieces
- glue
- Christmas cards

Finally, here's something to do with last year's Christmas cards! Banners are becoming more and more popular everywhere you turn. Your students are all familiar with the many sizes and styles of banners that are available. You can make multicultural banners as a holiday project right in your own classroom.

Have students select a cultural theme for their banner. Make a list on the board: Kwanzaa, Hanukkah, St. Lucia's Day, Mexico, Hawaiian Joyeaux Noel and so on. On paper, sketch an idea for the banner. Encourage your students to use a symbol for their theme, such as a menorah, palm tree or a crown of candles.

Using the Christmas cards and fabric pieces, begin to cut and assemble the pattern for your banner. Use words and pictures from the cards. When your cultural picture is complete, be ready to glue it to your piece of felt. First fold over the top of the felt to make a pocket for the dowel rod, and secure it in place using glue. When the glue has dried completely, slide the dowel rod through. Now glue your cultural theme onto the felt to complete your banner. This activity is an ideal project for cooperative learning groups. Assign a leader for each group and allow the students to brainstorm before beginning. Make it a classroom contest. Hang the completed projects on a wall using pushpins under the dowel rods. You may also hang the banners with ribbon or string.

by Jo Jo Cavalline and Jo Anne O'Donnell

Home & School

Candy Letters

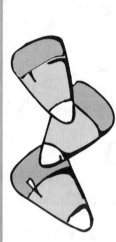

Candy corn can be glued to a black bulletin board background to make the caption "Trick or Treat." For a Valentine's Day caption, use red gummy hearts and inexpensive peppermints for Christmas displays. It is easy to find candies for most holidays. This idea also works well for borders when the candies are glued onto narrow strips. Adhere the candies with school glue and let lie flat 24 hours before putting up.

by Va Reane Hesse

Magnetic Pictures

Make magnetic pictures with old Christmas cards or old valentine cards. Cut special parts out of the cards or use the whole card. Laminate each one and add a magnetic strip to the back. Place them all on a magnetic board. Select one child each day to choose one special magnet until all students have received one. Children love to display them on their desks or at home. This idea could also be used as a countdown activity before a vacation or party.

by Karen Saner

KWANZAA

An African American Holiday

Kwanzaa is a nonreligious holiday honoring African American people and their past. Dr. Maulana Karenga, an African American teacher, first celebrated Kwanzaa in 1966. For seven days (December 26 until January 1), people learn more about the customs and history of Africa.

The term *Kwanzaa* means "first fruits of the harvest." This word comes from the Swahili language and represents all ethnic groups of Africa.

This holiday is for family and friends to spend time together and create their own customs. This celebration encourages learning more about Africa and the history of African Americans.

Food for Kwanzaa Celebrations

During Kwanzaa, help your students prepare African food in the classroom. Use the traditional foods of Africa to make a fruit salad for your Kwanzaa celebration.

2 lemons	2 apples
2 bananas	4 kiwi
$1/2$ pound seedless grapes	2 oranges, sectioned
1 cup nuts	$1/2$ cup coconut
2 cups cantaloupe or melon, cubed	$1/2$ cup sugar
water	

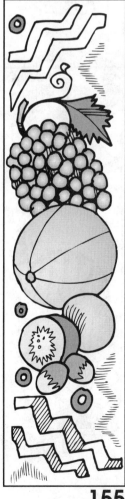

Cut the lemons in half. Squeeze the juice into a bowl. Set aside. Slice or cut the fruit in cubes. Combine in a large bowl. Sprinkle with the lemon juice.

Make a syrup of 2 cups water and $1/2$ cup sugar. Bring to a boil and cook for two minutes. Allow to cool and pour over fruit. Add coconut and nuts. Refrigerate until ready to serve.

by Carolyn Ross Tomlin

Kwanzaa Vest

While holding a Kwanzaa celebration in your class, allow the children to dress in their newly designed Kwanzaa vests. It is easy to make and here is what you need:

> brown grocery bag
>
> black, red, green and yellow paint
>
> scissors
>
> black, red, green and yellow yarn (optional)
>
> glue

Open the bag up fully. If there is an imprint on it, you may wish to turn it inside out when forming the vest. First cut a slit straight up the front of the vest. Then cut a round section for the neck. Place the bag around the child's shoulders and find the correct spot for the armholes. Cut two armholes so that the child can slip on the vest. Now allow the children to show their individuality and creativity by designing the vest for the Kwanzaa holiday. Make the paints and paintbrushes available to them. They can make stripes or designs using the Kwanzaa colors. If yarn is available, they can fringe the bottom of the vest by gluing yarn pieces of various colors to the hem.

by Jo Jo Cavalline and Jo Anne O'Donnell

156

Tu B'Shvat
The New Year of the Trees

Tu B'Shvat

Tu B'Shvat is a Jewish holiday that is celebrated in January or February. Its name means "the fifteenth of Shvat." Shvat is the fifth month in the Jewish calendar.

Tu B'Shvat is the New Year of the Trees. This holiday falls during the cold winter months in most of North America. In Israel, however, it marks the beginning of spring. At this time, almond trees are in bloom throughout Israel. Many people celebrate by planting trees.

In America, Tu B'Shvat has become a time to celebrate the environment. Some people observe the holiday with a special meal. They have readings, songs and prayers about nature. All kinds of fruits are eaten, especially those that grow in Israel.

Bean Tree

Purchase dry lentils, split peas, navy beans, kidney beans and any other large beans or seeds you can find. Provide each child with glue, beans and a sheet of stiff cardboard. Have students glue the beans onto the cardboard in the shape of a tree. They can use different colors for the trunk, the leaves and flowers. Keep the trees flat and allow them to dry thoroughly before displaying them in the classroom.

by Katy Z. Allen and Gabi Mezger

The Uses of Trees

Challenge students to think of the many ways in which trees are useful. With older students, have small groups work cooperatively to make lists and then share their ideas while you write them on the board. Have younger students simply suggest ideas. Remind students to think of uses in the natural world (such as providing places for birds' nests), as well as uses for people. How many ideas can they think of? Afterward, have each student pick one or two uses and draw a picture to illustrate it. Create a bulletin board with the title "The Uses of Trees."

The Lorax

Read the Dr. Seuss book *The Lorax,* or show the video. Afterward, discuss the story. Ask the following questions: Why do you think Dr. Seuss wrote this story? Do you think that what happened in this story could happen to our world? What can children do to help protect trees?

All Kinds of Fruits

Provide students with a variety of fruits with which they might not be familiar, such as carob, figs, dates, almonds, pomegranates, star fruit or whatever is available in your local supermarket. Take a survey to find out which fruits are the most popular.

Fruit People

Turn the fruit into people or animals. Give them eyes, mouths and noses.
Give them arms and legs. Color them.

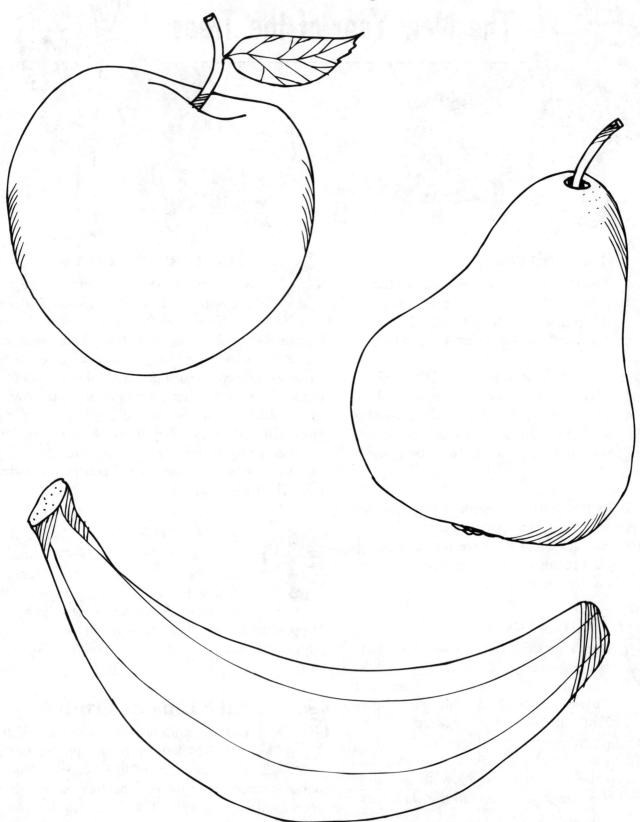

Math in Hebrew

The language of Israel is Hebrew. Hebrew is read from right to left. It has a different alphabet. In Hebrew, letters are also numbers. Below are 10 Hebrew letters and the numbers they equal.

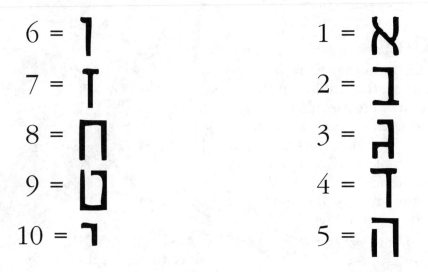

6 = ו	1 = א
7 = ז	2 = ב
8 = ח	3 = ג
9 = ט	4 = ד
10 = י	5 = ה

Try to do math in Hebrew. Add or subtract. Write the answer with regular numbers.

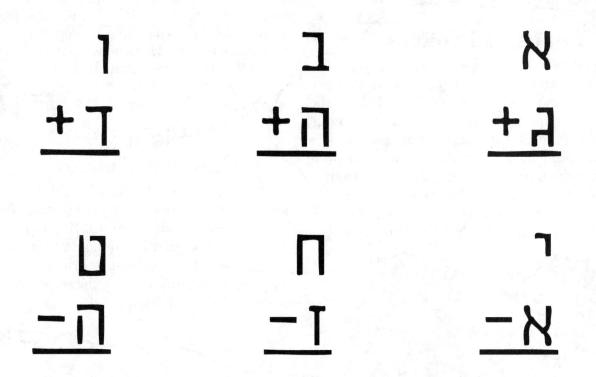

To Have a Dream

January 15th is the birthday of Dr. Martin Luther King, Jr., a man honored for his peaceful efforts to obtain equal political, social and economic rights for all groups.

Dr. King

Display a picture of Dr. Martin Luther King, Jr. or share pictures from a book. Ask the children if they know who he is. Have them contribute any ideas about why he is famous. Briefly discuss the term *rights* and prompt them for ideas as to what kinds of rights people in the United States have. Explain that Dr. King's dream or hope was that all people would be able to have the same rights. Ask the children for their thoughts on whether or not this dream has become a reality.

Differences

Introduce the concept of "different, but the same" by using inanimate objects, such as two pillows. Encourage the children to explain how they can simultaneously be different and the same. Have them search throughout the room for other objects that are also the same yet different and share their discoveries with the class. Relate the same idea to individuals in the class. Have them contribute observations about physical differences, even though they are all children.

Peaceful Progress

Explain to the children that Dr. King worked to change laws in peaceful ways such as speeches and marches. He was awarded the Nobel Peace Prize for his peaceful efforts towards change. Provide the children with paper, markers and scissors. Have them each create their own peace prize. Staple crepe paper streamers to each of their designs. Use safety pins to attach the peace prizes onto their chests to wear in honor of Dr. Martin Luther King, Jr.

Lights, Camera, Action

Invite individual children to role-play peaceful solutions to familiar situations. Suggestions: Two children wanting to play with the same toy. Someone borrowing a favorite toy, then losing it or breaking it. Someone being unkind to a sister, brother or friend.

by Marie E. Cecchini

Public Speaking

Share pictures of Dr. Martin Luther King, Jr. and others giving speeches from a *podium* or *lectern*. Introduce these words. Explore reasons why a speaker might use one. Have the children assist you in constructing a lectern from a cardboard box and brown paper. Tape a yardstick to the lectern for a microphone. Invite the children to take turns at the lectern and give a short speech about something they did that expressed kindness and fairness to another person.

If I Could

Ask the children to think about things they would like to do to make the world a better place for everyone to live. Provide them with paper and markers to make posters about Dr. Martin Luther King, Jr. or about the things they would like to do. Staple each poster to a sturdy cardboard stick. Have them march in their own peace parade, carrying their posters for a better world.

Dr. Martin Luther King, Jr.

Dr. Martin Luther King, Jr. had a special dream
(Put palms of hands together and rest cheek on them.)
That he wanted to share with others.
(Spread out arms.)
He wanted people to talk—not scream—
(Speak softly, cover ears on "scream.")
And all be sisters and brothers.
(Join hands with friends.)

All People

Share the following poem with your students and talk about what the last two lines mean.

Happy Birthday, Martin
Happy birthday, dear Martin.
Happy birthday to you.
We're learning to celebrate
All people, too.

Happy Birthday, Benjamin Franklin!

Just one of Benjamin Franklin's accomplishments would be enough to make him famous; it's amazing how many things this man invented and the achievements he made. He called himself a printer; however, his talents included that of a writer, diplomat, scientist, inventor, philosopher, educator and public servant.

Benjamin Franklin was born in Boston, Massachusetts, on January 17, 1706. He was the 15th child in a family of 17. His father, from England, was a poor soap and candle maker. Since education was expensive, Benjamin did not have much formal schooling after the age of 10.

In 1732, Franklin published his most famous work, *The Poor Richard's Almanac.* The almanac was a calendar and weather forecast for the year and contained jokes and proverbs. Franklin published under the pen name of Richard Saunders. Two famous proverbs of Poor Richard were "Early to bed, early to rise makes a man healthy, wealthy and wise" and "A rotten apple spoils his companions." Both the almanac and a newspaper he helped publish sold well. Franklin set up numerous print shops in other colonies and became wealthy enough to retire from business at the age of 42.

Benjamin Franklin was an active inventor throughout his adult years. He invented the Franklin Stove, which helped heat drafty homes. His most important work was done with electricity. He studied works of the European scientists where they stored electricity in special tubes. He tried these experiments himself and later published a book about electricity.

He conducted a famous experiment with his son, William, that intrigues all students. Franklin realized that lightning was a discharge of electricity from the clouds. The father-son team went out to a meadow and flew a kite during a thunderstorm. He attached a metal key to the bottom of the string. A charge of electricity went down the wet string, and as he placed his knuckle to the key, he saw an electrical spark. This proved his theory that lightning is electricity. He followed up this experiment by inventing the lightning rod to protect buildings from lightning bolts.

Benjamin Franklin organized a postal system. Before stamps were used, a person would collect his mail at the post office and pay for it. Because of unclaimed mail, money was lost. Franklin decided to print the names of people who had mail awaiting them. He set up a bookkeeping system. In 1753, Franklin was made Deputy Postmaster General for all the colonies. Mail was carried by stagecoach across the country; however, Franklin devised many ways to improve the system.

Franklin was an important statesman. He signed four important documents: the Declaration of Independence (1776), the Treaty of Alliance with France (1778), the Treaty of Paris (1783) and the Constitution (1787). He died on April 17, 1790. Today, look for Benjamin Franklin's picture on the U.S. $100 bill.

Try a few of the following classroom activities with your students as you study this famous man in the month of January.

by Tania Kourempis-Cowling

Deliver the Mail

Print each consonant on the front of an envelope. Give an envelope to each child in the classroom. Choose one child to be the letter carrier. This person carries a paper sack full of cards with pictures on them. The letter carrier pulls out a picture and tries to find the student with the correct envelope—the beginning sound of the object in the picture should match the letter on the envelope. Variations could be matching capital letters with lowercase; matching colors, shapes or numerals with dots on a card and so on.

Paper Plate Kite

Glue strips of crepe paper to one side of a paper plate. Tie a yarn handle to the opposite side of the plate. Let the students hold on to the yarn handle and run with the kite to make it fly. This is a great art project, as the children color and decorate the plates, and then take them outdoors for a fun running and flying experience.

Kite Picture

Copy a drawing of Benjamin Franklin. Cut out the drawing and glue it onto light blue construction paper. Make a kite out of colorful paper, fabric or wallpaper. Glue this onto the paper, along with string, to make a kite picture. Draw dark clouds and lightning bolts. Don't forget to attach a cut-out key shape.

Poor Richard's Proverbs

Match the beginning of the proverb with its ending
by placing the correct letter in the blank.

_____ An apple a day

_____ A bird in the hand

_____ Little strokes fell

_____ Look before

_____ Early to bed, early to rise

_____ An ounce of prevention

a. is worth two in the bush.

b. great oaks.

c. is worth a pound of cure.

d. keeps the doctor away.

e. you leap.

f. makes a man healthy, wealthy and wise.

National Handwriting Day
January 23

Practice writing *welcome* in different languages from other countries. See if you can copy the following writing samples. Get a taste of handwriting from around the world!

Korean 환영 합니다 ---------------------------

Hebrew ברוך הַבָּא ---------------------------

English Welcome ---------------------------

Russian Добро́ пожа́ловать ---------------------------

Arabic أهلاً وسهلاً ---------------------------

Chinese 歡 迎 ---------------------------

Japanese ようこそ ---------------------------

by Donna L. Clovis

Mardi Gras

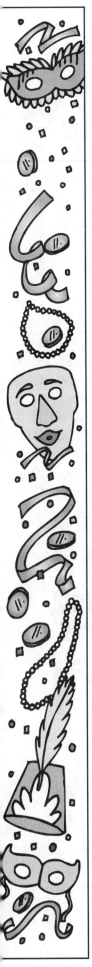

In the South, just say the words *Mardi Gras* and children, as well as adults, think of fun, fantasy, mystery and merriment. Explore the meaning and history behind the yearly carnival celebration.

The Beginning of Mardi Gras

Mardi Gras, or Carnival as it is sometimes called, is the celebration time of Christians before the season of Lent. The Christians were once required by their church to fast from meat, eggs and dairy products during the Lent period before Easter. The word *carnival* comes from the Latin words that mean "the taking away of meat." Therefore, before this fasting period began, the people celebrated heartily by indulging in rich foods, dance and masquerade.

Mardi Gras is celebrated all over the world. Its name is different in different countries. For example, the Germans call it *Fasching* and the Polish call it *Zapusty*.

Calendar Calculations

Mardi Gras is calculated by use of the Gregorian calendar and lunar aspects, as well. Easter occurs on the first Sunday after the first full moon, after the vernal equinox. That is why the date is different from year to year. The 40 days before Easter are called Lent. The last day before Lent is called Fat Tuesday, the most famous day of the Mardi Gras celebration. The festivities go on for a week or two prior to Fat Tuesday.

Mardi Gras Today

Mardi Gras is a time of merriment for all and is celebrated throughout the United States. However, big parades are seen and broadcast on television throughout Mobile, Alabama; New Orleans, Louisiana, and other towns along the Gulf Coast, even into the panhandle of Florida. Everyone is busy during this holiday season. Parade floats are constructed, costumes are sewn, trinkets are manufactured, cakes are baked and children are engaged in decorating their schools and the community with their artwork.

King Cakes

King Cakes are found in bakeries beginning in early January (Epiphany), officially starting the Mardi Gras season. In European countries, the Feast of Epiphany is celebrated to honor the coming of the Wise Men bearing gifts to the Christ Child. The baking of King Cakes has long been a custom. Europeans bake an almond inside, and the person who receives it in their piece of cake must portray one of the Magi, also receiving good luck. Today, Americans put a small plastic baby figurine inside, and the person receiving it must bake or bring the next King Cake to the parties. King Cakes are oval, ringed danish cakes filled with fruits and sweets. They are topped with icing in the royal colors of Mardi Gras—purple (justice), green (faith) and gold (power). King Cake season ends on Fat Tuesday, the day before Lent.

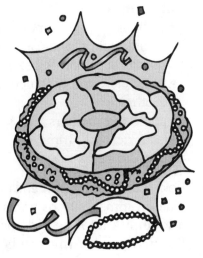

by Tania K. Cowling

165

Celebrating in the Classroom

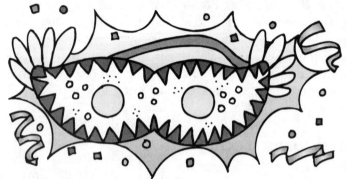

Mardi Gras Masks

Students can make their own masquerade masks from poster board. Cut out a mask shape. Collect decorating trims in the festive colors of purple, green and yellow (gold). Glue on sequins, feathers, glitter, lace and so on. Attach a piece of elastic to the back of the mask with a stapler so it will fit the child's head.

Toy Floats

Gather several boxes of different sizes (jewelry boxes are perfect for this project). Cover these with tissue or construction paper in Mardi Gras colors. Glue the boxes together to make a float replica. Add decorative trims, make paper flags, use stickers, attach plastic people or animals—all to make an authentic-looking parade float. Place the children's floats along a shelf to make a street parade display.

King Puppets
You will need:
- 1 shoulder pad (removed from an old sweater or blouse; colored fabric ones are best)
- round Styrofoam™ ball or Ping-Pong™ ball
- tacky glue or low temperature glue gun
- toothpick
- paint and markers
- lace, rickrack, trims, etc.
- chenille strips

Fold the shoulder pad ends to meet in the center. Glue these together to look like a robe. You can also glue on trims, buttons and so on to make the character. Paint facial features onto the round ball. Poke a toothpick into the ball and then insert this head into the top edge of the shoulder pad puppet. Glue this into place. Arms can be made by wrapping chenille strips (pipe cleaners) around the head portion and shaping these into arms. The child can then place their finger into the bottom edge of the shoulder pad to manipulate their puppet's actions.

King Cupcakes

Make cupcakes for the class according to package directions. This could be a class cooking project or brought in from home. The fun part is making the royal icing. Place confectioner's sugar into three bowls. Moisten the sugar slightly with water to make a frosting consistency. Add drops of food coloring to make Mardi Gras colors.

> Purple—drops of red and blue
> Green—drops of yellow and blue
> Yellow—drops of yellow

Spread this thin icing on top of each cake. Add multicolored sprinkles for a festive look.

Junk Jug Shaker

Make a parade even more festive by creating rattling sounds to go with the music. A homemade instrument that could add these sounds would be a "junk jug shaker." Each child will need an empty milk or juice jug with a handle. Then have fun collecting objects to place inside for noises. Items like wooden beads, jingle bells, dried beans, pennies, pebbles and so on could be used. Apply glue to the inside of the jug lid before screwing it into place. Have the children hold the jug by its handle and shake it up and down as they march around the room.

Bead Necklaces

There are two types of homemade necklaces that can easily be made in the classroom. You can make a clay mixture and roll beads, or string colorful pasta. Here is one recipe for salt dough (there are many others in art books). Mix 1 cup salt, $1/2$ cup cornstarch and $3/4$ cup water in a pan. Stir these ingredients over low heat. After the mixture has thickened, in about three minutes or so, place it onto waxed paper. Let the dough cool slightly and then proceed to knead it until smooth. Roll the dough into small balls and push a plastic straw through the center to make a threading hole. Allow the beads to air dry thoroughly.

Optional: Purchase multicolored pasta or tint regular pasta by using food coloring. Dip the pasta into a bowl containing water, food coloring and a teaspoon of rubbing alcohol. Leave the pasta in this mixture only long enough for the pasta to tint, and then quickly remove it to air dry on waxed paper. Thread the beads or pasta onto a length of yarn. Tie the ends together after measuring around the child's head for size.

Mardi Gras Resources

Coasting Through Mardi Gras—A Guide to Carnival Along the Gulf Coast by Judy Barnes, Jolane Edwards, Carolyn Lee Goodloe and Laurel Wilson. Copies can be obtained by writing to: Coasting, P.O. Box 25, Point Clear, AL 36564

Arthur Hardy's Mardi Gras Guide ($6.50). Write to: P.O. Box 19500, New Orleans, LA 70179

Tourist Information: Call (504) 566-5005
Computer Advice: http://www.nawlins.com

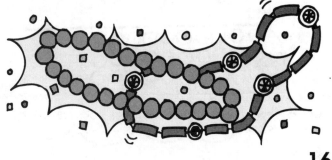

February
Children's Dental Health Month

by Jo Jo Cavalline and Jo Anne O'Donnell

Dental health is a very important part of a child's development. To encourage good dental health, discuss the proper care of teeth and the importance of seeing a dentist. Try the following activities during Children's Dental Health Month.

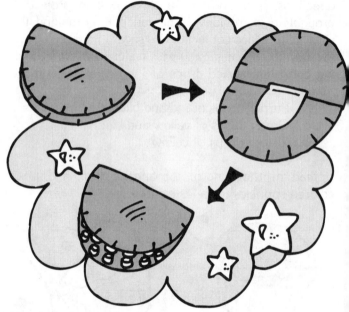

Davey Dentist's Mouth

Materials:
- paper plate (not Styrofoam™)
- red construction paper
- 32 white miniature marshmallows
- glue
- scissors

Fold the paper plate in half to create a mouth shape; then open it up again. Cut a tongue from the red construction paper, 3 1/2" x 2 1/2", and round one end. Glue the tongue in the center of the paper plate. Glue 16 marshmallows around the top of the plate and 16 marshmallows around the bottom of the plate for teeth. Have the children review their dental health lessons by making Davey Dentist's mouth open and shut like a puppet.

Toothbrush

Materials:
- poster board, 15" x 3"
- 30 foam packaging pieces
- glue
- scissors

Round the edges of the poster board as shown. Glue the foam pieces on one end of the poster board to form the bristles of the toothbrush.

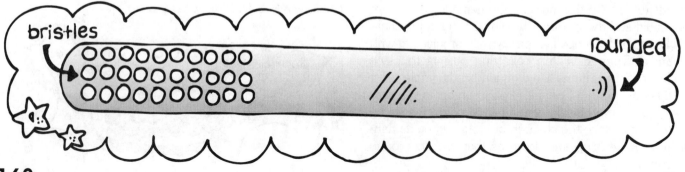

bristles

rounded

168

Tooth Poem

When I smile I want you to see
My teeth as white as they can be.
I brush them morning, noon and night
So they will stay shiny and bright!

Bulletin Board

Have the children bring in pictures of people showing their teeth when they are smiling. The pictures
can be from magazines, newspapers, food containers or from their family albums. The title of your bulletin board could be "Smile and the World Smiles
with You" or "Smile–It's Contagious" The bulletin
board will generate discussion and smiles.

Riddle: What is the longest word in the dictionary?

Smiles. There is a mile between the two Ss!

Brush Your Teeth Song

(To the tune of "Row, Row, Row Your Boat")

Brush, brush, brush your teeth,
  *(Use index finger and pretend to brush
  teeth.)*
Brush them every day.
  (Continue to brush.)
Brush them up and down and 'round.
  (Brush as stated.)
Brush in every way!
  (Brush in all directions.)

by Judy Wolfman

CHINESE NEW YEAR

Teacher Background

Chinese New Year is among the many holidays and customs of the Orient—it is probably the best known. At midnight on the 20th of February, the new year begins. This joyful and ceremonious holiday is celebrated with lion and dragon dances, fireworks, parades and eating special foods. The most common customs for families during this happy season are cleaning house, paying off debts, showing respect to older family members, giving and receiving money and sharing food with visitors.

Cleaning house is required to get rid of all bad fortune of the past, and it must be done during the last few days of the old year. Paying off old debts allows one to start the new year with a "clean slate." Food is important symbolically. Eating pink cake and red fruits means you will have good luck. Fish and pork symbolize a good harvest and that all wishes will come true. Excitement is in the air. Everyone wears new and colorful clothing to visit family members. It is customary for the children to receive money tucked away in red envelopes!

The worship of Buddha is part of the Chinese religion. It is said that he promised gifts to all the animals who came to pay him homage. Twelve animals came in the following order: rat, ox, tiger, rabbit, dragon, snake, horse, ram, monkey, cock, dog and boar. A year was named after each one. This makes up the 12-year Chinese zodiac. Each animal is used to identify a new year. The year is believed to have the characteristics of the animal it represents. Many believe that people born in a certain year will have some of the same characteristics of that animal and that the year will also determine what their life will be like!

Firsthand Experiences

If you know adults of Chinese background, perhaps one or several would be willing to be a guest speaker for the class. A field trip might be arranged to a local Chinese restaurant, where students could go "behind the scenes" and watch the preparation of different foods. Several Oriental cooking shows on television might be viewed.

Folk Wisdom

Philosophy can provide students with deep insights and understanding regarding different cultures through literature, the arts and the particular beliefs of that group. Read and discuss each of the following Chinese proverbs with students:

A lean dog
shames his master.

Even a bad coin
has two sides.

Done leisurely, done well.

After discussion, students can illustrate the proverbs. A class book might be started, adding sayings, stories and proverbs students find from other cultural groups.

by Teddy Meister

Chinese Zodiac

Year	Animal	Personality
1986	tiger	rebellious
1987	rabbit	happy
1988	dragon	lucky
1989	snake	wise
1990	horse	popular
1991	ram	charming
1992	monkey	mischievous
1993	rooster	aggressive
1994	dog	worried
1995	pig	gallant
1996	rat	nervous
1997	ox	patient

The cycle is repeated every 12 years.

Action Collage

Provide magazines and newspapers for cutting. Divide the class into 12 small groups. Assign each group an animal from the Chinese zodiac list and tell them to cut out pictures of that animal. Mount these on a large sheet of art paper, adding the year each represents. Display these as a colorful bulletin board collage.

Every Twelve Years

Make a copy of the Chinese zodiac chart for each student, or prepare one on a large chart for class use. The 12-year cycle starts with the rat. Have students identify which animal represents the current year. Next year? The year 2000? Can they determine the animal for the year they were born? The year they first started school?

Red Means "Good Luck!"

If you lived in China, the Chinese New Year celebration would be a very exciting day for you. At the end of all the day's activities, the children are tucked into bed . . . but that's fun for the Chinese children! While the children are asleep, their parents place money in a red envelope and put it under the children's pillows. Chinese families use red envelopes because red means "good luck."

Activities

- Surprise your children by slipping red envelopes in their desks while they are out of the room. If you don't want to use money in the envelopes, give certificates for special privileges (for example, lunch with the teacher, an extra recess, a classroom movie, free reading time, no homework).

- Have children make red envelopes and tuck a surprise inside for friends, parents or someone special. To make the envelope, cut out the pattern, trace on red paper, cut out, fold on the dotted lines and paste the edges. Place a surprise inside!

- Discuss the similarities between the red envelopes of the Chinese people and the Tooth Fairy which is popular in the United States.

by Jo Jo Cavalline and Jo Anne O'Donnell

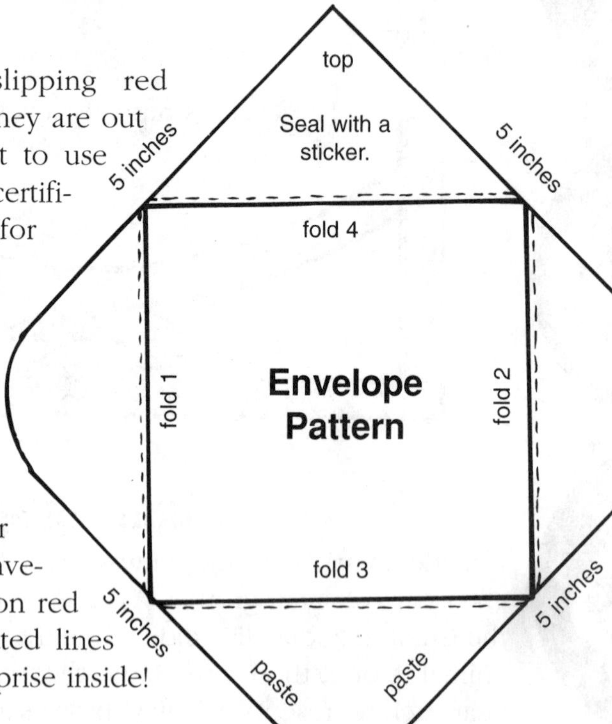

top

Seal with a sticker.

5 inches

5 inches

fold 4

fold 1

Envelope Pattern

fold 2

fold 3

5 inches

5 inches

paste

paste

It's Free!

As of this writing, the following address is current for requesting free information:

The Asia Society
112 East 64th Street
New York, NY 10021

It's Groundhog Day

The Groundhog

The groundhog comes out of the ground.
> *(With thumb and forefinger of left hand, make a circle.*
> *Stick forefinger of right hand through it.)*

First he looks up; then he looks down.
> *(Stick finger way up, then bring it down.)*

If he sees his shadow, he runs back inside
> *(Quickly bring finger out.)*

For six more weeks, where he stays and hides.
> *(Put finger behind back.)*

by Judy Wolfman

There are many vital statistics about the groundhog that can be quite interesting for you and your class to know and discuss.

Common Name: groundhog or woodchuck

Family: They are members of the rodent family and the largest species of the squirrel family. They are also related to gophers, which are also called prairie dogs and beavers.

Average Weight: Around 10-15 pounds

Average Length: 1 to 1½ feet long

Coloration: Brownish-black with yellow highlights

Life Span: About six years in the wild and between 10-15 years in captivity

Range: The types we see live in the eastern United States and in southern and eastern Canada.

Population: There is a large amount of these animals. There's as many woodchucks as there are raccoons and opossums, mostly in the rural areas rather than the city.

"To see or not to see its shadow" is the question of the day on February 2. It's officially Groundhog Day when this small creature predicts the upcoming seasonal weather. The legend states that if the groundhog comes out of his burrow and sees his shadow, we're in for six more weeks of winter. If no shadow is seen, spring is on its way.

Many years ago in England, Scotland and Germany, the folk belief was that hibernating animals would awaken in mid-winter to check the weather and decide whether to go back to sleep or stay up for spring. February 2 seemed to be the day of choice. This custom was brought to the United States by German immigrants in the late 1800s. They settled in an area of Pennsylvania called Punxsutawney, which is 100 miles northeast of Pittsburgh.

Punxsutawney Phil is the world's most famous groundhog. He is the one that television networks and national publications arrange to see and film. Phil lives the life of the rich and famous as he resides in a custom-designed den at the Punxsutawney, Pennsylvania, library. He is a tourist attraction, and once a year he treks up to Gobbler's Knob for the shadow ritual, which has been a tradition since 1886. If you need more information about famous Phil, use the following sources to find out what you want to know.

The Punxsutawney Chamber of Commerce 1-800-752-PHIL

Phil's Fan Club ($7.50 a year)
Punxsutawney Groundhog Club
Chamber of Commerce
124 W. Mahoning Street
Punxsutawney, PA 15767

A gift catalog of custom souvenirs is also available through the Chamber of Commerce.

Computer Web Site:
http://www.groundhog.org

by Tania K. Cowling

Lunch Bag Puppet

Duplicate copies of the groundhog above. Have the children color and decorate it. Cut out the two pieces and glue them onto the lunch bag to make a puppet. Then have children place their hands into the bags to manipulate the puppets.

Groundhog Art

Tell the children to pretend they are groundhogs. You have awakened and are looking outside your burrow. What do you see?

Have students draw and color a picture. Share each picture with the class.

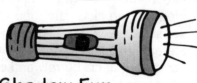

Shadow Fun

Use flashlights or spotlights to play these games.

1. Pick a spot on the wall or floor. Guess where to place your finger so that the shadow touches the spot.
2. Use various objects to create shadows. Does the object always cast the same shadow?
3. Make a big shadow. Make a small shadow. (Move close to or far from the light to create these images.)
4. Make your own shadow dance, wave, twirl around, fall down, jump and so on.

Shadow Partners

Have children pick a partner and pretend to be each other's shadow. The children face one another. One child moves, making obvious motions, while the other child tries to mirror what the first one is doing. Take turns trying both roles.

Pop-Up Puppet

Your students can make pop-up puppets using paper cups and tongue depressors. The paper or foam cups can be decorated with markers and stickers. On a tongue depressor, the children can draw the face of a groundhog. Cut a slit in the bottom of the cup and insert the stick. The children can raise or lower the groundhog by pushing the depressor up and down from under the cup.

174

Groundhog Day Bulletin Board

Ode to the Forecaster

Groundhog, Groundhog,
Please tell us what to do.
Should we wax our sleds?
Or will the sky be blue?

Groundhog, Groundhog,
Tell us what to do.
Please tell us, Groundhog,
We're counting on you!

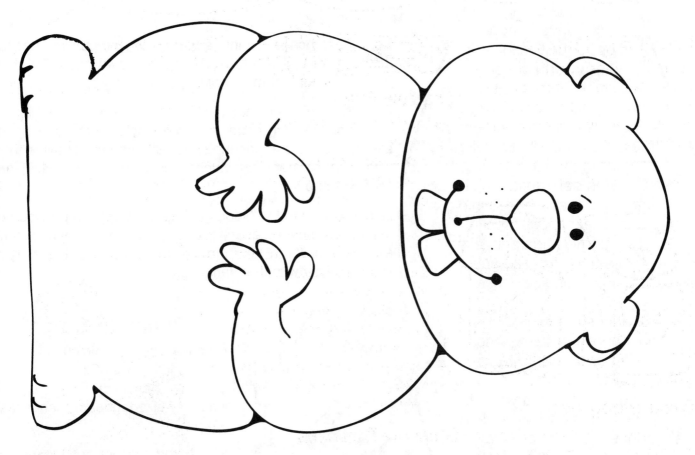

Make groundhog puppets on a stick. Use while reciting the poem. On February 2, when the groundhog makes his prediction, write his reply in rhyme. Example: No, no there won't be snow.
Right into spring we go!

You can also use this as a bulletin board activity as shown. Give each child a groundhog and let him or her predict if the groundhog will indeed see his shadow.

by Jo Jo Cavalline and Jo Anne O'Donnell

Quick, grease the griddle! Pancake Day is February 2, if you happen to live in France. In England, Shrove Tuesday is the day for flapjack festivities. In the U.S., there is a whole week during February. Pancake Day in France brings opportunities for a year's worth of good luck. Grown-ups challenge themselves to toss pancakes in the air and catch them in a pan, while holding a coin in the other hand. Children gain good luck by finding a thread baked into a pancake. Festivities in England include pancake races and pancake-eating contests.

Chances are that you would not choose to have pancakes flying and skillets waving in your classroom, nor would you wish to send your students home with stomach-aches, but Pancake Day can still be fun. Try these activities for a fun-filled Pancake Day.

by Gloria Trabacca

Pancake Mix Measuring

- complete pancake mix (just add water)
- zippered plastic bags
- measuring cups and spoons
- 1 penny for each child
- large bowl

Pour the pancake mix into a large bowl and provide measuring cups for children to use to fill their own bags. Tell them how many cups of mix to place in their bags.

For older children, make this activity more challenging by removing the one-cup measure and replacing it with assorted sizes of measuring cups and spoons. Provide them with measurement equivalents, such as 3 tsp. = 1 T. and 16 T. = 1 cup.

Tape a penny to the Good Luck card (directions provided on the following page), attach the card to the bag of pancake mix and have children take them home and share the story of Pancake Day with their families.

Pancake Catch

- smallest size plastic cups
- 18" lengths of string (one per child)
- quarter-size tagboard "pancakes"
- tape

Have students cut out a tagboard pancake. Tape the pancake to one end of a length of string. Tape the other end of the string to the inside bottom of the paper cup. Have fun trying to flip the pancake into the paper cup "pan."

Pancake Good Luck Cards

Make copies of the card pattern below. Provide tan crayons and brightly colored yarn. Punch holes where marked around the edges of the cover page, and at the top of the inside page. Students may first color their cards, and then lace yarn around the cover page. Have students begin and end the lacing at the top of the pan-cake. The final few stitches should pass through both pieces of paper to attach the front and back of the card. Or cards may be stapled at the top. In this case, omit holes from the second page of the card. Send Good Luck cards home with a pancake mix gift.

In France, today is Pancake Day,
with food to eat and games to play.
They flip a pancake in the air
and catch it if they may.
If they catch it, then good luck
will be theirs all year through.
So, I'm bringing you this card,
and you can try for good luck, too!

Books to Read

Pancakes for Breakfast by Tomie de Paola. Harcourt Brace Jovanovich, 1978.

The Pancake by Anita Lobel. Greenwillow Books, 1978.

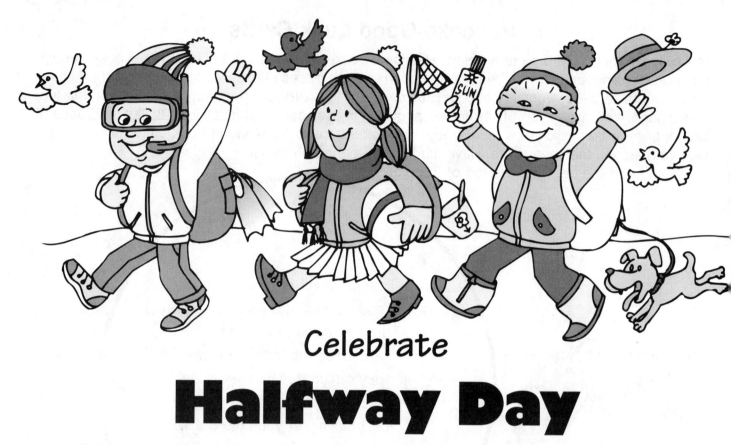

Celebrate

Halfway Day

February 4th is Halfway Day, the day when we are halfway through winter. Celebrate by "searching for the sun."

"Sun"glasses

Make "sun"glasses out of paper plates, paint, glitter and yarn. (Remember to make these a day ahead so they can be worn on Halfway Day.)

- paper plate halves with eyeholes precut
- yellow and orange paint
- gold glitter
- yarn in complementary colors

Provide each student with a paper plate half. They can first cut "rays," and then paint their sun bright orange and yellow. If desired, gold glitter may be sprinkled on the wet paint to help the sun shine! Punch one hole in either side of the sunglasses, thread with yarn and tie to fit each child.

by Gloria Trabacca

178

You Are My Sunshine

Sit in a circle and sing "You Are My Sunshine." Take turns choosing emotion and color words to substitute for *happy* and *gray*.

Seashell Hunt

Hide two or three sizes of seashell macaroni in your classroom and have a treasure hunt. Assign a number value to each size. Who has the most shells? Who has the least? Whose shells have the most or least value? Have the class choose different number values. Which answers will change? Whose shells have the most/least value now?

Beach Collage

- construction paper
- sand
- seashell pasta
- crayons
- glue

Make a beach collage, starting with crayons and torn paper. Add sand and seashell pasta to make a beautiful beach to take home.

Picnic at the Beach

Spread out beach blankets and have a sunny day picnic. Slice oranges into sunshine circles or serve pineapple rings with pretzel stick rays.

Sandcastles

Put damp sand in your water table, along with pails, shovels and various containers for making sandcastles (margarine tubs, yogurt cups, etc.). Challenge students to build a two-story castle or a tunnel that doesn't collapse.

HAPPY BIRTHDAY, ABE!

Abraham Lincoln's birthday is celebrated in many of the United States. Some celebrate the anniversary of his birth on February 12th, his actual birthday. Others celebrate it on the first Monday in February. Still others include Lincoln's birthday in their Presidents' Day celebration on the third Monday in February. By including a celebration of Abraham Lincoln's birthday in your February schedule, you can help students learn more about this great man.

Named After Lincoln

Many buildings, parks, streets and towns are named after Abraham Lincoln. Find out if anything in your town is named for him. Use an atlas to find out how many United States cities and towns are named Lincoln. Which state is called the Land of Lincoln?

If I Were President

Abraham Lincoln was the sixteenth President of the United States. Two important things that he accomplished during his presidency were freeing the slaves and keeping the United Sates together. Ask students to share what they would do if they were President.

Heads and Tails

Look at the tails side of a penny. What building is pictured? The first Lincoln head cents did not have the Lincoln Memorial pictured on them. The memorial was added in 1959 to celebrate the 150th anniversary of Lincoln's birthday.

Examine the picture of the Lincoln Memorial. Can children see the statue of Lincoln? The Lincoln head cent is the only United States coin with the same person pictured on the front and back.

Have the students design a coin with their picture on the front. What would be pictured on the back? What would be the value of their coin?

Abe's First House

When Abraham Lincoln was born, his family lived in a small, one-room log cabin. What toy used for building is named after Lincoln? Invite students to construct log cabins from this toy, or from sticks and twigs.

Abe's Coin

Ask students which United States coin has a picture of Abraham Lincoln on it. Tell them that the first Lincoln head cents were made in 1909 to celebrate the anniversary of Lincoln's 100th birthday. Give each student a penny. Show them where to find the date that tells when that penny was made. Who has the oldest penny? How many years old is it? Challenge them to find an older penny. Warn them not to take pennies out of someone's coin collection. Each time someone brings in an older penny, figure out how old it is.

Work Charades

During his lifetime, Lincoln had many different jobs. As a child and young man, he worked on his family's farm and split rails. When he left home, he worked as a ferryman, a store clerk, a postmaster, a surveyor, a lawyer, a politician and was President of the United States.

What kinds of work do the students do at home? What kinds of work would they like to do when they grow up? Invite them to act out jobs they'd like to do when they are adults. Challenge the other students to guess the job being acted out.

Suggestions for a Party

Bake gingerbread for a birthday cake. Back in Lincoln's day, gingerbread was a special treat.

Read *Abe Lincoln's Hat* by Martha Brenner. Have a hat race. Give the first person on each team a large hat stuffed with papers. That person runs to a designated place and back, then gives the hat to the second person, who does the same. If the hat falls off or any of the papers fall out, the person must stop and replace them before continuing the race. The first team to finish wins.

It's been said that Abe Lincoln would walk 20 miles to borrow a book. Celebrate his birthday with a book exchange. Ask everyone to bring in a used book.

Bibliography

Brenner, Martha. *Abe Lincoln's Hat.* Random House, New York, 1994.

Bruns, Roger. *Lincoln.* Chelsea House Publishers, New York, 1986.

D'Aulaire, Ingri, and Edgar Parin. *Abraham Lincoln.* Doubleday & Company, Inc., Garden City, New York, 1939.

Davis, Norman M. *The Complete Book of United States Coin Collecting.* Macmillan Publishing Co., Inc., New York, 1976 (pp. 45-49).

Fritz, Jean. *Just a Few Words, Mr. Lincoln.* Grosset & Dunlap, New York, 1993.

Kunhardt, Edith. *Honest Abe.* Greenwillow Books, New York, 1993.

Miller, Natalie. *The Story of the Lincoln Memorial.* Childrens Press, Chicago, 1996.

Monchieri, Lino. *Abraham Lincoln.* Silver Burdett Company, 1981.

Reed, Mort. *Cowles Complete Encyclopedia of U.S. Coins.* Cowles Book Company, Inc., New York, 1969 (pp. 97-106).

Richards, Kenneth. *The Story of the Gettysburg Address.* Childrens Press, Chicago 1969.

The World Book Encyclopedia, Vol. 12, World Book, Inc., Chicago, 1993 (pp. 329).

by Carolyn Short

Abraham Lincoln's Log Cabin

Help Abraham Lincoln cut some logs for his log cabin home. Which logs would Lincoln choose? Find the logs that tell something about Lincoln's life. Cut out the logs. Look for the places where they fit on the cabin. Then paste the logs on the cabin. Color the picture.

by Sister Mary Yvonne Moran

Read what each log says. Find the ones that state true facts about Abraham Lincoln and his life, then color those logs. Cut the logs out and paste them in the place where they fit on the cabin.

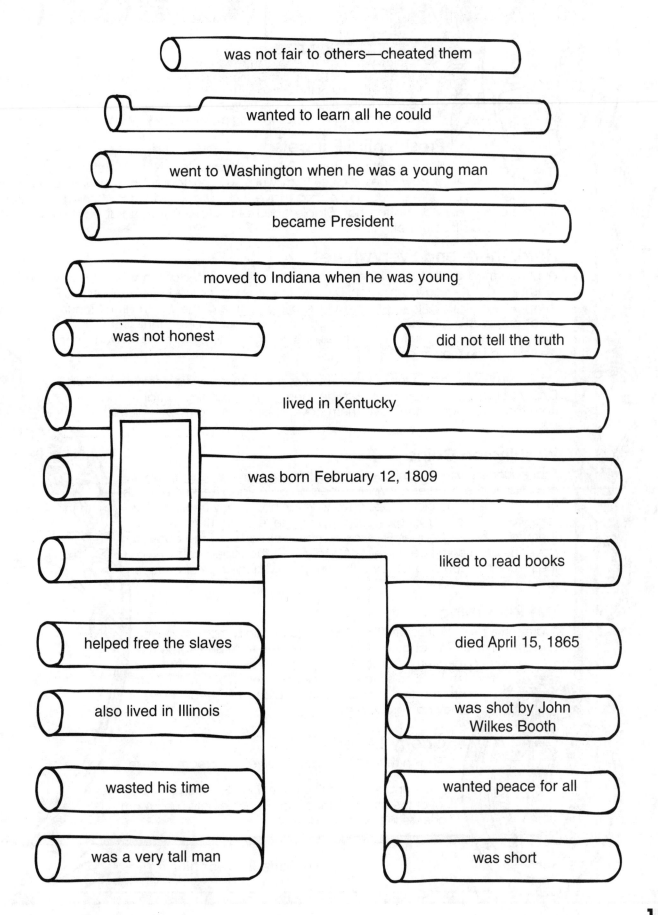

was not fair to others—cheated them

wanted to learn all he could

went to Washington when he was a young man

became President

moved to Indiana when he was young

was not honest

did not tell the truth

lived in Kentucky

was born February 12, 1809

liked to read books

helped free the slaves

died April 15, 1865

also lived in Illinois

was shot by John Wilkes Booth

wasted his time

wanted peace for all

was a very tall man

was short

George

George Washington is one of the two famous United States Presidents honored on Presidents' Day. As the first Commander in Chief of the United States Army and the first President of the United States, he helped establish the United States as an independent nation. Explore several ways in which we remember George Washington by sharing the following activities with your class.

Presidential Puppets

Display several pictures of George Washington. Note the style of his hair and clothing. How does it differ from what we see today? Provide the children with paper plates, markers, glue and cotton. Have them draw and color Washington's face on the plate and glue on cotton hair. Staple each plate to a sturdy cardboard stick and turn George into a stick puppet.

Here, There and Everywhere

Display a map of the United States. Show the children the state in which they live. Point out Washington state and Washington, D.C., which are both named after the famous President. Do they live near to or far from each? Next, share a picture of the Washington Monument, which is located in Washington, D.C., and was built to honor our first President. Compare the height of the monument to any surrounding trees or buildings in the picture. Has anyone in the class ever visited the monument?

Have the children make their own replicas of the monument from thin cardboard. Empty cereal boxes work well. Provide them with a pattern to trace and cut from the cardboard; then have them cover their monuments with aluminum foil.

Washington Coins

Share quarters with the children. Notice the size, color and shape of the coin. Name the pictures and/or numbers on both sides. Read the words on both sides to the class. Does anyone know how many cents a quarter is worth? Place a piece of rolled tape on several quarters and stick them to a sheet of paper. Be sure to show both sides of the quarter. Have the children place a sheet of paper over the taped coins, hold the paper in place and rub over the quarters with the side of a crayon to make coin prints.

The Real Thing

Share some real cherries with the class. Try to obtain some with leaves and stems intact. Talk about where cherries come from and name the parts (leaves, stems, fruit). Slice one open. Talk about what you find inside. Slice several more open. Allow the children to taste the fruit and have them plant the seeds to see if they can grow trees.

Cherry Letters

English muffins   sliced cherries   cream cheese

Slice and toast the English muffins. Spread cream cheese over the muffins. Place sliced cherries into the cream cheese in the shape of a W.

by Marie E. Cecchini

Washington

Cherry Tree Legend

Discuss the following legend of George Washington and the cherry tree. As a boy, George receives a new hatchet which he tries out on one of his father's cherry trees. When his father questions the felled tree, George tells the truth and is not punished. Have the children share their thoughts on the story. Next, provide them with paper, brown markers, cotton swabs, red and green paint. Ask them to draw a tree trunk and branches on the paper with the brown marker. Then have them add cherries and leaves with the paints and cotton swabs.

Cherry Magnet

Have the children trace and cut out a small circle from thin cardboard. Color it brown. Cut brown pipe cleaners into 3" lengths. Have each child count out two pipe cleaner pieces; then glue one end of each piece to the cardboard circle. Have them glue a red pom-pom to the opposite end of each pipe cleaner piece. Provide them with green paper, markers and scissors to draw and cut out three leaves. Let them glue their leaves to the brown cardboard. Allow to dry. Then glue a magnet strip to the back of the cardboard.

Note: Do gluing on waxed paper. This makes the project easier to move for drying, and the waxed paper will peel easily off of any excess glue.

George Washington

When George Washington was a little kid,
(Show size of a small child.)

He was just like you and me.
(Point to others and self.)

One of the naughty things he did
(Put up index finger for "one.")

Was cut down a cherry tree!
(Pretend to swing an axe.)

His dad was mad and made George cry,
(Rub eyes.)

And George was very sad.
(Show a sad face.)

Then he said, "I cannot lie."
(Look up–serious and brave look.)

And both of them were glad.
(Smile broadly.)

by Judy Wolfman

Washington Bills

Share single dollar bills with the children. Who is on the front? Can they see his tiny name? Note the pictures on the back. Read the large word *one* and have the children name the letters. Count how many times the word appears on the front and back of the bill. Count how many numeral 1s are on the front and back of the bill. Explore the relationship between quarters and dollars.

Holiday Classroom Decorations

Profiles of Great Americans

During the months of January and February, America honors three great men: Abraham Lincoln; George Washington and Dr. Martin Luther King, Jr. As you teach about these leaders, make a profile of each man and place on the bulletin board or in the hallway near your room. Also include profiles of students and place on the same bulletin board.

To make profiles, have each student sit on a stool with a large sheet of white paper attached to the wall behind him or her. Shine a large flashlight on the student. Quickly draw the outline with a black marker. The students copy this on black construction paper and then cut it out and paste on white paper.

by Carolyn Ross Tomlin

14 Fabulous
Valentine Projects

Here are fourteen fun ideas for February 14th—Valentine's Day!

1. Picture Cards

Take a snapshot of each child, or have each child bring in a small self-photo. Glue their pictures to white paper. Provide each child with one red and one pink pipe cleaner. Have them twist the colors together and bend the pipe cleaners into a heart shape. Glue the heart shapes around the pictures. When the glue is dry, trim off the excess white paper with scissors. Tape or glue a yarn loop to the back of each heart for hanging. Mom and Dad will love this special valentine treasure.

2. Heart Matching

Prepare several 9" x 12" sheets of paper or poster board with heart shapes of various sizes that you draw or stamp on. Prepare a number of individual hearts to match each size. Place the heart cards and a container of heart shapes in your math center. Show the children how to place a heart from the container on top of a size match on the card. Have the children make use of these during independent time.

3. Broken Heart Matchups

Cut out several red and/or pink poster board heart shapes. On the hearts, write or draw either upper and lowercase letters, numerals and the corresponding number of dots, or letters and beginning sound pictures. As you prepare the cards with letters, numerals or pictures, leave space between each pair of objects for cutting. After you prepare the cards, cut each one apart in a slightly different way. Place the cards in a related center area for the children to match on their own.

4. Sequential Snack

Prepare red gelatin and refrigerate until it reaches a jelly-like consistency but is not firm. While the children wait for the gelatin, have them use plastic knives to help you slice strawberries, cherries and red grapes. Place each fruit in a separate bowl. Save one whole strawberry for each child. Add a little strawberry juice to whipped cream and stir until pink. When the gelatin is ready, give each child a clear plastic cup and a red spoon. Have them alternate layers of gelatin and fruit. Specify the order in which the fruit is to be layered. Top each parfait with pink whipped cream and a whole strawberry. Now lick your spoons. Refrigerate until firm; then enjoy your treat.

by Marie E. Cecchini

Red-Letter Day

5 Supply each child with a white Styrofoam™ tray and a pink crayon (washable marker tends to rub off). Have them color a frame around the edges of the tray. Punch two holes at the top of each tray and thread with pink yarn for hanging. Have the children make a large V on their trays with the pink crayon. Let them trace their Vs with glue, then place red milk jug lids along their glue lines. Allow to dry. Ask them what they think the V stands for. Can they guess the sound V makes?

Heart Mobile

6 Cut several 3" squares of clear, self-adhesive paper. Peel the backing off of one for each child and have the children decorate the center of their squares with glitter, sequins, buttons, feathers or dried flowers. Cover their designs with a second piece of clear, self-adhesive paper and seal around the edges. Use a pattern and an ink pen to trace a heart shape around their designs. Have them cut out their hearts. Let them each make three. Punch a hole at the top of each heart, thread with a yarn length and knot. Punch three holes in a small, plastic margarine tub lid and tie the opposite ends of the yarn lengths through these holes. Tape a yarn loop to the center of the plastic lid for hanging.

Giant Heart "Cookies"

7 These "cookies" will look good enough to eat, but don't! Have the children cut a large heart shape from a Styrofoam™ tray. Let them paint the hearts red or pink. Allow the paint to dry; then have the children dribble glue here and there on their hearts. Sprinkle the glue with colored sugar and cake decorations or glitter and colored rice. Yum!?!

Valentine Breeze Catcher

8 Have the children wrap bath tissue tubes with red or pink tissue paper. Secure with tape. Let them each cut out two paper hearts and decorate with glitter. Let the glue dry, then staple the hearts to opposite sides of the tube. Tape or staple three red or pink crepe paper streamers to the bottom of the tube. Punch two holes on either side of the tube top and thread with red yarn for hanging.

Fold-Over Heart

9 Have the children trace and cut a large white paper heart. Provide them with cotton swabs and red and white paints. Let them dab both colors of paint onto their hearts. Before the paint dries, help them fold their hearts in half and smooth them out with flat hands. Carefully re-open the hearts. Did anyone make a new color?

Card Carriers

The children will love carrying their valentine card collections home in these cute little totes. Have them cut the top off of a paper lunch bag and help them fold down the new edge. The bags should be about half their original height. Provide the children with old valentine cards, glue and scissors. Let them cut designs, pictures and words from the old cards and glue them to the outside of their bags. Cut strips of thin cardboard and have the children decorate these with markers. Staple these handles to either side of the bag top.

"Candy" Hearts Basket

Twist the ends of a pipe cleaner through either side of a small, plastic produce basket to make a handle. Have the children trace and cut white Styrofoam™ hearts that are 2" to 3" across. Let them color both sides of the hearts with crayons, placing their hearts into their baskets as they are colored. Share some messages from real candy hearts, such as **yes, hug me** and **hi.** Help them use a narrow-tipped marker to write messages on their pretend candy hearts.

Heart Angels

For this project, each child will need one large heart, one small heart, two medium-sized hearts, a cardboard strip, a red pipe cleaner, markers, glue and tape. Place the large heart upside down (body), then glue the point of the small heart (head) to the point of the large heart. Glue the points of the medium-sized hearts (wings) to either side of the large heart. Decorate the cardboard strip with markers and staple it to the bottom of the body. Draw a face on each angel. Shape a circle at the top of the pipe cleaner and fold it forward to form a halo. Tape the bottom of the pipe cleaner to the back of the head.

Heart Flowers

Let the children each make two heart flowers by gluing a red or pink heart to the top of two pipe cleaners and two leaf shapes to either side of each pipe cleaner. Set these on waxed paper to dry. Help them make a vase by gluing an inverted Styrofoam™ cup onto a piece of cardboard for stability. Have an adult use a ballpoint pen to carefully poke two small holes in the cup. When the glue dries, help the children push their flower stems through the holes of their "vases."

Party Place Mats

Have the children cut a large heart shape from white paper. Let them edge the heart with red or pink marker. Cut several vertical slits, about 1" apart, in their hearts. Provide them with red and pink paper strips to weave through the slits in their hearts.

Trim any strips that hang over the edge of the heart. Secure the ends of each strip with tape.

Valentine Verses

A couplet is a verse with two rhyming lines. Each line has the same number of syllables. Help the children make valentine cards featuring original couplets. The completed cards may be sent to classmates, members of their family, friends, residents at a retirement home or children in a hospital.

Before the children begin to write, introduce and reinforce rhyming words and syllables.

1. As you read stories by Dr. Seuss, have the students supply the rhyming words.

2. Present the verse, "Roses are red, violets are blue . . ." Write it on the board. Draw a line under each syllable. Clap the number of syllables in each line and count them.

3. To practice rhyming and rhythm, write the following couplets on the board. Leave blanks so the children may supply missing words. Accept any reasonable responses.

   a. Roses are red, violets are blue.
      Everything's fine when I'm with _____.

   b. Stop! Don't be a _____!
      Will you be my valentine?

   c. My heart jumps like a kangaroo,
      When I am _____ after you.

   d. I am climbing up a vine,
      _____ for my valentine.

4. Brainstorm a list of words that rhyme with *blue*. Have the students compose other endings for the "Roses are red, violets are blue" verse.

Writing the Couplet

Write an opening line. Brainstorm a list of rhyming words. Write a second line that ends with a word from the list and has the same number of syllables as the first line.

Creating the Card

Materials: You will need white paper (4½" x 6" or 6" x 9"), felt-tipped pens, small sponges, heart-shaped stencils, paint and pencils.

Procedure: Complete the cards using any of the suggestions below.

1. To add background color, dip a sponge in paint and lightly dab it over entire surface.
2. Use the stencil and sponge to make heart patterns.
3. Carefully copy the verse onto the paper. Trace over the letters with a felt-tipped pen.
4. Add a border of hearts or colorful designs to highlight the couplet.
5. Don't forget to sign your name.

by Patricia O'Brien

190

Cooking with Kids

Hearts Delight

Ingredients:

2 large boxes of red gelatin
2 pints whipping cream
2 cans crushed pineapple (drained)

Have the children make the gelatin as directed on the package. You may wish to use the pineapple juice in place of water. Allow the gelatin to partially set. Whip the cream. Combine the pineapple, whipped cream and gelatin. Stir until well mixed. Refrigerate about an hour. Spoon into small paper cups and enjoy!

Crackers with Heart

Ingredients:

snack crackers   frosting (or cream cheese)
red food coloring   large marshmallows
cinnamon hearts   tongue depressor sticks

Give each student a snack cracker. Add a couple drops of red food coloring to the frosting or cream cheese; stir until blended. Have the students use a stick to spread some frosting or cream cheese over their cracker. Place a big marshmallow on top of the frosting. Add a little more frosting to the top of the marshmallow. Stick a cinnamon heart on top.

Happy Hearts

Ingredients:

1 cup butter   1 cup sugar
1 egg   3 T. milk
1 tsp. vanilla extract 3 cups flour
$1^1/2$ tsp. baking powder $^1/2$ tsp. salt
vanilla frosting   cinnamon hearts
red shoestring licorice icing tube
heart-shaped cookie cutter

Cream butter and sugar together in medium-size mixing bowl. Beat in egg, vanilla and milk. Stir in flour, baking powder and salt until well mixed. Preheat oven to 400°F. Roll out dough, $^1/3$ at a time, on a floured surface to $^1/8$" thickness. Using cookie cutter, cut into heart shapes. Place 1" apart on ungreased baking sheets. Bake for 5-8 minutes (until golden brown).

Once cookies have cooled, fill icing tube with frosting and have children outline the inside of their cookie heart. Have them put a small squirt of icing where the eyes, nose and mouth would go. Place a cinnamon heart on the two spots for the eyes and for the nose. Cut 1" pieces of licorice and put on the frosting spots for the mouth and eyebrows. Have a heart and enjoy!

by Teresa E. Culpeper

Heart Mobile

Here's a lovely way to decorate your classroom on Valentine's Day. Cut 1" strips of 12" x 18" red construction paper. Repeat this procedure using white and pink construction paper. Next, trim 2" from the top of the white strips and 4" off the top of the pink strips. Finally, cut out a 3" red heart for the center.

To begin assembly take one red strip, one white strip, one pink strip and a 3" red heart. Fold each strip in half and staple the bottom.

Place all the top edges together and curve inward to form a heart.

Staple all six strips together at once. You should have three colored hearts that are nested inside each other.

Have the child write his or her name on the 3" heart, and then suspend it from the center of the nested strips. Hang these mobiles around your room for a lovely Valentine's decoration.

by Ann Scheiblin

Hooray for Winter

CHINESE NEW YEAR

INK

Happy Valentine's Day!

"Bee" Mine

Clip Art for Hanukkah

NUN   GIMMEL   HAY   SHIN

OLIVE

OIL

Creative Ideas
for Clip Art

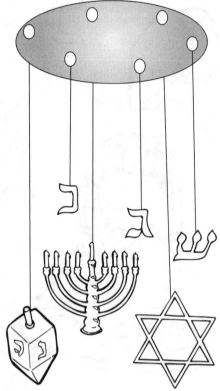

Mobile

Here are two suggestions for you to make a mobile using the clip art on pages 194 and 195.

Use a sturdy paper plate and punch holes around the outer edge of the plate. Use string or yarn to attach the clip art. You may want to enlarge or reduce art depending on what you need. Cut out the patterns and color them. (Note: You may want to laminate them for longer use.)

Another suggestion is to use sturdy tagboard. Cut a rectangle shape approximately 3" x 20" and write a message on it lengthwise. (Or use a piece 3" x 32" and staple the ends together to form a circle.) Punch holes around the outer edge of the plate. Use string or yarn to attach the clip art.

Happy Hanukkah

Different Uses for Clip Art

- Bulletin Board Decorations
- Tabletop or Desktop Decorations
- Party Favors
- Take-Homes for Parents
- Refrigerator Magnets
- Ceiling Decorations
- Window/Door Decorations
- Greeting Cards
- Portfolio Pieces on Folders

(Note: You may want to reduce or enlarge the art according to your needs.)

by Kim Rankin

Seasonal Borders

Use the months of January, February and March to make creative borders for holiday or seasonal bulletin boards. You'll teach the skills of cutting and following directions in the process.

Cut one 8$\frac{1}{2}$" x 11" sheet of paper into three equal strips. Fold accordion-style as shown. Cutting one pattern makes four shapes. Make enough strips to outline a bulletin board for this holiday or season. Students may choose an appropriate color or decorate creatively.

January—snowman
February—tooth for Dental Health Month
February—heart for Valentine's Day
February—top hat for Lincoln's birthday or Presidents' Day
March—shamrock for St. Patrick's Day
March/April—bunny or duck for Easter

by Carolyn Tomlin

←11"→

2$\frac{13}{16}$"

8$\frac{1}{2}$"

then

←2$\frac{3}{4}$"→

fold

then

Tape pattern on top and cut around...

then

(Don't cut here!)   (Don't cut here!)

then

Decorate!

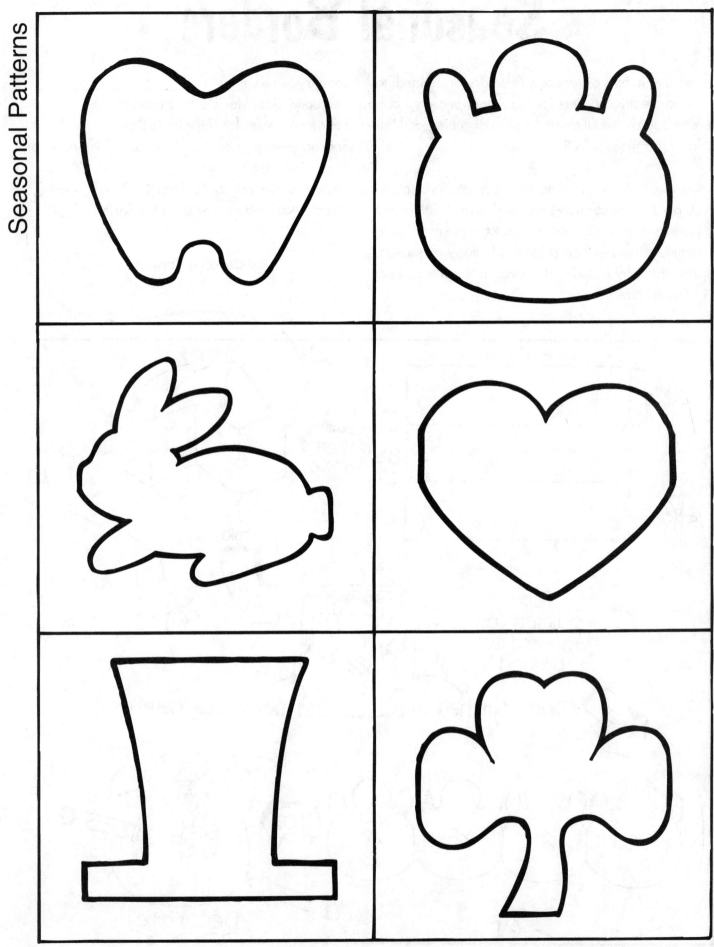

Signs of Spring

Mama bird, mama bird,
What do you see?
I see a juicy worm
Waiting for me.

Fuzzy rabbit, fuzzy rabbit,
What do you see?
I see a field of clover
Waiting for me.

Tadpole, tadpole,
What do you see?
I see a tiny bug
Waiting for me.

Baby chick, baby chick,
What do you see?
I see a grain of corn
Waiting for me.

Firefly, firefly,
What do you see?
I see a starry night
Waiting for me.

Bullfrog, bullfrog,
What do you see?
I see a snapping turtle
Waiting for me.

Young colt, young colt,
What do you see?
I see a stack of hay
Waiting for me.

Little mouse, little mouse,
What do you see?
I see a piece of cheese
Waiting for me.

Spotted calf, spotted calf,
What do you see?
I see my mama
Waiting for me.

by Carolyn Tomlin

Directions: Print the story on lined chart paper. Discuss top to bottom, and left-to-right movement. Use a wand to focus on each line as you read. Children will enjoy "reading" this seasonal story that uses repetition. Ask follow-up questions later. Allow time for students to draw an animal mentioned in the story.

It's not raining!

Sun's out!

What to Do with Umbrellas
if It Is Not Raining

Collect umbrellas from your closets and ask students to bring in their old ones from home. And when "April showers bring May flowers . . ." use them in your classroom.

Compound Words

Suspend an umbrella from the ceiling using fishing line. Sew the line or cord into the umbrella. Have students write compound words on raindrop-shaped pieces of paper. Attach the raindrops to the umbrella using tape or staples.

Book Reports

Umbrellas can display a book report by writing the book title on the handle and book characters on index cards hanging from the umbrella. Write a sentence on the story cards.

Learning Centers

Write questions on boot shapes, raindrops or cats and dogs! Learning centers can reinforce math facts, English skills, beginning sounds, reading vocabulary words, science units or social studies units.

Extra Umbrella Ideas

Use umbrellas to display good work or special projects.

A big umbrella would make a good silent reading area. Hang raindrops from the umbrella.

Bulletin Board

Cut out a large umbrella shape from construction paper or poster board, and attach it to the bulletin board. Fasten book jackets around the umbrella. Write this rhyme on the bulletin board:

It's raining;
It's pouring;
Reading is never boring.

by Jo Jo Cavalline and Jo Anne O'Donnell

200

Spring and Summer

Kid Space is a place of school yard (and backyard) beginnings. It is an ever-changing, fascinating place where children can connect with the natural world and enjoy opportunities not readily available inside. Kid Space is a stage for school yard (or backyard) adventures. It is a safe place where kids can explore freely and make first-hand discoveries. Make the most of the smells, the colors, the textures, the sounds, the excitement, the freedom and the peace.

Feel the Weather

Experience the weather using all of your senses in nature's classroom! Children see and feel the weather around them every day. The wind, water and heat from the sun create an endless cycle of changing weather that can be observed, felt detected, measured and recorded.

You Need (for each child):
- the outdoors
- weather-appropriate attire
- cassette recorder
- blindfolds

What to Do:
1. Take students to an outdoor location in various kinds of weather.
2. Encourage children to observe the weather by looking at it up close and at a distance. Discuss what they see. Did they observe anything they had not seen before?
3. Encourage children to listen to the weather by closing their eyes or wearing blindfolds. Have they taken the time to listen to the weather before?
4. Encourage children to feel the weather by lying on the ground or touching it with their hands. How does the pavement or grass feel?
5. Ask children to smell the weather. Do they notice any smells? What are they? Which direction is the wind blowing?
6. Use a cassette recorder to record sounds of the weather and children's responses to the weather on particular days. Compile a "Weather Wise" recording that includes weather facts, songs and sounds.

by Robynne Eagan

Mud Murals

Use a natural medium of earth tones to create a masterpiece. Kids can't take this artwork home to hang on the fridge, but they will have a story to tell when they get home!

You Need:
- old paintbrushes or painting instruments made from natural objects (try leaves, grasses, sticks, plants or stones)
- a wet, muddy puddle
- a paved or concrete surface (a school yard or sidewalk works well)

What to Do:
1. Provide each child with a painting instrument or instructions to search for one.
2. Be sure each child has access to a puddle and a painting surface.
3. Offer words of encouragement, inspiration and praise to the young artists as they create.
4. Take a photograph of the completed mural and the young artists.

Sunny Days

The Art of Evaporation

The sun's heat will cause water to vanish before your eyes! It doesn't actually vanish; it evaporates or changes form. The sun's heat causes particles at the water's surface to vibrate fast enough to escape into the air in the form of a gas called a vapor. Watch evaporation in action with this simple activity.

You Need:
- a puddle of water on a paved surface
- a sunny day
- chalk or tempera paint

What to Do:
1. Find or make a puddle of water on a paved surface on a sunny day.
2. Trace the puddle with chalk or tempera paint.
3. Watch what happens as the sun's heat beats down on the puddle.

Sun Versus Shade

You Need:
- a shady spot
- a sunny spot
- two bowls
- four ice cubes of the same size
- stopwatch
- two thermometers

What to Do:
1. Put two ice cubes in a bowl and put the bowl in the sun.
2. Put two ice cubes in a bowl and put this bowl in the shade at the same time.
3. Start the stopwatch, and observe the bowls every few minutes.
4. How long does it take for the ice cubes to melt in the sun? In the shade?
5. Place one thermometer in the sunlight.
6. Place the other thermometer in the shade.
7. Take hourly readings of each thermometer.
8. Graph the hourly temperature differences for the day.
9. Discuss the differences in the melting times and temperatures for the sun and the shade.

Sun Prints

Use the sun's energy to create a print and encourage children to observe the interesting shapes found in nature.

You Need:
- construction paper or recycled fax paper
- Plexiglas™ cover to hold objects in place (if necessary)
- a piece of heavy cardboard, slightly larger than the glass
- a flat work space
- objects found in nature—leaves, seeds, feathers, grasses, pebbles

What to Do:
1. Place the paper on the cardboard.
2. Arrange your items in an interesting pattern on the paper.
3. Cover the paper and objects with the Plexiglas™ to hold objects in place.
4. Leave this in the sun for an entire day, or until all exposed areas of the paper are faded by the sun.

Try This:
Glue your sun print to a cardboard frame. Attach a string on the back for hanging the sun's artwork.

Shadow Art

Children can learn about the sun and their shadow while having fun!

You Need:
- a sunny day
- paved surface
- chalk

What to Do:
1. Go outside first thing in the morning, and have each child choose a partner.
2. Have each child mark an X on the pavement, several feet away from any other Xs.
3. Each child will stand on their own X and have their partner trace their shadow.
4. Take children outside again at noon, and then as late as possible in the daylight, to trace their shadows again.
5. Note and discuss the differences in the shadows.

Your Shadow Knows

Most children are well aware that the sun's rays can be harmful to their skin. Help children to recognize the time of day when the sun is most intense by looking at their shadows. A child's shadow is at its shortest when the sun is at its strongest. Use this little rhyme to teach this important lesson.

When your shadow is small, stay out of the sun. When your shadow is tall, go out and have fun.

Earth Day in Kid Space
Make an Air Pollution Indicator

On Earth Day, help students learn about the pollution in the air around them. This simple experiment will illustrate the amount of particulate matter in the air.

You Need:
- two sturdy paper plates
- two pieces of scrap wood or sticks
- nail and jaw clip or tape and clothespins
- petroleum jelly

What to Do:
1. Nail jaw clips or tape clothespins to the end of each of the sticks. Attach paper plates.
2. Spread a thin layer of petroleum jelly on the paper plates and place the sticks in two somewhat protected outdoor locations.
3. Leave the Pollution Indicators in place for several hours and then observe.
4. Observe again after one day and then after one week.
5. Record results by pasting them on a chart for all to see. Have students record descriptions and reaction under each spot.

Try This:
If the air is very clear in your area, you may need to use a microscope and slides smeared with petroleum jelly to detect the particulate matter. Discuss the differences between natural particulate matter in the air and pollutants that can be harmful to our environment and health.

Environment Friendly Clothes Dryer

Help students discover how to use the energy of the wind and sun—naturally!

You Need:
- sunny day
- string or rope
- two poles or locations to tie the rope ends
- clothespins
- wet cloth

What to Do:
1. Tie the rope between two locations.
2. Soak various colors of cloth and wring them out.
3. Hang the cloth samples on the clothesline and observe what happens. How long did it take to dry the cloth? Did any one color of cloth dry quicker than the other samples? What caused the cloth to dry? Was more than one factor involved?

Try This:
- Set drying lines in various locations. What factors affect the drying of the cloth?
- Lead children to discover the environmental benefits of using this method of drying clothes over the use of a clothes drying appliance.

Spring Book Nook

Celebrate the spring season with our exciting array of books and activities. *Four Stories for Four Seasons* by Tomie de Paola (New York: Simon & Schuster, 1977) is the perfect book to welcome spring or any season of the year! This charming book is a collection of four seasonal stories featuring four animal friends—dog, cat, frog and pig. Your class will enjoy the lovable characters and amusing stories.

It's play time! *Small Plays for Special Days* by Sue Alexander (New York: Ticknor & Fields, 1977) features short holiday plays for two actors. "Roar! Said the Lion, a Play for the First Day of Spring" will get your spring season off to a roaring start! "The White House Rabbit," a perfect play for the Easter season, can be found in *Special Plays for Holidays* by Helen Louise Miller (Boston: Plays, Inc., 1986).

Poems, please! *Celebrations* by Myra Cohn Livingston (New York: Holiday House, 1985) is a wonderful collection of holiday poems enhanced by the beautiful illustrations of painter Leonard Everett Fisher. Easter, St. Patrick's Day, Columbus Day and Thanksgiving are among the holidays "celebrated" in this book. After sharing some of the poems in this book, have your class write and illustrate their own springtime holiday poems.

The Easter Egg Farm

Auch, Mary Jane. *The Easter Egg Farm.* New York: Holiday House, 1992.

Pauline is no ordinary hen. The eggs she lays are such a work of art, that her owner, Mrs. Pennywort, decides to start an egg farm. A lady wants to buy some eggs for an Easter egg hunt. When the day before Easter arrives, everyone is in for a big surprise—the eggs start hatching. Find out what happens next!

- Design a billboard to advertise Pauline's "eggs"traordinary eggs.

- Extra! Extra! Read all about it! Write a news story about Mrs. Pennywort's "eggs"ceptional hen. Remember the five *W*s: *Who? What? Where? When?* and *Why?*

- Pretend that you have a hen like Pauline. What would you do with the eggs?

by Mary Ellen Switzer

It's April Fool's Day

Kroll, Steven. *It's April Fool's Day.* New York: Holiday House, 1990.

Uh oh! It's April Fool's Day and Alice is getting tired of Horace's mean tricks. She decides to teach him a lesson and play a few tricks on him. Will her idea change Horace's outlook on playing pranks?

- Think about it. Horace and Alice decided to become good friends. What are some outdoor games they could play to have fun? Write a list of four outdoor games you enjoy playing with your friends.

- Write three adjectives to describe your best friend.

- Design a special trophy for your best friend. Include pictures on the trophy that would show what your friend is interested in.

How Spider Saved Easter

Kraus, Robert. *How Spider Saved Easter*. New York: Scholastic Inc., 1988.

Oops! When Ladybug's Easter bonnet is accidentally ruined by a melting chocolate bunny, Spider comes to her rescue. Spider weaves her a beautiful new spiderweb hat. But will Ladybug be able to win the best bonnet contest at the Easter parade?

- Design your version of a spiderweb hat. Draw a picture of what your hat would look like.

- Help! Write a story about a hero who saves a melting chocolate Easter bunny.

- Those amazing arachnids! Use an encyclopedia or reference book to find information about spiders. Create a poster report with pictures and facts about spiders.

Arthur's April Fool

Brown, Marc. *Arthur's April Fool*. Boston: Little, Brown and Company, 1983.

That lovable Arthur is back with some magic tricks up his sleeve for the April Fools' Day school assembly. But will he be able to remember the tricks with that bully Binky Barnes bothering him?

- Meet the Fabulous Magician! Design a sign that Arthur could use in the April Fools' Day school assembly.

- Tell about the April Fools' "trick" that Arthur played on Binky Barnes.

- Draw a picture of a magician's top hat. Abracadabra . . . Draw what comes out of the hat when you wave a magic wand. Now write a story about your picture.

The Mother's Day Mice

Bunting, Eve. *The Mother's Day Mice*. New York: Ticknor & Fields, 1986.

It's Mother's Day, and the three mice brothers go exploring in the meadow to find that "perfect" present for their mother. When a big black cat foils Little Mouse's plan to give his mother some honeysuckle, he decides on something even better—a special Mother's Day song!

- Surprise! Think of a "perfect" Mother's Day gift that you could make. Draw a picture of your gift and describe how to make it.

- Design a Mother's Day trophy for "The World's Best Mom." Draw a picture of what your special trophy would look like.

- On Mother's Day, we often think about other women who are special to us. Write a few sentences telling about another woman who is important to you. Draw a picture of that person.

Home & School

Easter Eggs

Collect small plastic Easter eggs (those that open). Write a sentence strip for each egg, such as: 1. Pass out treats. 2. Water the plants. 3. Feed the fish. 4. Sharpen the pencils. Hide the eggs in the room. Several times throughout the day, ask a student to look for an egg. Use for behavior modification or when students are "on task."

Faces in Our Garden

Paper cupcake/muffin liners create flowers with a three-dimensional effect. Cut petals, stems and leaves from bright colored construction paper. Paste liners in center of flowers, with school pictures of students in the center.

Circle Learning

Learn about life within a circle by placing a Hula-Hoop™ (or a rope circle with a three-foot diameter) in a grassy area. Using magnifying glasses, search for insects. Identify by looking up different species in a children's reference book.

by Carolyn Ross Tomlin

Henri's

Henri was a caterpillar. Not a striped caterpillar. Not a fuzzy caterpillar. Just a plain old ordinary caterpillar. Henri's mother was a beautiful butterfly. She loved Henri very much, and she could see that he was really very special.

Henri was a happy little caterpillar. He smiled at the sun, and he danced in the rain. He sang with the birds, and he raced with the beetles. The most wonderful thing about Henri was that whenever he was happy, Henri glowed with joy. Henri's glow was bright purple, and when anyone saw it, it always cheered them up. Since Henri had so much fun doing so many different things, he glowed purple most of the time. You can imagine how many people were happy because Henri was around!

Unfortunately, as Henri grew older, something terrible happened. Henri forgot how happy he was. He was grumpy when the sun woke him up. He was grouchy in the rain. He thought that the birds gave him a headache, and the beetles bothered him. Henri didn't glow anymore, and he forgot that he was special.

"I'm just a plain old BORING caterpillar," said Henri, and pretty soon people started to believe him. Only Henri's mother remembered how special he really was.

One day, Henri had enough. "I'm going to find some treasure," he said. "Then I'll be someone special!" His mother watched sadly as Henri packed to leave. She kissed and hugged him good-bye; then Henri walked slowly down the path.

The sun was beginning to go down by the time Henri came to the meadow. He slept there under a leaf and woke up with the sun. Henri searched all day in the meadow, but he didn't find any treasure.

The next day, Henri trudged to a stream. He looked up the stream. He looked down the stream. He looked down into the water and thought—just for a moment—that he saw a treasure sparkling there, but it turned out to be just his own reflection. Henri was getting discouraged.

by Gloria Trabacca

Treasure

On the third day, Henri walked slowly to the forest. He looked in the trees. He looked under the bushes. He even searched through the moss, but there was no treasure to be found. Henri was sad and very tired. "I might as well give up," he thought. "I will never find my treasure." So Henri began to spin his cocoon. He worked very hard until the cocoon was like a tiny room that went all the way around him. Then he tiredly closed his eyes.

Henri fell asleep right away, but something woke him up! It was sharp, and it was poking him right in the back! He couldn't seem to find a place to put it in his tiny cocoon, so Henri picked up the sharp thing and held it. Soon he went back to sleep. Before too long, something else bumped into Henri's head. He woke up just long enough to pick it up, too.

It seemed like Henri had just gone back to sleep when OUCH! a whole bunch of very hard, pointed things bumped right into his stomach! "I don't remember leaving anything sharp in this cocoon," the sleepy caterpillar thought as he began scooping up the pile of uncomfortable things. Poor Henri. He was so tired. At last he gathered up all the hard, pointed things, and even though he was having trouble holding them all, Henri fell asleep. He slept for a long time.

One day, Henri woke up very suddenly. It was hard to breathe and hard to move! He struggled to tear a hole in his cocoon and broke out into the warm sun. Henri stretched his wings and looked at them closely. The hard pointed things that he had held while he was sleeping had stuck to his wings! Now that he was in the light, Henri could see that they were jewels! They were many different colors: yellow, red, blue, green . . . even purple! Henri had found his treasure.

The little butterfly was so happy that he began to glow purple with joy—just like he had when he was a happy little caterpillar. He fluttered home as fast as he could go—through the woods, over the stream, across the meadow and up the path. Henri was eager to show his mother that now he *was* a treasure.

But she had always known.

Flying High

Caterpillars and butterflies are standard springtime fare, but children never seem to tire of their magic. This year, ad
some new ideas to your butterfly unit, and watch it fly!

Caterpillar Clues

(To the tune of "Twinkle, Twinkle, Little Star")

Caterpillar on the ground,
Short and fat or long and round.
Some are striped,
Some are brown;
All hang, funny; upside down.

Funny little, crawly guy
Turns into a butterfly.

Crawly, Creative Crunchies

miniature round crackers
zucchini rounds
raisins
napkins
plastic knives or craft sticks

carrot rounds
creamy peanut butter
stick pretzels
aprons or paint shirts

Offer a variety of round foods. Let children assemble caterpillars, using peanut butter as "glue." Add raisin eyes and pretzel antennae, if desired. As an additional activity, have each child chart how many stripes of each ingredient are on his caterpillar. Eat and enjoy!

Flights of Fantasy

Read "Henri's Treasure" to the children. Have children imagine that they are crawling into a very special chrysalis. Its magic can turn them into whatever they want to be—whatever they treasure. As them what they will turn into. Have everyone dra a picture of the "treasure" that they will be.

If your children have a rest time, try readir "Henri's Treasure" before nap, asking them to crav into their magic chrysalis when it is time to la down. Let their imaginations run wild while the rest, and complete the activity when rest time over.

Magic Chrysalis

Designate a quiet corner in the clas room as the magic chrysalis. Childre may choose to use this area whe they wish to gain control of behavic and emerge as beautiful butterflies.

Surprises for Henri

Prepare a bag containing items o various shapes and textures Blindfold a child and have her reach into the paper bag cocoon. See if she can identify the "gems" in her cocoon, using only the sense o touch.

Butterflies on Parade

In your dress-up area, have scarves available that can be pinned to the shoulders and wrists of clothing. These make wonderful, colorful butterfly wings!

Butterfly Mobile

Materials

- toilet paper tubes
- paint or pretty paper (gift wrap, pictures from gardening catalogs)
- construction paper
- yarn
- glue, scissors, hole punch, stapler

Have each child decorate a cardboard tube with paint or paper. While these dry, have each child color and cut out five butterflies.

When tubes have dried, punch two holes directly opposite each other on the top edge of the tube. Punch five holes along the base of the tube. Attach yarn in the following lengths: 2-3"; 1-3 1/2"; 2-4"; 1-4 1/2"; 1-5". Attach yarn through each of the bottom five holes. (These can be knotted and stapled on; omit punched holes.) Staple one butterfly to the end of each string. Attach a 12" piece of yarn, one end through each of the upper holes. Make a small hanging loop, and knot 1" from center top.

Metamorphosis
in C Major

Verse One

A lit-tle ca-ter-pil-lar worm crawl-ing next to a fern, de-cid-ed
there must be more to life, Than crawl-ing on the ground feel-ing
damp and down, and he knew right then he want-ed to fly.

Chorus

He want-ed to fly, yes he want-ed to fly
High up in the sky. To be filled with glee, to drink
nec-tar you see. He want-ed to be a but-ter- fly.

He had a fuzzy wuzzy coat with a spot on his throat
And three or four upon his dusty back,
Tears filled his eyes as he said with a sigh,
Will I ever learn to fly before I die?
Chorus:

He had heard others say that there might be a way
For a worm to fly high in the sky
You must spin a small room, it's called a cocoon,
But some said if you did you'd surely die.
Chorus:

He must take a chance he crawled high on a branch
A small cocoon room did he make.
While praying for the best his chin fell on his chest,
This caterpillar had what it takes.
Chorus:

And to his surprise, one day the light filled his eyes
Something new upon his back
A lump filled his throat, then he saw his new coat
He spread his wings and became a butterfly.
Chorus:

by Don Mitchell

Weather WISE

Weather is a constant source of intelligent questions from curious kids. The ever-changing weather of early spring provides the setting for scientific exploration of many things. Try these Weather WISE activities to help kids learn about the weather and its effects on their natural environment. Simple procedures and the use of everyday materials make the Weather WISE activities simple and easy for children and educators. Encourage young learners to formulate questions, investigate their environment, make discoveries and become weather wise!

Report the Weather

There's no better time than early spring to keep track of the weather. It's exciting, ever-changing and fascinating to talk about.

As part of a language arts program, ask students to research and give the weather reports. It is an important task that can be presented on a daily basis along with the calendar. Have students observe, study and research the weather to help them prepare a statement to communicate particular conditions at a particular place and time. Young children can merely look out the window and report what they see. Students in grades one or above are capable of studying the classroom weather station (if you have one), checking the newspaper, or listening to the news to help them prepare their weather reports. Encourage students to use weather maps, technical information, props and creativity in these reports.

Weather Walk

(Discussion questions can be adapted to suit any grade level.)
What better way to understand the weather than to take a walk in it. Take walks on days which offer varying weather conditions.

Encourage students to observe and discuss the weather they experience.
- How does the sky look? What types of clouds can be seen?
- Is there any precipitation? What kind? How much?
- How does the air feel? Is it damp or dry?
- Does it feel cold or warm? What is the temperature?
- Is there wind? Which direction is it blowing?
- Is there evidence of any animals? How will this weather affect them? How will this weather affect people you know?
- What people are most affected by the changing early spring weather? What effects will the weather have on farms, gardens, waterways, roads, travel and special events?

by Robynne Eagan

Rainbows

Early spring is a perfect time to take a look at one of the wonders of nature—the rainbow. Seize the moment when there's a rainbow in the sky to present your lesson on rainbows!

Rainbow Recipe

Do you know what is needed to make a rainbow? Sometimes the weather conditions have just the right ingredients to make a rainbow: sunlight and droplets of water. When do these conditions generally occur? Ask students to keep a Rainbow Record—to record the weather conditions when rainbows were sighted. Discuss their findings.

Make Your Own Rainbow

How can you make your own rainbow? Talk about the ingredients that are needed—sunlight and water. On a sunny day, you can add your own water droplets to the air by using a hose with a spray nozzle set for the finest spray. Spray in a direction away from the sun and have children stand by you. If children stand in just the right place, they will be able to see the tiny rainbow. Rainbow gazers may need to move up and down or to the side to catch sight of the rainbow. Allow each child to make a rainbow.

What Causes the Rainbow?

Sunlight, or white light, is really a mixture of many colors. When the sunlight shines through a concentration of water droplets at just the right angle, the ray of light is bent and breaks into the colors we see in the rainbow.

R - O - Y - G - B - I - V

What on Earth can these letters stand for? Roy-g-biv is one way of saying it. These letters represent something to do with the rainbow. Can your children figure out the mystery? Red - Orange - Yellow - Green - Blue - Indigo - Violet, of course. The colors of the rainbow always appear in this order. Have your students make up memory aids to help them remember this sequence.

Paint a Rainbow

Use poster paints and large paintbrushes to paint a rainbow with the right colors in the right order.

• Indigo is a dark violet-blue color.

Have You Ever Seen a . . .

Double rainbow?
Moonbow?
Sun dog?
Pot of gold at the end of the rainbow?

Finish the Sentence

At the end of the rainbow there is . . .

Winter's Over: A Spring Tally

In the Northern Hemisphere, spring officially begins on or around March 20th or 21st when the spring equinox occurs. On this date, day and night are of equal length everywhere in the world. The Earth is at a point in its revolution around the sun when the sun seems to cross the equator.

Spring may officially begin on this date, but in many places it doesn't feel like it. Discuss the quarterly official changes of season and the arrival of seasonal weather. When does spring really arrive in your Kid Space? Venture into the great outdoors to look for signs of the arrival of spring weather.

Complete the spring tally sheet below to determine when spring weather has arrived.

_____ The temperature gets warmer.

_____ The days get longer.

_____ The nights grow shorter.

_____ People wear less clothing.

_____ The snow melts.

_____ The landscape, lawns and school yard turn green.

_____ The shoots of flowers and bulbs peek through the earth.

_____ Buds appear on the trees.

_____ Birds return.

_____ People prepare to celebrate Valentine's Day, St. Patrick's Day, Passover, Groundhog Day, April Fools' Day and Easter.

_____ Children play more outdoor games and sports.

The Snow and Rain Quiz

1. Precipitation is the stuff that falls from the clouds onto our heads. Circle the things that fall from the clouds.

   rain   leaf   hail   snow   dogs   sleet

2. Choose words from the word box to fill in the blanks below.

   a. High up in the sky it is cold, and water vapor that is in the air condenses and forms tiny droplets of _____.

   b. Water droplets gather together in the sky to form _____.

   c. When the water droplets get too heavy, they fall as _____.

   d. When the weather is _____, the droplets fall as rain.

   e. When it is cold enough, tiny droplets will freeze to form ice _____.

   f. Ice crystals gather together to form _____.

Word Box

snowflakes   warm
water
crystals
rain
cold   clouds
wind

Irish Green

When March winds welcome St. Patrick's Day, invite your students to experiment and create with the color green.

The Sharing of Green

Declare one day as Green Day. Ask that each child wear something green and bring in a green item from home to share at circle time. As the group discusses their green contributions, note the varying shades of green. Have the children suggest ways in which they think these different greens are made.

Sorting Shamrocks

Cover three coffee cans with white paper. Glue a different-sized green shamrock to the outside of each can (small, medium and large). Provide the students with several green poster board shamrocks of each size. Have them sort the shamrocks and drop them into the appropriate containers. Help them count how many they found of each size. Which group(s) has more, less or the same number of shamrocks?

Experimenting with Green

1. *Water Moves:* Pour a small amount of water into a clear plastic cup. Add a drop or two of green food coloring. Cut a strip from a coffee filter and place one end into the water. Observe the green water as it "crawls" up the white filter paper.

2. *The "Un"-Making of Green:* Pour a small amount of water into a clear plastic cup. Cut a second strip from the coffee filter. Color a narrow band of green, with washable marker across the strip, about one or two inches from the bottom. Place one end of the strip in the water. Observe the water as it climbs the paper strip and moves into the marker band. Continue to watch as the water separates the green. Help the children note the yellow and blue coloring as it appears.

by Marie E. Cecchini

Green Wall Hanging

Provide each child with glue and a strip of green paper about four inches wide. Poke two holes at the top of the paper and thread with green yarn for hanging. Supply a variety of green items, such as buttons, leaves, fabric scraps, pipe cleaners, beads, jug lids, yarn and sequins. Have them each create a green collage.

Green Sweep

Place two cardboard boxes on their sides, several feet away from the children. Two at a time, have the children use housekeeping brooms to sweep a green balloon across the floor and into one of the boxes.

Shamrock Places

Prepare one large and several small green felt shamrocks. Place the large shamrock on the flannel board. Ask individual children to select a small shamrock and give them specific directions for its placement on the flannel board. Suggestions: far from, next to (near), above, below, left, right, behind, in front of and so on.

Painting with Water

For this experiment, you will need three clean measuring cups, yellow and blue food coloring, a stirring spoon, water, white paper and cotton swabs. Fill two measuring cups with water. Add a few drops of yellow food coloring to one, and add blue to the other. Stir to mix in the color. Have the children observe as you pour part of each color of water into the empty measuring cup. What happens when the colors mix? Let the children use cotton swabs dipped into these watercolors to create pastel pictures on white paper.

Count and Search

Prepare a few paper shamrocks with varying numbers of dots. Place the shamrocks in a bag. Ask individual children to pull a shamrock out of the bag, count the dots, then search the room and point out the same number of green items. Place the shamrock back in the bag and give the bag a shake before the next person's turn. Encourage the children to choose green objects that have not already been "found."

Dancing Belts

Have each child cut out two green shamrocks. Help them trace the edges of each shamrock with white glue; then sprinkle gold glitter over the glue. Allow the glue to dry. Next, provide each child with a length of ribbon, heavy yarn or a fabric strip. Help them staple a shamrock to each end of their ribbons and tie these ribbon belts around their waists. Now gather the group into a circle and ask them to place their hands on their hips. Play some Irish dancing music and have them do a jump-kick dance. You may also want to try a "pattern dance" such as three jumps, two kicks.

Slimey Limey

For a manipulative material with a texture all its own, try this.

> 1 T. white glue
> 1 T. water
> green food coloring
> 2-3 tsp. Borax™ mixture*

*Borax™ mixture:

> 1 T. Borax™
> 1 c. warm water

Mix the white glue thoroughly with the water. Add a few drops of food coloring. Dissolve Borax™ in warm water. While stirring the glue mixture, slowly add two to three teaspoons of the Borax™ mixture until a ball is formed. Store in a plastic sandwich bag. **Note:** 1 T. glue and 1 T. water make enough for about two children.

Try stretching the green ball quickly, then slowly. Try bouncing it. Try holding one end of it up and see how it stretches.

Name Necklaces

Provide small pre-cut shamrocks for the children. Have them count out as many shamrocks as there are letters in their names. Help them write each letter on a separate shamrock with white glue; then sprinkle green glitter over the glue. When the letters are dry, provide children with green yarn and large blunt needles. Show them how to string their shamrocks from side to side to spell their names. As they complete their necklaces, tie the yarn ends to secure.

Green Is My Garden

Make individual planting trays by cutting several green Styrofoam™ egg cartons into two half-dozen sections. Provide the children with their own planting trays and allow them to place soil in each section. Supply seeds to grow "green things." You may want to refer to the fruit and vegetables from the "Green Food" tasting. Make a small sign for each garden, to label whose it is and what was planted. Tape the sign to a toothpick and insert it into one of the cups.

Sprinkle Paint

Fill old saltshakers and spice bottles with blue and yellow tempera paint. Provide the children with these paint shakers, white paper and spray bottles filled with water. Have the children sprinkle both paint colors onto the white paper. Then spray the papers with water. Note any color mixing.

Shamrock Flag

Let the children use a green marker to trace a large shamrock pattern on a 9" x 12" sheet of white paper. Have them sponge paint the shamrocks green. When dry, tape each flag to a cardboard paper towel tube.

Shamrock Shakers

Help the children use tape and green tissue paper to cover a bath tissue tube. Let them cut two circles from a brown paper bag. Secure one circle over an end of the tube with a rubber band. Have the children count out four or five dried peas and drop them into the open end of the tube. Secure the second circle over the open end with a rubber band. Provide shamrock stickers for the children to use to decorate their shakers.

Now put on some St. Patrick's Day music and have a parade with your flags and shakers.

Shamrock Puzzle

Supply the children with green paper, markers, scissors, a heart-shaped pattern and a triangle-shaped pattern. Have them each trace and cut out three hearts and one triangle. Display a picture of a shamrock and have the children fit their puzzle pieces together to form their own shamrocks. Provide them with envelopes for their pieces.

Shamrock Puzzle Math

Prepare several cards with a green triangle shape. On each triangle, write a different numeral. Prepare several heart shapes with a varying number of dots. Help the children select the correct hearts, by counting the dots, to place with each triangle so the numeral will equal the number of dots.

Green Food

Ask parents to contribute to a sampling session of green foods. Possibilities include: fruits, vegetables, jelly, juice, gelatin, ice cream and pudding. Help the children with naming any foods unfamiliar to them. Let them sample what they choose. Note if the green fruits and vegetables are also green on the inside.

Dish Garden

Cut shamrock shapes from green sponges. Have the children moisten the sponges and set them in plastic lids. Provide them with grass seed to sprinkle on top. Keep the sponges moist and observe as the grass grows.

St. Patrick's Day

Kid Space is a place of school yard beginnings. It is an ever-changing, fascinating place where children can connect with the natural world and learn all kinds of things. Kid Space is a safe place where kids can explore freely, embark on adventures and make learning discoveries all on their own. Make the most of the smells, the colors, the textures, the sounds, the excitement, the freedom and the peace and quiet.

eland is famous for its lush green rolling hills. What etter place to celebrate this holiday than out in the eenery!

g on the Green

e lively Irish Jig is a traditional dance of Ireland. ave children follow these easy instructions for some op and jig fun. This activity is great for concentra- on, coordination and endurance. It might take a tle practice, and not everyone will catch on, so low a little creative license for children to hop and oint and stamp to their own drummer! Take the opping and jigging out to the green for some ctive, outdoor St. Patrick's Day fun.

1. Stand straight and proud with your feet placed together.

2. Put your hands on your hips—or for added effect, place the backs of your hands on your hips with your palms facing outward.

3. Put your left foot slightly forward and to the side and tap your heel on the ground once while you hop once on the right foot.

4. Hop once again on the right foot, but this time bend your left knee and point your left foot so the toes tap the ground in front of the right foot.

5. Hop for a third time on the right foot and bring the left foot back to the side with heel down on the ground.

6. Hop on the right foot for a fourth time and land with a bit of a stomp with both feet back together again.

7. Repeat the hopping-heel-toe process again, hopping on the left and then the right and so on.

• Add to the fun by bringing a portable music player out to the green with some lively Irish tunes.

Gold in the Greenery

There's nothing quite like a hunt for gold on St. Patrick's Day and no better place for it than in the greenery!

Hide shiny pennies, gold foil-wrapped pennies or gold-wrapped chocolate coins in a designated area of the school yard. Have students drop the coins they find in the "pot." Make this a cooperative exercise by asking students to find 100 coins in five minutes. Hide more coins than you ask the children to find. Have students drop the coins in the pot as they find them. The pot of gold can be used as manipulatives for math exercises and then shared by all.

Leprechaun's View

Have students get down to the leprechaun's level. How does nature look from down there? Do children notice anything they had not seen from their vantage point?

by Robynne Eagan

Search for the Four-Leaf Clover

Host a hunt for a four-leaf clover. Encourage children to talk about the sights, smells, sounds and textures as they hunt through the foliage. The shamrock is a clover leaf—or trefoil—made up of three parts. The shamrock was considered a sacred plant by the early Irish settlers called the *Celts*. The four-leaf clover—which is very difficult to find—is thought to bring luck to those who find it.

Make a Lucky Charm

If you are lucky enough to find a four-leaf clover or can piece one together, you can make your very own Irish lucky charm.

You Need:
- four-leaf clover or reasonable facsimile
- two sheets of plain white paper
- flower press or heavy book
- white tagboard or construction paper
- clear adhesive plastic sheet
- scissors
- glue
- tweezers
- small paintbrush
- single hole punch
- green yarn

What to Do:
1. Place the four-leaf clover or two three-leaf clovers between the sheets of white paper. Place the white paper in a flower press or between the pages of a large, heavy book. Leave the clover to dry and press for three to four days.
2. Cut a circle from the white tagboard, large enough to frame your clover with a border edge.
3. Cut the clear adhesive plastic piece to extend about 1/8" around the edges of the tagboard.
4. Carefully paint glue on the back of the clover and place the four-leaf clover, or arrange the three-leaf with an extra petal, on the tagboard. Allow the arrangement to dry thoroughly before continuing.
5. With adult assistance, remove the backing from the plastic covering and carefully place over the tagboard and clover.
6. Cover the back of the tagboard with the second piece of covering.
7. Trim the edges to make them straight, and punch a hole in the top of the tagboard.
8. Thread green yarn through the hole so you can wear your lucky charm as a necklace or hang it as an ornament.

Did you know that clover is a sign of a healthy school yard? Clover fixes nitrogen in the soil, attracts beneficial insects and makes lawns appear very green.

Cooking with Kids

Paddy's Parfaits

Ingredients:

green gelatin
pistachio-flavored instant pudding
clear plastic glasses

1 pint whipping cream
green gummi candy

Have students make up the gelatin according to the package directions. (You may want to make this the day before you plan to use it.) Refrigerate until set. Make up the pudding according to package directions. Whip the cream. Put a couple of spoonfuls of gelatin in each glass. Add a couple of spoonfuls of pudding on top. Place a spoonful of whipped cream on top of the pudding. Top it off with a green gummi candy. Enjoy!

Hoppy's Happy Salad

Ingredients:

red and green leaf lettuce
1 cup raisins
1 1/2 cups mini marshmallows
1/4 cup orange juice
1 1/4 cups light salad dressing

2 medium carrots (shredded)
3/4 cup chopped walnuts
2 medium apples (chopped)
1/4 cup honey

Have students wash the lettuce and tear into bite-size pieces. Shred carrots; peel and chop apple into bite-size chunks. Mix lettuce, carrots, raisins, walnuts, marshmallows and apples together. In separate bowl, mix together orange juice, honey and dressing. Pour over salad and toss until well blended. Serve up and nibble away!

Shamus' Shanty

Ingredients:

limeade
your favorite ice cream
green maraschino cherries
clear plastic glasses, straws and spoons

Scoop a couple of spoonfuls of ice cream into each glass. Fill glass with limeade. Top with a maraschino cherry. Top of the mornin' to you! (You can substitute ginger ale or lemon-lime soda for the limeade, but my students enjoyed the refreshing taste of the limeade.)

Bunny Ears

Ingredients:

1/2 banana per student (cut in half lengthwise)
chocolate sauce
2 pints whipping cream
2 white cake mixes
9" x 13" pans
chocolate sprinkles

Prepare cake mixes according to package directions. Set aside until cool. Whip cream; slice bananas in half lengthwise. Cut cake in lengths about 2" wide. Each student receives one length of cake on a small plate. Cut each length in half widthwise (so student has two pieces of cake). Trim the top end of each piece slightly so they look like rabbit ears. Place a banana slice on each "ear." Dribble chocolate sauce over the entire ear. Spoon whipped cream on top. Sprinkle with chocolate sprinkles.

by Teresa E. Culpeper

Busy Little

SUMMER IS HERE

Summer is here!
Winter is done.
I'm going to have
A lot of fun.

I'm going to fish,
(Pretend to cast a line.)
And ride my bike.
(Ride a bike.)
Maybe I'll camp,
And take a hike.
(Hike around.)
I know I'll swim
(Pretend to swim.)
When the sun gets hot.
(Wipe brow.)
I'll rest a little
(Place both hands to cheek and "rest.")
And play a lot!
(Jump rope, bounce a ball, etc.)

APRIL FOOL!

Little bears have three feet,
(Hold up three fingers.)
Little birds have four.
(Hold up four fingers.)
Little cows have two feet,
(Show two fingers.)
And girls and boys have more.
(Show five fingers.)
Do you believe my story?
(Point to "you"; point to own temple, then head.)
Do you believe my song?
(Point to "you," temple and throat.)
I'll tell it only once a year,
(Hold up index finger.)
When April comes along.
(Clap hands to express pleasure.)
APRIL FOOL!

LITTLE RAINDROPS

This is the sun, high up in the sky.
(Form large circle with arms up.)
A dark cloud suddenly comes sailing by.
(Move hands through the air in a parallel motion.)
These are the raindrops,
(Bring arms down; flutter fingers.)
Pitter, pattering down.
(Flutter fingers.)
Watering the flower seeds
That grow under the ground.
(Slowly bring hands up; cup to form flowers.)

Fingers

BAKE A MATZOH

Bake a matzoh. Pat! pat! pat!
(Slap hands together on each "pat.")
Do not make it fat, fat, fat.
(Slap hands together on each "fat.")
Bake a matzoh. Flat! flat! flat!
(Slap hands together on each "flat.")
Bake a matzoh just like that!
(Snap fingers on "that.")

THE PASSOVER TABLE

Let all who are hungry come and eat.
*(With right hand, gesture to others to
    come.)*
Let all who are hungry come for a treat.
(Gesture with left hand.)
Matzohs and latkes and nuts and wine—
They fill the table at Passover time.
(Use both hands to indicate the table.)

SPRINGTIME

(Use appropriate actions.)
Skates we bring.
Push the swing.
Play See-Saw
Margery Daw.
Roll the hoop.
Jump the rope.
Climb the slide.
Ride astride
On a horse.
(Stick, of course!)
Gallop fast.
Home at last.
Windy March.
April showers.
Children pick
May's wild flowers.

FIVE LITTLE EASTER EGGS

Five little Easter eggs,
(Show five fingers.)
Lovely colors they wore.
Mother ate the blue one,
(Pretend to eat the egg.)
Then there were four.
*(Bend one finger down; show
    four.)*
Four little Easter eggs,
Two and two, you see.
(Show four fingers.)
Daddy ate the red one,
(Pretend to eat the egg.)
Then there were three.
*(Bend one finger down;
    show three.)*
Three little Easter eggs,
(Show three fingers.)
Before I knew,
Sister ate the yellow one,
(Pretend to eat the egg.)
Then there were two.
*(Bend one finger down;
    show two.)*
Two little Easter eggs,
(Show two fingers.)
Oh, what fun!
Brother ate the purple one,
(Pretend to eat the egg.)
Then there was one.
*(Bend one finger down; show
    one.)*
One little Easter egg,
(Show one finger.)
See me run!
(Hide finger behind back.)
I ate the very last one!
*(Pretend to eat the egg; then
    show there are none.)*

by Judy Wolfman

April 1 has long been known as April Fools' Day or "All Fools Day." It has roots in many cultures. Some say it may be related to the spring (vernal) equinox, when nature fools people with unpredictable weather. The ancient Hindus could have begun this custom when they celebrated the Feast of Holi, a spring festival held between March 25 and April 1, featuring tricks and pranks. Some trace this day back to a French king in 1856 who made changes in the calendar. Anyone resisting this change was fooled by pranksters and called an April Fish.

Today it is celebrated in much the same way in the United States, Canada and Europe. It is a day for playing practical jokes, with the victim called the April Fool. It's a great day in school to set up silly and harmless activities to play on friends and teachers.

April Fools' Day

Crazy Dress Day

Use April 1 as your crazy dress day. Tell the children to come to class dressed in a foolish way. Examples would be socks that don't match, shoes worn on the wrong feet, different earrings, or shirts and pants worn inside out. Sit at circle time and have each child stand as the others decide what is unique about his/her dress.

April Fish

The children in France try to attach a paper fish to a person's back on April 1. This victim is called an April Fish. Cut out fish shapes from construction paper. Place a piece of rolled masking tape to the back. Let the children walk around the classroom and try to attach these fish on each other's backs. Yell out, "April Fish!"

Mirror Magic

Make signs on poster board or construction paper, printing the letters backwards. Then stand in front of a mirror, and watch the correct words appear like magic. Use simple words or the children's names.

226

Foolish Art

Supply a small brown bag for each student. Inside, place scraps of colorful construction paper, yarn, buttons, sequins, toothpicks, craft sticks, etc. Create a silly invention or creature. End the session with a wacky show and tell where the children discuss their projects.

No Peek Drawings

Give each child a sheet of paper and a crayon. At a signal, name an object for children to draw behind their backs. Hold up the pictures to see who drew the funniest one!

The Fool "Says"

Play a Simon Says-type game using rather silly movements and positions. Choose a child to be "it." He demonstrates a foolish position for the class to try. A few examples would be to hop backwards, walk forward with one eye closed, skip forward holding onto your nose, etc. Dream up other silly ideas for the game.

Silly Sandwiches

Spread filling between two square slices of bread. Provide other edible items to use as decorations while creating a silly person or creature sandwich. Lettuce leaves extending beyond the side of the bread make great hair. Provide things like carrot sticks, olives, pickles, small rounds or squares of cheese, pimentos, cucumber slices, etc. Have a contest for the "funniest" sandwich creature!

Backwards Greetings Game

A child walks up to the chalkboard and introduces himself to the class by saying, "Good-bye, my name is _____." He then writes a word spelled backwards for the class to unscramble. After they identify the correct word, the student returns to his seat, greeting the class with an expressive "Hello!"

by Tania Kourempis-Cowling

Listen Up for April Fools' Day!
Charlie's Challenges

Skills: listening for details
Materials: blank paper, pencil

Put your name at the top of your paper. Draw a line across the middle of your paper to divide it into a top half and a bottom half. I am going to read you a story. Listen carefully for April Fools' tricks. On the top half of your paper, make a tally mark each time you hear a trick. The tally marks will help you count.

Story: Charlie woke up as usual to the sound of his alarm clock. When he reached to turn it off, he re-alized something was wrong. He always set his alarm for seven o'clock, but now it was only 6:00. Someone had made him get up one hour early! Charlie decided to make the most of his extra time and take a walk before breakfast. He quickly pulled on his clothes. When he tried to put on his left shoe, his foot got stuck. Charlie found a wad of newspaper stuck in the toe of his shoe! After fixing that problem, he went down to get his jacket. But when he tried to slide it off the hanger, he found the jacket was inside-out and zipped up. Here was another challenge to straighten out!

Finally, Charlie did step out of the house for a walk. He strolled down the driveway and unlatched the iron gate. Yuck! There was something sticky all over the handle. He first sniffed, then licked his finger. Honey! Someone had put honey on the gate latch! Charlie wiped his hand on the grass as best he could and walked on.

When he arrived back home, his mom greeted him with breakfast. Charlie gulped down his orange juice, then sprinkled sugar and poured milk on his oatmeal. Oops! The sugar was really salt. After a few salty swallows, Charlie's mom kindly let him eat some toast instead. By this time, Charlie was beginning to wonder why he was having so many problems and who was responsible. But before he could say anything to his parents, the phone rang. Charlie jumped up to answer it. It was the school principal. He asked Charlie to come in right away because he was in BIG trouble! Charlie was really scared. Dad offered to drive him to school. It was a very quiet ride. Suddenly, Charlie's dad stopped the car in front of a bakery.

"Hey, Dad, what's this?" asked a surprised Charlie.

"APRIL FOOLS', SON! You're really not in trouble at all. I planned that trick, along with the others you found this morning. How about a doughnut before school starts?"

"Sure, Dad!" Charlie laughed as they entered the bakery.

Now check to see how many tally marks you made. Write that number on the top half of your paper and circle it. On the bottom half, draw a picture of one of the tricks in the story.

by Ann Richmond Fisher

April Fools' Math

Skills: addition, subtraction, following directions
Materials: reproducible (see page 230), pencil

Put your name on the top of your page. Look at the April Fools' Math problems. You will notice a lot of mistakes. Listen carefully and follow these directions.

1. In Row A, circle the problem with the backwards number.

2. In Row A, draw a box around the one problem that is correct.

3. In Row A, put an *X* on every problem where the answer should be six.

4. In Row B, circle *every* answer that is correct.

5. In Row B, draw a line to connect the two problems that should have the same answer.

6. In Row C, one problem has no answer. Write in the correct answer.

7. In Row C, put an *X* on all the incorrect answers.

8. In Row D, all the answers are correct, but the addition and subtraction signs are missing. Add the correct sign to each problem.

9. In Row E, all the problems should equal 10. But one number from each problem is missing. Write in the correct number.

Calendar Clues

Skill: months of the year
Materials: lined paper, pencil

Write your name at the top of your paper. Number your paper from 1 to 10. Three months of the year come before April, and eight months come after April. For each number on your paper, I am going to say the name of a month. If that month comes before April, write a *B*. If that month comes after April, write an *A*.

1. May
2. January
3. September
4. August
5. March
6. November
7. July
8. February
9. October
10. June

April Fools' Math

A.
$$\begin{array}{r} 3 \\ + 1 \\ \hline 4 \end{array}$$
$$\begin{array}{r} 2 \\ + 3 \\ \hline 4 \end{array}$$
$$\begin{array}{r} 4 \\ + 2 \\ \hline 7 \end{array}$$
$$\begin{array}{r} 1 \\ + S \\ \hline 4 \end{array}$$
$$\begin{array}{r} 1 \\ + 5 \\ \hline 7 \end{array}$$

B.
$$\begin{array}{r} 4 \\ + 4 \\ \hline 7 \end{array}$$
$$\begin{array}{r} 3 \\ + 3 \\ \hline 6 \end{array}$$
$$\begin{array}{r} 2 \\ + 2 \\ \hline 4 \end{array}$$
$$\begin{array}{r} 4 \\ + 3 \\ \hline 6 \end{array}$$
$$\begin{array}{r} 1 \\ + 3 \\ \hline 5 \end{array}$$

C.
$$\begin{array}{r} 8 \\ - 3 \\ \hline \end{array}$$
$$\begin{array}{r} 6 \\ - 1 \\ \hline 5 \end{array}$$
$$\begin{array}{r} 7 \\ - 2 \\ \hline 5 \end{array}$$
$$\begin{array}{r} 8 \\ - 4 \\ \hline 5 \end{array}$$
$$\begin{array}{r} 9 \\ - 5 \\ \hline 4 \end{array}$$

D.
$$\begin{array}{r} 7 \\ 4 \\ \hline 3 \end{array}$$
$$\begin{array}{r} 5 \\ 2 \\ \hline 7 \end{array}$$
$$\begin{array}{r} 3 \\ 3 \\ \hline 0 \end{array}$$
$$\begin{array}{r} 6 \\ 2 \\ \hline 8 \end{array}$$
$$\begin{array}{r} 5 \\ 3 \\ \hline 8 \end{array}$$

E.
$$\begin{array}{r} 6 \\ + \underline{} \\ 10 \end{array}$$
$$\begin{array}{r} 5 \\ + \underline{} \\ 10 \end{array}$$
$$\begin{array}{r} 3 \\ + \underline{} \\ 10 \end{array}$$
$$\begin{array}{r} 8 \\ + \underline{} \\ 10 \end{array}$$
$$\begin{array}{r} 1 \\ + \underline{} \\ 10 \end{array}$$

Celebrate Passover

uring passover, Jews all over the orld will sit down to a special meal lled a seder to celebrate their free- om.

lany years ago, Jews lived in Egypt, here the King was very cruel. The ews became his slaves and worked ard making bricks for the King's uildings.

young man, Moses, felt sorry for e Jews, and went to the King many mes to ask him to let the Jewish aves go free. But the King refused, d made them work harder.

od helped Moses by bringing on 10 agues to the King. The tenth one rought the angel of death, who killed e firstborn in every Egyptian home ut passed over the homes of the ews. (This is where the name assover comes from.)

he King finally let the Jews go. Toses told them to pack quickly, led em out of Egypt, the land of slavery,

to a land of freedom.

The *seder*, which means a particular order of service that goes with the meal, has special foods that help today's Jews remember the story of Passover.

The *matzoh* is like a cracker and is very flat. It reminds the Jews that they left Egypt in such a hurry that their bread didn't have time to rise and bake properly.

Moror, or bitter herbs like horseradish, reminds the Jews of how bitter it was to be slaves.

A mixture of apples, nuts, cinnamon and wine, called *charoses* is a reminder of the mortar and bricks the Jews made for the King.

Parsley, a reminder of spring, is dipped in salt water to make the Jews think of the tears that

were shed when they were hardworking slaves.

Two other foods, a roasted egg and a roasted lamb bone, recall the special sacrifices that were made.

While families enjoy this religious dinner together, they read from a special book called the Haggadah. Everyone participates as they share the story of Passover.

Charoses

- 1 cup apples, peeled and chopped
- 1/4 cup chopped nuts
- 1 teaspoon honey
- 1 teaspoon cinnamon
- grated rind of 1/2 lemon (optional)
- 2 tablespoons of red wine (or grape juice)

Mix all of the ingredients together in a bowl. Serve with matzoh or crackers. Makes a tasty snack!

You may need someone to help you chop the apples and nuts.

by Judy Wolfman

Hildy

My hen, Hildy, has a secret
Of the most amazing kind,
For Easter she laid patterned eggs
That she, herself, designed:
Eggs with diamonds,
Eggs with stars,
Eggs with twinkly-winkly bars,
Eggs with crescents,
Eggs with flowers,
And two eggs with rainbow showers!

My hen, Hildy, is a marvel.
She's a darling and a dear.
Best of all, she's promised me
To lay them every year!

by Jeanene Engelhardt

Hop into Spring

Welcome the spring season with our "eggs"citing array of seasonal activities.

Spring is in the air! Spark up the springtime season by creating a "Spring Fling" collage with your class. Brainstorm with your students and make a list of things they enjoy doing in the spring—such as flying kites and playing baseball. Ask them to cut out magazine and newspaper pictures of people enjoying these activities. Glue the pictures to a kite-shaped piece of colorful butcher paper to make your collage. Display on a bulletin board in your classroom.

Calling all kids! Climb to the very top of our egg tree by completing all the activities below. Decorate an egg on the tree for each activity you finish. Start coloring the eggs at the bottom of the tree first.

- Let's pretend! Imagine that you wake up one morning and find a tree with colored eggs growing in your yard. Draw a picture showing your pretend tree. Tell what you would do with the colored eggs.

- Be an author! Write a story about the day it rained polka-dot eggs.

- Spring is here! Make a list of things you enjoy doing in the spring.

- Write a funny poem about an egg named Eggbert. Draw a picture to go with your poem.

- Math time! Write a yummy word problem about chocolate bunnies.

- Give a four-carrot salute! Write a tall tale about Astro Bunny—the first rabbit in space.

- Be an inventor! Create a spaceship for Astro Bunny called the Galaxy Eggspress. Draw a picture of your invention, and label the parts.

- Pretend you are on an egg hunt at the park and find a REAL golden egg. Tell what happens next.

- Congratulations! You have just been hired by Sherlock Rabbit Detective Agency. The Acme Candy Store needs your help—all of their lemon jelly beans are missing! Can you solve the mystery?

- Imagine that you are planning the first Easter egg hunt on the moon. Write a news story telling all about your special event.

by Mary Ellen Switzer

Easter Basket Surprise Dot-to-Dot

Connect the dots and you will find out what's inside the basket.

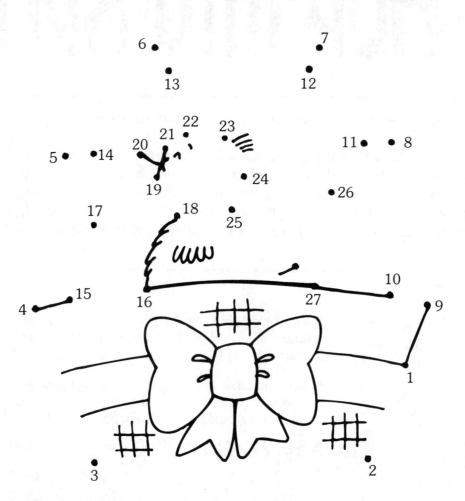

What I named my "surprise": _____

Tell what happened when you took your "surprise" to school for show and tell.

_____

_____

_____

_____

_____

_____

TLC10100 Copyright © Teaching & Learning Company, Carthage, IL 62321-001

Be a Hat Designer!

Help! Randa Rabbit needs a new hat for the Easter Parade. Design a hat that all her friends will rave about.

Design an Egg

Calling all sports fans! Design an egg for your favorite sports figure.

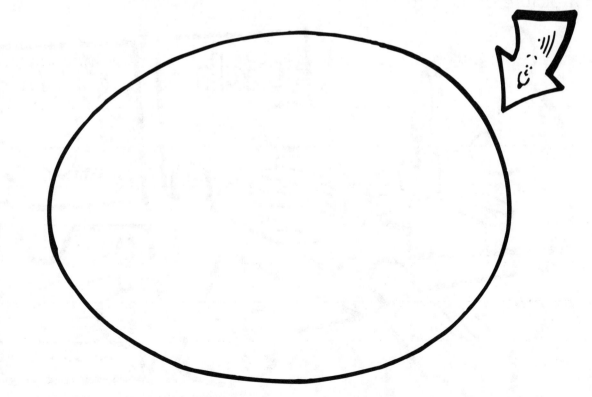

Hidden Picture Fun

Here's an egg hunt that's full of surprises! Find the 10 hidden eggs in the picture—and that's not all! See if you can find the hidden chocolate rabbit, too!

It's Puzzle Time!

What bird lays the largest egg? Cut out the puzzle shapes and put them together to make a picture of the bird.

Create-a-Tree

Draw a tree and label the parts. Include the roots, trunk, leaves and branches in your drawing.

Be a Tree "Eggs"pert

Find out all about trees. Use an encyclopedia or reference book to help you. Write your interesting facts you have learned.

1. _____

_____

2. _____

_____

3. _____

_____

4. _____

_____

Umpteen Egg Ideas for Easter

If you're looking for some "eggs"citing ideas for Easter, look no further. Here are some crafts, decorations, games and science ideas sure to give your class some "eggs"tra fun for the holiday.

Easter Egg Exchange

The old Pennsylvania Dutch tradition of exchanging beautifully decorated Easter eggs can come to your classroom.

Have each student decorate a plastic berry basket and a hard-boiled egg. This can be done at home and brought in, or you can choose to do this as a class project. Make sure students understand that their egg and basket will be a gift to another student, so they should do their best decorating.

During your class party add a few candies to each basket; then have students draw names to see which basket they get to take home. This project is also lots of fun when different classes exchange eggs.

Mr. Egg

This project requires blown eggshells. This isn't hard for children to do, as long as you remind them not to pretend they are a hurricane.

Have each student carefully poke a tiny hole in the small end of an egg. Have them poke a larger hole in the bigger end. Over a sink (or bowl, if you wish to keep the egg's insides), have the child *gently* blow on the small end until the egg's yolk and white slide out the larger hole. Wash the empty eggshell carefully.

Mr. Egg is made by first decorating a toilet tissue tube with construction paper clothes. You can add buttons, rickrack or other materials.

Next paste facial features on the eggshell or draw them on with markers. Add some yarn for hair. Then attach the eggshell to the cardboard tube. These make cute puppets. You might consider using them in a springtime skit.

238

Hatching Chick

Glue one half of an eggshell to a small square of poster board. In the center of the shell, glue a large yellow pom-pom. On top of that, glue a smaller yellow pom-pom. Add two wiggly eyes and an orange paper beak, and you have a cute baby chick ready for Easter.

Harry, the Egg Man

Harry is a simple but fun project. Carefully chip away the large end of an egg and drain out the contents. Wash the egg and decorate it with facial features. Fill the egg with potting soil, add grass seed, water it and place the egg near a window. Eggs can be kept in an egg carton for easier handling.

As the grass seed sprouts, it will create Harry's hair. After a couple of weeks, children enjoy giving their "Harry's" a haircut.

Eggshell Plant Pots

Collect and crush at least 12 empty eggshells for each student. Spread glue on the sides of a metal can. Roll the can in the eggshells and allow it to dry completely. Paint the can with acrylic paints, fill it with dirt and add a pretty plant.

by Donna Stringfellow

Egg in a Bottle

Here's a neat "eggs"periment sure to fascinate your class.

Set a shelled hard-boiled egg on the mouth of a bottle (a Tropicana™ orange juice bottle works well), and show your students that the egg will not easily fit into the bottle. Remove the egg and drop some burning paper into the bottle. Quickly replace the egg on the mouth of the bottle. Now the air pressure inside the bottle will easily pull the egg inside.

To remove the egg, tilt the bottle and blow into it. Take the bottle away from your mouth and watch the change in air pressure push the egg out.

Pass-Along

This game is fast and crazy. To play, have children form a circle. Give one child an egg–plastic, hard-boiled or raw (if you're brave). Have the children begin passing the egg. Add a jelly bean to the game and start passing it in the opposite direction. Keep adding eggs and jelly beans (eggs going one way, jelly beans the other) until hands are flying, trying to keep up with the passing items.

In the mass confusion, items will get dropped and that's the name of the game. Whoever drops an item is out of the game. The circle becomes smaller, and the game continues until one person is left safely holding an item.

Decorated Eggs

Students can decorate eggs using white glue and many common household products.

1. Cut out several of the egg shapes from cardboard using the pattern on the right. Students will use this to trace.

2. After students trace the egg shape on white paper, they can decorate it by drawing lines, circles, faces, zigzags or other designs.

3. Apply white glue (the kind in a squeeze bottle works best) to one part of the design. Sprinkle one of the suggested items on the glue. Let that dry and shake off the excess. Apply glue to another section of the design and sprinkle another item on that section. Continue until the eggs are completely decorated.

4. Students can cut out the finished eggs after they dry and hang them from a tree or use them as classroom decorations.

Note: This project can be rather messy. You might want to spread newspaper over a large table and let students work together in one area rather than at individual desks.

Items to use for decorating eggs:

seashells

uncooked rice

colored sand or gravel

Cheerios™, Rice Krispies™ or other types of dry cereal

sunflower seeds or other small seeds

uncooked macaroni or other noodles

various colored dried beans

popped popcorn

colored sugar

peanuts

by Cindy Barden

240

Once upon an Easter

"Oh, woe," sighed Easter Bunny.
"I don't know what to do.
My ears hurt; my feet hurt.
I think I have the flu."

"And tomorrow is Easter morning,"
The Easter Bunny said.
Mrs. Bunny answered,
"You belong in bed.
Have some nice hot carrot soup,
And rest a little while.
Everything will be all right,"
She murmured with a smile.

Easter Bunny closed his eyes
And soon was sound asleep.
Mrs. Bunny quietly crept
To where the bunnies keep
Easter eggs and fluffy chicks,
And candy in a bin.
Mrs. Bunny whispered,
"I think I should begin
Delivering Easter baskets
To every house in town."
So she hopped throughout the night—
Up the streets and down.

She didn't know which houses
Had some girls or boys,
So every house got baskets
With candy, eggs and toys.

Grandpa Jones, awakening,
Could not believe his eyes.
He said, "I'm very happy
With my Easter Day surprise.
First time Easter Bunny's come
Since I was nine or ten.
Do you think next Easter,
He'll visit me again?"

by Mabel Duch

Easter Bunny's Book Nook

Swing into the spring season with our exciting array of books.

Peter Cotton Tail's Easter Book by Lulu Delacre (New York: Scholastic, Inc., 1991) is full of Eastertime surprises. Follow Peter Cottontail as he delivers his colorful eggs, and you can learn about the many symbols of the Easter season. Have fun singing an Easter version of "Itisket, Itasket," and try an old-fashioned egg roll. Directions for dyeing some sensational eggs are also included.

For Easter decorations galore, *175 Easy-to-Do Easter Crafts*, edited by Sharon Dunn Umnik (Boyds Mills Press, 1994), is the perfect book for you. Seasonal baskets, eggs, greeting cards and other holiday treasures will delight your class. Some of the crafts include Chick Finger puppet, Bunny Party Cups and Easter Place Mats. There are even directions for a felt board egg hunt game and a glitter egg mobile.

Winnie the Pooh's Easter

by Bruce Talkington; illustrated by Bill Langley and Diana Wakeman. New York: Disney Press, 1996.

Wow, what an egg! Winnie the Pooh and his friends gather around a giant-sized Easter egg that Pooh has found. When Rabbit tells them that an Easter egg can talk, Pooh and his friends try some plans to make the silent egg speak.

• Surprise! You find the *biggest* Easter egg in the world. Draw a picture of what the egg looks like. Tell what you would do with it.

• Do you know what bird lays the largest egg? It's the ostrich. Find out more about this amazing bird. Look in an encyclopedia or book about birds to help you. Create an *Amazing Ostrich* book with pictures and facts.

Happy Easter, Dear Dragon

by Margaret Hillert; illustrated by Carl Koch Cleveland: Modern Curriculum Press 1981.

Come along and join a boy and his pet drago as they enjoy the Easter season. Making necklace of spring flowers, decorating eggs an marching in an Easter parade are some of th highlights of their holiday.

• "D" is for dragon. Make a list of all th words in the story that begin with "d." Nov put your list in alphabetical order.

• Happy birthday! You get a most unusua birthday gift this year—a pet dragon. Drav a picture of your new pet. Tell how yo would take care of it.

• You decide to take your dragon to a neigh borhood Easter egg hunt. It's a day you wi never forget! Tell what happens.

by Mary Ellen Switzer

242

The Big Bunny and the Easter Eggs

Steven Kroll; illustrated by Janet Stevens. New York: Scholastic, Inc., 1982.

Wilbur the Easter Bunny is all ready to deliver Easter baskets. The eggs are all painted, and there's lots of jelly beans and chocolate candy. Seems there's just one problem—Wilbur has a cold. Can he still deliver the Easter baskets?

• Poor Wilbur! It's time for him to deliver Easter baskets and he has a cold. Write a story telling how you came to his rescue.

• Help Wanted! Pretend that the Easter Bunny needs a new artist to paint eggs. Write an ad for this new job.

• Cartoon caper. Create a comic strip version of this story.

Bunny Trouble

by Hans Wilhelm. New York: Scholastic, Inc., 1985.

Easter is coming, and all the bunnies are hard at work decorating eggs for the big day. Everyone except Ralph is busy that is. All he wants to do is play soccer. Ralph soon finds himself in trouble when he practices his dribble in a farmer's cauliflower field.

• Happy Easter, Ralph! Design a special Easter egg for Ralph with a soccer theme.

• Calling all soccer fans! Create a brand-new game using a soccer ball. Write directions for playing your game.

• Think of a catchy name for your new game. Draw a billboard sign to advertise this amazing game.

The Great Big Especially Beautiful Easter Egg

by James Stevenson. New York: Greenwillow Books, 1983.

In this humorous Easter tale, a grandfather reminisces with his grandchildren about his journey many years ago to hunt for the world's greatest Easter egg. The children are in for an Easter surprise when they discover that the egg is still around after all these years.

• When he was younger, the grandfather traveled to the Frammistan Mountains in search of the world's greatest egg. Draw a picture of one event during his journey.

• You have all heard the old saying "An apple a day keeps the doctor away." Now finish this one: "An egg a day ____."

Easter Parade

by Mary Chalmers. HarperTrophy, 1988.

Join a lively group of animals as they gather to collect Easter baskets for a special parade. When there is one tiny basket left, the animals search everywhere to find the missing animal. Who can it be?

• Draw a picture of your favorite animal in the Easter parade. Write two sentences about the animal.

• Make a list of all the words you can think of using the letters in *Easter parade.*

• Plan an Easter parade that everyone would rave about. Draw a picture showing what your parade would look like.

Egg-a-Thon Book Week

The Easter season is a perfect time for an Egg-a-Thon Book Week. Delight your students with books and activities featuring an egg theme. Here are some "eggs"cellent read-aloud favorites your class will enjoy:

Chickens Aren't the Only Ones by Ruth Heller. Grosset & Dunlap, 1981.

Egg Story by Anca Hariton. Dutton Children's Books, 1992.

Green Eggs and Ham by Dr. Seuss. Random House, 1960.

Horton Hatches the Egg by Dr. Seuss. Random House, 1940.

Rechenka's Eggs by Patricia Polacco. Philomel Books, 1988.

The Easter Egg Artists by Adrienne Adams. Charles Scribner's Sons, 1976.

The Easter Egg Farm by Mary Jane Auch. Holiday House, 1992.

The Golden Egg Book by Margaret Wise Brown. Golden Book, 1947.

The Most Wonderful Egg in the World by Helme Heine. Atheneum, 1983.

The Surprise Family by Lynn Reiser. Greenwillow Books, 1994.

Billy Bunny's
Easter Surprise

Early Easter morning, Billy Bunny heard a strange sound. He had never heard a noise like this before. "What could be making that pecking sound?" he wondered.

He decided to find out where it was coming from. He grabbed his basket. He put on his coat and shoes and went outside.

First he looked up in a tree. He looked up through the branches to the bright blue sky. But all he saw was a mother robin feeding her babies. "I'm glad I'm not a bird," thought Billy. "I don't like worms for breakfast."

Then he looked under a rock. But all he found was a little green snake. He watched as the snake wiggled off in the grass. "I'm glad I am not a snake," thought Billy. "Someone might step on me."

Finally, he looked in his Easter egg basket. That's where he should have looked first.

by Carolyn Ross Tomlin

That's where he found the baby chicks! They were pec[k]ing their way out of their shells.

One, two, three, four . . . five babies. "Oh, no," said Bil[ly.]

The chicks looked at Billy. Billy looked at them. But th[ey] looked so cuddly, he couldn't be angry.

Billy Bunny scratched his fuzzy head. He wiggled his lo[ng] ears. He twitched his whiskers.

A soft, yellow chick flapped his wings. The chick made [a] little pecking noise.

Billy Bunny said, "If you're going to be surprises f[or] Easter, you'll have to be quieter. Okay?"

The chicks settled down in the basket.

Then he hopped down the road. And instead of eggs, [he] gave all his friends a just-hatched chick for Easter.

Flannel Board Characters

Use these characters (pattern included) on a flannel board as you read the story "Billy Bunny's Easter Surprise." Place a strip of Velcro™ on the back of each shape. Place each character on the board when you come to that part of the story.

back view of puppet

stick

Egg Questions and Answers

Help children recall the sequence of events in the story by writing each question below on an egg made from pastel-colored construction paper. Copy the sentences. Place the eggs in an Easter basket filled with artificial grass. Children may remove an "egg" and answer the question. Use this activity for small group or center time.

- What did Billy Bunny hear? (a strange sound)
- What items of clothing did he put on? (a coat and shoes)
- Where did he look first for the sound? (in a tree)
- What lived in a tree? (a mother robin and her babies)
- Where was the next place he looked? (under a rock)
- What was hiding under a rock? (a snake)
- Where was the last place he looked? (in his Easter egg basket)
- What was in the basket? (baby chicks)
- How many baby chicks did he count? (five)
- Describe how Billy Bunny appeared. (He had a fuzzy head, long ears and whiskers.)
- Why was Billy Bunny surprised when the chicks hatched? (He thought they were only Easter eggs.)
- What did he tell the chicks they would have to do? (be quiet)
- How did the story end? (He gave his friends baby chicks instead of Easter eggs.)
- What was your favorite part?
- Did you like the way the story ended?
- Were you surprised about the eggs hatching?
- Have you ever had a surprise like Billy Bunny?
- Would you rather have Easter eggs or baby chicks? Why?

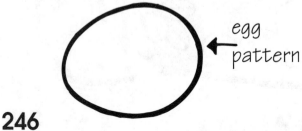

egg pattern

Bunny Cake

Make a bunny cake as a cooking and decorating project during this season. Bake a packaged cake mix according to the direction using two 8-inch round pans. Line a large cookie sheet with foil Cool and remove the cake from the pans. Place one round cake on the bottom of the cookie sheet. Cut the other cake into two ear and a bow tie (see diagram) and place on the sheet. Spread with prepared frosting. Sprinkle coconut on the frosting. Use jell beans for eyes, nose and mouth; licorice for whiskers.

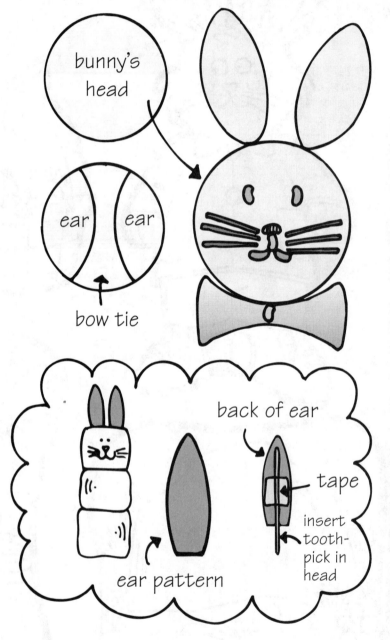

Bunny Favors

Place three large marshmallows together with toothpicks. Cut pink ears from construction paper. Attach with extra toothpicks. Use red felt-tip pen to draw a face. Do not eat but use as an art project

LIFESAVERS®
FIVE FLAVORS

in a Shopping Bag
An Easter Story

don't know what old people like," complained Matthew. "Besides, I don't see why we should have spend our spring break working. Why can't we st have fun?"

Because," said his mother, in the same pitiful tone f voice that Matthew had used with such skill, "it n't just spring break. This is the week before Easter, special time for us."

Special like big chocolate rabbits and hunting for ggs in the park?" asked Matthew. He had perked considerably.

imagine there will be some of that," smiled his other. "But there will be something more."

More treats!" exclaimed Matthew, doing a little ance.

More *treating* other people," finished his mother.

Like visiting the old folks' home," sighed Matthew. e had stopped dancing and started slumping over e basket that his mother had been packing.

found the bars of soap," a cheerful voice wafted to the room. Behind it came Mrs. Anderson and er daughter, Ashlynn. Matthew and Ashlynn were e same age, nine years old; and their families ere close friends.

Rose-scented and honeysuckle-scented soap will erk up our friends at the County Rest Home," niled Mrs. Anderson. Matthew peeked into her ulging shopping bag; even he had to smile at the elightful scents!

Ashlynn added, "We found some of the softest washcloths to put in the basket, too. They'll feel nice on the older folks' delicate skin." Ashlynn had been to the County Rest Home before, and she knew how much the residents enjoyed the small gifts.

While the two moms packed their baskets and bags, Ashlynn and Matthew moved outside to load a dozen small pots of mums into the mini van. The mums made a bold, springtime rainbow on the van floor: lavender, yellow and peach-colored.

by Dr. Linda Karges-Bone

247

"These flowers are going to brighten up the rooms," noted Ashlynn. "And they could use some color."

"Why don't they just buy some paint and pictures and stuff, like *we* do to decorate?" asked Matthew.

"It's not that simple, Matt," Ashlynn told her friend. "The folks in the County Rest Home don't have much money, or hardly anyone else to take care of them. Their monthly checks are just enough to pay for their beds and food."

"Is that why my mom and your mom and some of the people at the church go out there . . . to bring stuff that they can't buy? Is that why we're bringing all these bags and baskets?"

"That's it . . . partly," answered Ashlynn. "But it has to do with helping others because you want to, because it is the right way to live." Ashlynn emphasized her words, too, but they didn't sound quite the same as Matt's grumbling.

Matthew thought about this all the way to the County Rest Home.

He and Ashlynn pulled down a red wagon, and loaded it with the potted blooms of color. Pulling it into the cool, dark hall of the nursing home, Matt noticed how bright the colored mums looked against the pale walls and grey floor.

In the day room, Mrs. Anderson and Matt's mother greeted the nurse who was on duty. Ashlynn walked over to greet a lady who was sitting in a wheelchair. She hugged the lady and smiled.

"Little boy!" a quavering voice called.

Matt turned around. He saw an older gentleman, wearing a plaid shirt, khaki pants and a baseball cap.

"Did you bring any LIFE-SAVERS®?" asked the old man. Matt looked around for his mother, but she was busy unwrapping a bunny cake that had an ear problem. *Somebody* had jabbed

at the icing with his finger, stealing a taste, and th ear had lost its hold on the bunny cake.

Guiltily, Matt turned around. "LIFESAVERS®? Do yo mean me?"

"The colored ones, different colors in a roll. I can get those kind here."

Matthew remembered the brown shopping bag le in the mini van. "Hold on a second," he yelled an ran outside.

Dragging the bag back to the day room, Ma plucked out a shiny new roll of candy. "Here yo go."

"Darn these fingers," fussed the old man. "Arthrit has got 'em bad. Can't do a thing." He fumble with the paper wrapping.

"I'll do it," Matthew offered. He unwrapped th candy and handed it to the old man. A red disk wo first in the roll.

"Don't care for the red ones. You take it, boy urged the old man.

Okay." Matt popped the red one into his mouth."

"I'll take that yellow one," piped in a lady wearing a flowered robe and pink slippers. Matt carried it over to her, since she was leaning on a metal walker.

"Now, the green one. My favorite," declared the old man. He placed the green candy in his mouth and smiled. Matthew smiled, too.

"How come you can't get LIFESAVERS®?" he asked his new friend.

"Nowhere to go for them and no money to buy 'em if I could get away," he replied. "You get tired of not having your own things around you or being able to do when you want to."

"I like to get on my bike and ride to the store," agreed Matthew. He was beginning to understand.

The old man (his name was Mr. Ruppert Dawson) began telling Matthew about a bicycle that he had ridden 50 years earlier. "During the war, that would be World War II, gas was rationed, so I rode my bicycle to town when we needed something."

The old lady in the walker, Miss Helena, scooted over and told about her bicycle that once had a large wicker basket on the back. She had ridden the bicycle, using the basket to hold her books, to get to her teaching job in a one-room schoolhouse. That happened 60 years earlier. Miss Helena, he found out, was 82 years old.

Matthew, Mr. Ruppert Dawson and Miss Helena talked about bicycles and finished off a whole roll of LIFESAVERS® before they heard some lively music coming from across the day room. Ashlynn was playing "Camptown Races" on the piano. All around the day room, people were nodding and smiling. One lady, who wore dark, thick glasses, clapped her hands.

The smell of honeysuckle, a splash of rainbow-colored flowers and the sound of tinkling music had transformed the dark room. "It feels," thought Matthew, "like springtime has come inside." Something had changed, in the room *and* inside Matthew. "Just like the springtime changes the world around us. It's not just bringing beautiful baskets; it's *why* you bring the baskets that counts."

As they drove home from the County Rest Home, Matt reminded his mother, "Don't forget to get more LIFESAVERS® for our next visit and some raisins. Mr. Ruppert Dawson misses raisins in his oatmeal in the mornings."

From then on, LIFESAVERS® in a shopping bag, not chocolate in a basket, made Matthew think of Easter.

Teaching Across the Curriculum with "LIFESAVERS®"

Language Arts

1. **Flavor Word Brainstorm:** Use a blank piece of chart paper and scented, colored markers to record the children's responses to the prompt: "How many flavors or flavor words can you think of?" Here are some to get you started: chocolate, raspberry, malt . . . .

2. **Sweet Adjectives:** Use the LIFESAVERS® candy pattern and provide three to six colored construction paper pieces of candy for each child. Use the disks to write adjectives that describe pleasant tastes. String the adjective candies into necklaces to wear or to adorn the room. Here are some examples of appropriate adjectives: sweet, tasty, delicious . . . .

3. In many ways, the "LIFESAVERS®" story is one of contrasts. This makes it a good choice for introducing or reinforcing antonyms, words that mean the opposite of each other. Create an Opposites Attract game by using the LIFESAVERS® candy pattern to make pairs of antonyms from the story, as well as others. Randomly select children and tape an antonym LIFESAVERS® to their backs. Let the children mix and mingle until they have found their "match." Each pair can be rewarded with real LIFESAVERS® candies. Examples: old-young, dark-light, sweet-sour, wrinkled-smooth.

Creative Arts Activities

1. **LIFESAVERS® Designs:** Use inexpensive rolls o colored disk candies, colored and plai toothpicks and white art paper to set up center for designing creative pictures. Th stark contrast between the jewel-like car dies and the plain paper, and the simpl addition of the toothpicks as connector gives the children many varied opportunitie for design. Supply white glue to fasten th designs onto the paper.

2. **LIFESAVERS® Collages:** Use the LIFESAVERS candy pattern to reproduce multicolored "candies" for the children to cut out an arrange in interesting patterns on butche paper or freezer paper. Then select maga zine or newspaper photographs of older an younger people and create a "people co lage" on top of the existing LIFESAVERS mosaic for a sort of "stained glass" effec (Note: Use the magazine and newspape pictures from the social studies activity. This a logical enrichment or follow-up.)

Social Studies and Science

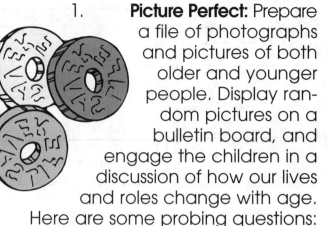

1. **Picture Perfect:** Prepare a file of photographs and pictures of both older and younger people. Display random pictures on a bulletin board, and engage the children in a discussion of how our lives and roles change with age. Here are some probing questions:

- Is life easier or more difficult when one is older/younger? Why?

- How do you treat older people? How *should* we treat older people?

- Why should we respect older citizens? How can we show them that we respect and care about them?

- What can younger people learn from older friends?

2. **Scents Alive:** Many of the incidents in the story contain descriptions of how we use our senses to interpret the world around us. Collect objects such as scented soap, a soft washcloth, raisins and others. Place these objects into a brown paper bag, and then invite individual children (blindfolded) to touch and smell the objects in the bag. How did they feel? Use the following observational checklist to complete the activity. Then place it in your science portfolios.

Mathematics and Problem Solving

1. LIFESAVERS® and raisins are easy and fun to use to introduce grouping concepts such as multiplication or division. Give each group of four children a paper cup of LIFESAVERS® or raisins and challenge them to solve the following problems. Small chalkboards are nice to use for recording the results. The group recorder can write the answer and hold up the board for instant checking.

- Matthew and Ashlynn want to bring two friends each to help out on their next visit to the rest home. How many children can we count on?

- The red wagon can hold seven plants. How many trips will Ashlynn and Matt have to make if they have 10 plants?

- Matthew's mom included 15 bars of scented soap and 18 washcloths in her basket. How can you figure out how many extra washcloths she packed?

Bunny Land

Invite your children to hop on over to "Bunny Land" for some fun-filled Easter activities.

Bunny Breakfast

Begin your day the healthy way by creating a delicious "bunny" dish.

What You Need:
English muffins
soft cream cheese
sliced melon
strawberries
red grapes
blueberries
raisins

What to Do:
Toast the muffins. Spread cream cheese on a muffin half and set it on a plate. Cut a melon slice in half and place the halves above the muffin head for ears. Slice a red grape in half and press the halves into the cream cheese for eyes. Slice a strawberry in half and place one half below the eyes for a nose. Position rows of raisins on either side of the nose for whiskers. Give your bunny a smiling, blueberry mouth.

A Bunny Tail

Draw a rearview picture of a rabbit on a cardboard box. Draw a circle to mark the tail position. Glue several strips of Velcro™ inside the circle. Provide the children with sock balls or foam balls. Have them take turns tossing the balls at the box. When a ball sticks to the Velcro™, the bunny will have its tail. (gross motor skills)

Bunny Bracelet

Cut several 1" circular strips from a cardboard tube. Slice each strip so it will open. Provide the children with white paper, scissors, markers and a small bunny pattern. Have them trace, color and cut out their bunnies. Staple each bunny to a cardboard strip. Open the strip and slide it onto the child's wrist.   (scissor skills)

Box Garden

Make use of shoe box lids, green paper and garden catalogs to "plant" a garden fit for a rabbit. Cut the green paper into strips. Have the children use scissors to fringe the strips for grass. Glue this grass around the edges of the lid, forming a framed, rectangular garden area. Let the children cut fruit and vegetable pictures from the garden catalogs to plant in their gardens with glue. (scissor skills)

Note: Bunny patterns for the various activities on these pages are located on page 256.

by Marie E. Cecchini

Bunny Faces

Draw and color a bunny head outline on a piece of cardboard. Cut out the face section. Have the children take turns placing their faces in the bunny head. Take a picture of each bunny-child. Frame the pictures to make Easter cards for their families.   (take-home card)

Bunny Math

Ask the children to bring in stuffed bunny toys from home. Have them introduce their bunnies to the class.

Bunny Sorting: Provide color-coded boxes or baskets for the children to use in sorting the stuffed animals by color. Tabulate the sorting results on a color graph. For each bunny in each color basket, place one rabbit sticker in the correct graph column. What color are most of the bunnies? Which color has the least number of bunnies?

Bunny Sizes: 1. Make use of several different-sized bunnies. Have the children arrange these from largest to smallest, mix them all together again, then arrange them from smallest to largest.
2. Separate the stuffed rabbits into three piles: small, medium and large. Count to see which group has the most/least rabbits. Do any groups have the same number of rabbits?

Bunny Count: Carefully count the whole bunny collection. Write the number on a sheet of paper. Where else can we find this same number? Can you find it on the clock or on the calendar?

Baby Bunny Baskets

Baskets: Punch a hole in both sides of a one-pound margarine tub. Fasten the ends of a pipe cleaner through the holes to make a handle. Let the children decorate the containers with Easter stickers. Place Easter grass in each basket.

Baby Bunny: Glue two cotton balls together, one on top of the other, to form a bunny head and body. Glue two small pink ears to the back of the head. Add two black hole-punch eyes, a pink triangle nose, yarn-snip whiskers and a yarn snip mouth. Place the baby bunny in its basket to dry.   (small motor skills, following directions)

Bunny Trail Tricks

Have the children pretend to be bunnies delivering eggs as they move through a bunny trail obstacle course. You might have them jump over a block, crawl under a table, walk a wavy length of yarn on the floor, shimmy through a cardboard box and walk in and out through a row of chairs. Let them each carry one small, plastic egg to be deposited in a basket at the end of the trail.   (gross motor skills)

B Is for Bunny

Color and cut out two large bunny shapes. Attach one to a bulletin board and tape the other to a cardboard box. Display a card showing upper and lowercase B. Talk with the children about the sound "B" makes. Have them listen for it when you say *bunny*. Ask them to contribute any other "B" words they can think of. Invite them to become sound detectives for the week. Ask them to look for objects and pictures with "B" names. Have them place the collected objects in the box and glue any pictures to the bulletin board bunny. As a group, check the box and bulletin board each day for any new additions.

Bunny in a Hole

Cut oatmeal or salt boxes in half. Cover the cylinder with green paper, poke a hole in the bottom and fill with Easter grass. Have each child cut out a small bunny from pink or white paper and color it. Tape the bunny to the top of a drinking straw or craft stick. Slide the opposite end of the straw or stick through the hole under the grass. The children can then hold the box in one hand and move the straw or stick with the other hand to make the bunny hop into and up from the grass.

Bunny Beenies

Provide the children with disposable plastic bowls to decorate with Easter stickers. Poke a hole in both sides of the bowl, thread with elastic cord and tie to fit under each child's chin. Have the children color and cut out their own bunnies. Tape each bunny to the top of a pipe cleaner. Poke the opposite end of the pipe cleaner through the hat and tape it to the inside. The bunnies will wiggle and hop when the children wear their beenies.

Bunny Cups

Make cute Bunny Cups for storing tiny treasures or colorful jelly beans. Supply the children with Styrofoam™ cups, pink paper, pink pom-poms, black pipe cleaners, scissors, glue and markers. Have them draw eyes on the cup and cut out two pink ears to glue at the top. Let them glue on a pom-pom nose and cut out a pink mouth to glue at the bottom. When the glue is dry, poke both ends of a pipe cleaner from the inside of the cup to the outside on either side of the nose for whiskers. Bend to shape. Add a second pipe cleaner in the same manner.

What Rabbits Do

(to the tune of "Frere Jacques")
I'm a rabbit. I'm a rabbit.
See what I do. See what I do.
Here at school, here at school.
I can munch a carrot.
I can munch a carrot.
Here at school.
Here at school.

(Variations: hop on one foot, hop on two feet, wrinkle my nose, bend my ears, wiggle my tail)

Snack Hop

Place a container of carrot sticks on a chair a few feet from the children. Mark a starting line. Have individual children begin at the starting line and hop to the carrots, counting how many hops each takes to receive a carrot. Remind them to sit while they munch their carrots. Bunnies cannot hop and eat at the same time.

Bunny Parade

Invite the children to use doll clothes and dress their bunnies for a parade. Help with any buttons, snaps or zippers as necessary. Play music as they march around with their animals. Have them line up the animals single file and clap to the music while the animals have their own parade.

Bunny Habits

Let the children take turns leading the group in imitating rabbit actions to the song above.

Bunny Bags

Draw several rabbit faces. Staple each to the top front of a paper lunch bag. Write a different number on each bag. Fasten the back of each bag to a bulletin board. Provide the children with a container of orange manipulatives such as marker lids, jug lids or beads. These are the pretend carrots. Have individual children read the numbers on the bags; then feed the bunnies the correct number of carrots by dropping manipulatives in the bags.

Clip Art for **Bunny Land**

MISSING
The Lost Easter Bonnet

Help! Tansy Turtle has lost her new Easter bonnet, and she can't seem to find it anywhere! Grab your crayons and finish the "Missing" poster, using these instructions:

1. Color the bonnet yellow.
2. Draw 2 big orange and 3 small pink flowers on the bonnet.
3. Draw 4 green leaves on the flowers.
4. Draw a blue butterfly on the bonnet and color the bow red.
5. Add any other items to Tansy's bonnet that you wish.

Bonus: Write a story telling how Tansy's animal friends help find her missing bonnet.

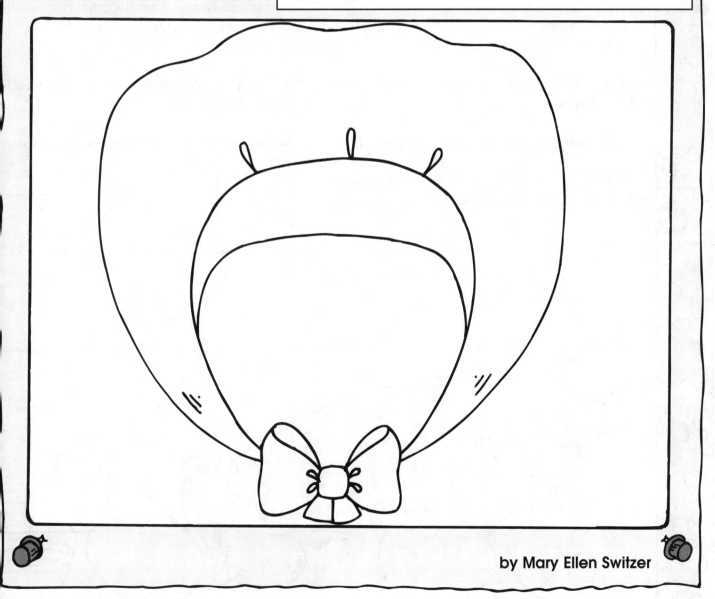

by Mary Ellen Switzer

No Eggs

by Phyllis Brubaker Pyle

"I'm not going to color any eggs this year," Bunny announced one early spring day.

The hens in Bantam Henhouse stood up in their nests and opened their beaks in astonishment.

"Last year I sat in the pot of blue dye," complained Bunny. "I spilled red dye on my foot and accidentally colored my whiskers green. Then I got my nose too close to an egg I had just painted yellow. Painting eggs is just too much trouble."

"But it wouldn't be Easter without colorful eggs," objected Hattie Hen.

"What will you put in the baskets?" asked Harriet Hen.

Happy Hen was too astonished to say anything.

"I'll fill them with candy eggs," explained Bunny. "I won't have to worry about breaking *them*."

"No real eggs for Easter!" exclaimed Hattie Hen.

"The children will be disappointed!" sighed Harriet Hen.

"Their parents will be upset!" cackled Happy Hen, even though she was still astonished.

"Oh, no," said Bunny. "The parents will be glad. Candy wrappers don't make a mess like eggshells. Now I must be going. Easter is just two days away, and I have lists to make." With these words, Bunny went hopping away to the room behind the henhouse where he had his workshop.

"We can't let Bunny ruin Easter this year!" exclaimed Hattie Hen.

"We've got to do something!" sighed Harriet Hen.

"We'll put our beaks together and think of a plan," cackled Happy Hen. She did not sound very happy.

The hens hopped down from their nests. They gathered in a circle and tilted their heads this way and that as they thought and thought.

Soon Hattie Hen began to cackle. Harriet Hen cackled louder. Happy Hen got very excited and cackled loudest of all.

After Bunny had gone home to bed, the hens marched into his workshop.

Hattie Hen moved the eggs by rolling them with her beak.

Harriet Hen mixed the dyes together.

Happy Hen used the tips of her wing feathers to splash the colors on the eggs. Sometimes she splashed the eggs. Sometimes she splashed herself and Hattie and Harriet Hen.

Bunny came to the workshop the next morning. "What have you done?" he cried when he saw the spots of gold, brown, red and blue dye all over everything.

"We couldn't let you ruin Easter!" exclaimed Hattie Hen.

"We colored the eggs for you!" sighed Harriet Hen.

"I'm afraid we colored ourselves, too," cackled Happy Hen.

Bunny looked at the baskets of colored eggs. "These are the most beautiful eggs I've ever seen," he said. "I can't wait to deliver them."

The three hens fluffed their many-colored feathers as they cackled happily.

And ever since that day, all Bantam hens in the henhouse have been speckled with many different colors.

Holiday Classroom Decorations

Paper Plate Easter Bunny

Simple materials help little hands become creative. Ordinary paper plates become an unusual Easter Bunny.

Materials:
- 2 paper plates
- 3 chenille stems
- felt-tip markers
- scissors
- glue

Use one plate as the bunny's face.

Cut the other plate into two ears and a bow tie. Draw eyes, mouth and nose.

Cut small slits and insert the chenille stems.

Staple the ears and bow tie on the head.

Use these bunnies as room decorations during the Easter and spring season. Or read a story about rabbits and use them as puppets.

by Carolyn Ross Tomlin

Hatching Out Numbers

Cover the bulletin board with light blue paper and corresponding border. Make a nest from a large brown grocery bag. Cut off and discard the top half. Open and cut 4" strips down from the top of the remaining bag. Add Easter grass to the nest. Staple to the board. Using pastel-colored construction paper, cut 24 eggs from the pattern. Number the eggs according to the grade level. Place several baby chicks (see pattern) near the nest. Use with small groups.

Change the board each day by putting up different directions. For instance, put an egg in the nest that shows:

- an even number
- an odd number
- a number greater than ___
- a number less than ___
- a number between ___ and ___
- the smallest number in your set
- the largest number in your set

baby chick pattern

egg pattern

by Carolyn Tomlin

Hatching Out Numbers

Put all the eggs that show an even number into the nest.

Paste here.

Fold

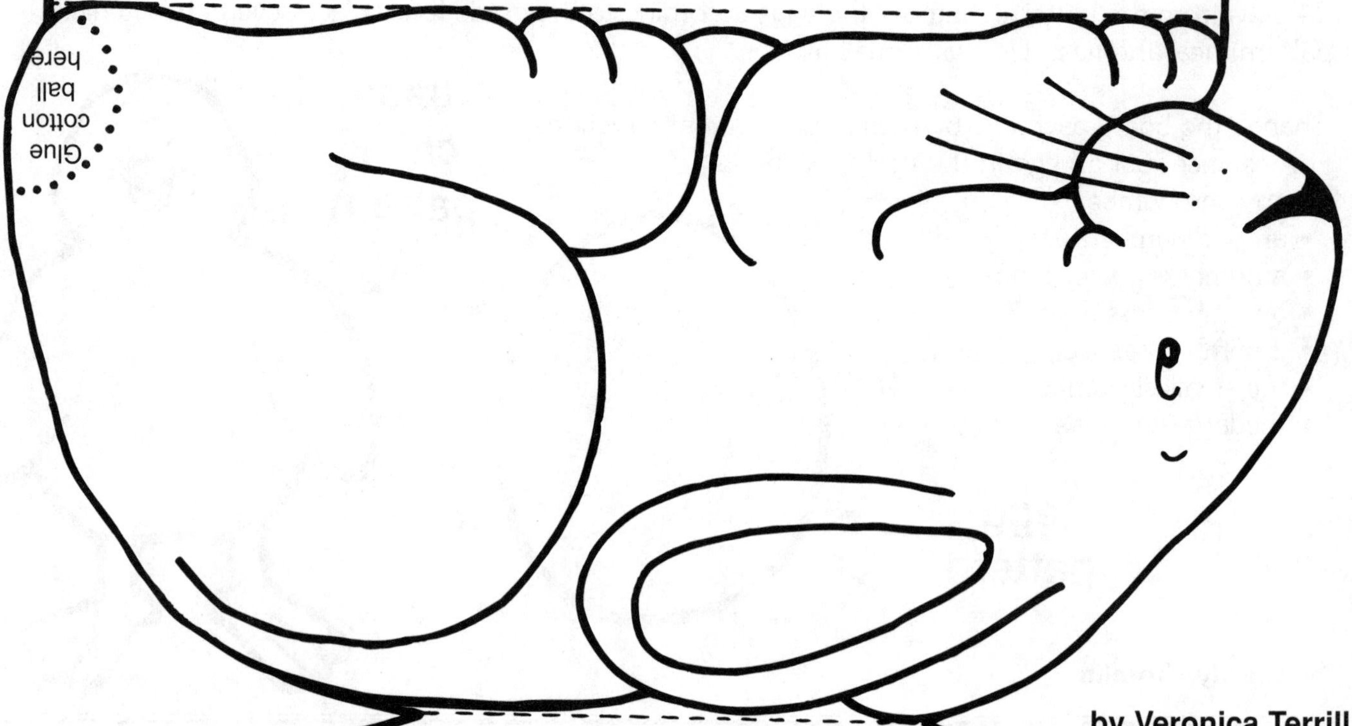

Glue cotton ball here.

by **Veronica Terrill**

Happy, Happy Easter!

Name _____

Fold

Paste to opposite side to form topper.

Arbor Day

Long, long ago there was a man
Named Johnny Appleseed.
He was a very kindly sort,
As everyone agreed.

He traveled all around our land,
Where trees were never found;
And in those empty spaces,
He sowed fruit seeds in the ground.

Years later apple blossoms grew,
And ripe fruit in the fall.
The deed he did so long ago
Was perhaps the best of all.

Each year on Arbor Day in spring,
We think of all our trees
And how very bare the world would be
Without such gifts as these.

So the next time you admire trees
And their products that we need,
Remember a stalwart pioneer
Named Johnny Appleseed!

by Jean Conder Soule

"Tree"mendous Arbor Day

By planting and caring for trees, we insure our own survival and our future. Julius Sterling Morton helped establish a holiday to remind us to plant and care for our trees. He started the first official Arbor Day in Nebraska on April 10, 1872. The movement grew, and Arbor Day became a legal holiday in many other states. In honor of Morton's contribution to the holiday, the date was moved to April 22, Morton's birthday.

Trees clean the air, return water moisture to the atmosphere, provide food and materials for much of the world, and give us critical medicines. Arbor Day is a time to plant, study and appreciate the beauty and usefulness of the trees.

"Tree"ific Tree Facts

1. The tallest tree is taller than a thirty-story building.

2. Trees continue growing as long as they live.

3. Trees can live to be thousands of years old.

4. The record for the thickest tree trunk is held by the Montezuma bald cypress at 40 feet around.

5. The tallest tree is the California Redwood which grows to a height of around 360 feet or 110 meters high.

6. There are six main groups of trees: broadleaf, needle leaf, palms, cycad, tree ferns and ginkgo.

A Tree or Not a Tree Product

Locate the objects or materials listed below. Ask students to guess which products come from a tree. (All of them do.)

almonds	pecans
walnuts	chocolate
coffee	maple syrup
olives	cinnamon
cloves	rubber
paper	charcoal
cork	

Barking up the Right Tree

With charcoal, crayons or colored chalk have your students do rubbings of different tree bark. With the leaf samples they collect, try identifying the trees from an encyclopedia.

"Tree"eats!

As an Arbor Day snack, plant your own "tree"eats. Fill small individual paper cups with about 1" of chocolate pudding for the dirt. Crumble chocolate sandwich cookies over it for topsoil. To make the trees, insert straight pretzels into gumdrops. The gumdrops will keep the pretzel standing upright as well as look like the balled roots of the tree. Plant your trees in the pudding and enjoy!

A Tree's Life

Obtain a slice of a tree trunk. The annual rings will tell the story of the tree's life. Rings that are close together show a period of lesser growth. There might have been a shortage of rainfall during those years. The amount of moisture can also be shown in rings which are spaced farther apart, as the abundance of moisture allowed the tree to grow faster. Count the rings and see how old the tree was when it died. Compare that lifespan to a human's.

by Terry Healy

264

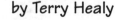

Bulletin Board Ideas

Cut out a large tree and place on a bulletin board. Cut out white apple-shaped paper. On the apple shapes, ask your students to write or illustrate ways in which trees and the Earth can be saved. To get your students started, remind them of the 3 Rs: *reuse, recycle and reduce*. Arrange the apple shapes on and around the tree. Title the bulletin board "Tree"mendous Ideas to Save Our Planet."

The Roots of Learning

As your students begin learning about trees and Arbor Day, discuss what they know and what they want to learn. On an outline of a tree, record what they know at the roots. The trunk will be the place to list what they want to know. On the fruit or the leaves, write what your students have learned as the study progresses. The tree can act as an illustration that learning is rooted in what you know and grows with the desire to learn more. The fruit is the new knowledge that you gain.

Science Sorting

Recognizing Patterns: On a walk or from classroom samples of branches, ask the children to classify the leaves. You may want to help begin the classification by asking them to find those branches which fit the following patterns:

1. Alternating leaf arrangements versus opposite arrangement.
2. Simple leaves versus compound leaves.
3. Palmate veins (looks like a hand) versus pinnate (like a feather). (The ginkgo trees have a third category of veins called parallel veins, but this is fairly rare.) Other ways to classify the leaves would include size, general shape and coloring.

An extension of this activity would be to place two or three circles of string on the floor. The string circles would overlap on one side, like Venn diagrams. Leaves could be sorted into the different circles or categories.

Suggestions for Arbor Day Celebrations

1. Interview a forester.
2. Visit a nearby arboretum.
3. Hold a poster contest urging people to plant trees.
4. Start a recycling box in your classroom or school.
5. Write articles for your local paper telling what you have learned about trees.
6. Collect money through recycling or other projects and buy a tree to plant at your school.
7. Make a tree map of your playground or a local park, showing the location and type of trees that can be found there.

Earth Day
Ways Students Can Help Clean Up the Earth!

Information: As our world population continues to grow, it is extremely important that students are aware of our resources and how they are used.

The first Earth Day was celebrated in April 1970, to increase public awareness of our endangered environment. Gaylord Nelson, a former United States senator, identified the perilous condition of our planet and single-handedly instigated the idea of Earth Day. April 22, 1995, was the 25th anniversary of Earth Day.

Touring My Home

Ask each student to take a tour of their home with an adult. Have them go from room to room listing or drawing all the items they see that use electricity. Have them label each room on a chart and record their findings under each category.

Light Bulbs Galore!

How many light bulbs do you have in your home? Have students count the number of light bulbs they find at home. An adult should be present to help with the counting, depending on student ability levels. Tell them not to forget that there are even tiny lights in VCRs, clock radios and microwaves!

Turn, Turn, Turn Those Off

How many times do we leave a room and forget to turn off the lights, TV, stereo or other appliances when they are not being used? Students can create family reminders on self-stick papers or note cards and place them in strategic spots around the house.

Wonderful, Wet Water

Discuss brushing teeth and taking baths and showers. Can students recall the exact steps in each process? Do they turn off the faucet while brushing teeth? Is the bathtub filled with only the amount of water needed? Does the shower run extra long for "play" instead of washing?

by Teddy Meister

Colorful Collages

Gather stacks of old magazines in advance. Tell students to cut out pictures of transportation methods that use fossil fuels (coal, oil and gas) as energy sources and paste them on art paper.

Poetry Passages

Create a class poem about the importance of Earth Day. Put it on a large chart for the bulletin board, and have students draw illustrations for the poem. More-able students might want to compose additional Earth Day poems individually or in small groups.

Terrific T-Shirts

If students can bring old T-shirts to school, they can create an original Earth Day logo of their own. If T-shirts are not available, use large sheets of white art paper cut to actual student size. These can be decorated on both sides.

Place the Place Mat Properly

For Earth Day celebrations, give students art paper the size of place mats. A border design can be used and an illustration showing one important aspect of Earth Day created for the center. Of course, *Earth Day* should be written somewhere on the mat. These can be used when students have lunch that day.

How Can I Help Clean Up the Earth?

Brainstorm a list of everyday things students can do to help keep the Earth cleaner. The list might include picking up trash on the school grounds or interior hallways, keeping litter out of their desks, not wasting paper, and using the water fountains for only a few seconds. Other suggestions might form a second list for things that can be done at home.

Open and Close in a Flash

Ask students to time themselves at home whenever they open the refrigerator. Do they stand and think about what they want to get before or after the door is open? What do other members of the family do? It is good to have a mental picture of what is already in the refrigerator, then open it, get it and close it in a flash!

Before implementing Earth Day activities, you might want to send for free materials to enhance the curriculum. At this writing, all addresses are current.

- Your local electric or gas utility companies.
- Your local county cooperative extension office.
- National Renewable Energy Lab., 16127 Cole Blvd., Golden, CO 80401-3933
- U.S. Department of Energy, Office of Public Inquiry, PA-5, 1000 Independence Ave., Washington, D.C. 21858
- U.S. Department of Energy, Office of Scientific and Technical Information, P.O. Box 62, Oak Ridge, TN 37831
- National Energy Information Center EI-231, Room 1F-048, Forrestal Bldg., 1000 Independence Ave., SW, Washington, D.C. 20585
- Johnathon Porritt, Special Advisor to Friends of the Earth C/O FREEPOST, 56-58 Alma Street, Luton, Beds, LU1 2YZ United Kingdom (Organization in England for "Friends of the Earth")

Earth Day Certificate

Read this certificate aloud to your class. Then let students fill in their name and color with crayons. Congratulate each child on their decision to protect the Earth as you date and sign each certificate.

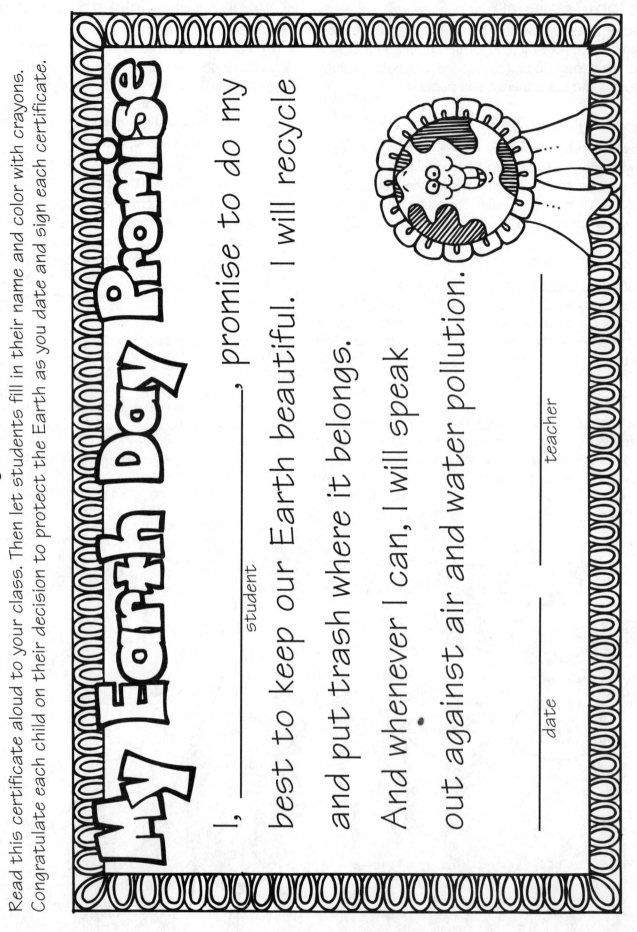

My Earth Day Promise

I, _____, promise to do my
          student

best to keep our Earth beautiful.   I will recycle

and put trash where it belongs.

And whenever I can, I will speak

out against air and water pollution.

_____
teacher

_____
date

by Becky Radtke

Caring for Our Earth

Cover a bulletin board with white paper and divide it in half. On one side, draw green grass, trees, a clear blue sky, clear blue water and sunshine. On the other side, color the sky light grey; glue candy wrappers, trash paper, empty soft drink cans and a dead tree. Omit grass. Talk with students about how each one has a responsibility to care for our Earth. Ask which picture shows the kind of place where they would like to live.

Celebrating
May Day

May Day, celebrated May 1, is a spring holiday that marks the revival of life: the coming of spring. It has been stated that this day originated with the ancient Romans who honored Flora, goddess of fruits and flowers. Later, the English celebrated this event by dancing around a "Maypole" which was erected in the middle of a village or town. The Maypole was decorated with long trailing ribbons that hung from the top. The dancers held the ribbons, and as they danced they wove the ribbons into patterns. A May Queen was chosen to reign over the festivities.

Traditionally, the people went out early in the morning of May 1 to gather fresh flowers and tree branches. This was called "bringing in the May." These flowers were used in baskets which decorated the homes. Today, children in the United States make baskets, fill them with spring flowers and present them to family, friends and neighbors. The ritual is for the child to leave the May basket on a person's doorstep, ring the bell and quickly run around the house before he/she can be caught and kissed.

Conduct your own classroom celebration of May Day this year. Activity ideas are included to help you prepare for this event.

by Tania Kourempis-Cowling

Maypole Dance

If you have a flagpole or tetherball pole in your playground, decorate it with colorful crepe paper. With very young children, it would be best if they danced around the pole without holding onto streamers. It avoids children getting caught and twisted amongst the ribbons. Play some music or beat a drum and give the children signals to walk, skip or hop around the pole. Changing directions as they circle is fun and educational; circle to the right, then about-face and circle to the left.

270

Hide the Flower

Pick one child to be it. This child covers his/her eyes while the teacher or another child hides a real flower in the classroom. It opens his eyes and searches for the flower. If he gets close to the hidden spot, the children clap their hands and continue clapping. If it gets too far from the flower, the students stomp their feet on the floor. These clues need to be explained to the children before the game begins. The "clapping and stomping" are discovery tools to this game.

Sing a Song of May

(Tune: *"Row, Row, Row Your Boat"*)
May, May, May is here,
Flowers everywhere.
Dance around the pole today,
May Day's here; let's cheer!

Waltz of the Flowers

Children love to find the opportunity to get up and dance. With all the emphasis on flowers, create costumes that are colorful and represent petals on flowers. You will need a piece of elastic to fit around the child's waist, a stapler and many strips of fabric. Crepe paper streamers could also be used as a simpler variation. Measure the child's waist and cut the elastic to fit. Staple the ends together. Attach the strips of paper or fabric with staples around the waistband. Have the children wear these flower costumes as they dance. "The Waltz of the Flowers" from *The Nutcracker Suite* is very appropriate.

Individual Maypoles

Give each child a cardboard paper towel tube. Encourage them to decorate these with colorful crayons, markers, tissue paper and other materials. Staple crepe paper, ribbon or fabric strips to one end. Gather the children to sing and dance to their favorite springtime music and move freely with their miniature Maypoles.

Giant Sunflower

Cut wedges from the edges of a small paper plate. Paint the plate yellow. After it's dry, glue sunflower seeds in the center of the plate. Attach a green construction paper stem and leaves. Voilá, a gigantic sunflower to admire!

Lei Day

On May 1, the people of Hawaii celebrate Lei Day, which is very similar to May Day. Children and adults make and wear colorful leis of fresh flowers around their necks. Leis are presented to people to express a feeling of friendship and love. Verbally you are welcomed with an "Aloha."

Lei Day is celebrated on all of the islands. Pageants, contests, music, singing and dancing fill the air. Hula dancing is the most popular form of dance, expressing words of song with the dancer's hands. The girls wear floral leis and grass skirts. They swing their hips to the rhythms of drums and musicians who play ukuleles. The Hula dance usually tells a story of the beautiful facets of nature, such as the sea, sky, beaches, mountains and palm trees.

A Hawaiian feast called a luau is planned for Lei Day. It is held outdoors with a whole pig roasting in a ground pit. Other favorite foods are bananas, pineapple, mangoes, papayas, yams and poi (mashed taro root).

Plan a Lei Day festival in your classroom with a few of these ideas:

MAKING A LEI

Have each child make a lei to wear during the class festival. Cut out flowers using this pattern from construction paper in all colors. You will need a dozen or more flowers per lei. Punch a hole in the center of each flower with a hole punch. Next, cut short pieces of drinking straws. With a length of yarn, thread the flowers and straws one after the other until you have the entire lei completed. Make sure it will fit over the child's head and knot the ends together.

HAWAIIAN TOSS GAME

Draw 10 shapes on a large sheet of cardboard to place on the floor. These shapes should include symbols of a Hawaiian festival, such as flowers, pineapples, palm trees, coconuts and bananas. Number these pictures from 1-10. Standing back a few feet, have each child toss a beanbag five times onto the gameboard. Add up the scores. After the entire class has had a turn, see who has the highest score.

ARTISTIC BEACH SCENES

Give each child a sheet of construction paper. Let them draw a beach scene with crayons, including the sun, palm trees, people, beach balls, umbrellas, chairs, etc. For texture, brush on glue and spread a thin layer of sand for a true beach effect. If you do not live near a body of water, white sand can be purchased at a nursery or hardware store. Small shells would also make a nice addition, if available.

by Tania Kourempis-Cowling

FANTASTIC FISH

Each child will need one plain paper plate. Cut out one "pie piece" shape from the plate and staple this to the opposite side of the plate for the fin. Explain to the children how colorful tropical fish can be. Let them color the fish with crayons, markers or paint. To enhance the art, glue on glitter, sequins or faux jewels.

PIN THE PINEAPPLE ON HAWAII

Make two small construction paper pineapples for each member of your class. Attach a rolled piece of masking tape to the back. Tape a map of the world on the wall. Discuss with the students where the Hawaiian islands are located. Blindfold each player and turn them toward the map to attach their pineapple. See who comes the closest to Hawaii.

COCONUTS

Pass a coconut around the classroom for the children to examine. Coconut is a very popular food in Hawaii. First pierce a hole in the coconut and drain out the milk. Let the children try a taste. Next, saw the coconut in half (adults only). Remove the meat and break it into small pieces to eat. To make a musical instrument, let the children take turns sanding down the coconut halves to make them smooth. These shells can be decorated with paints if desired. Holding one coconut half in each hand, tap the cut edges together to create hollow wooden sounds. Have the children walk, march, skip and gallop to the sounds of the clapping coconuts.

SUGAR CUBE PICKUP

This game is played with the same concept as Pick Up Sticks. Since sugar is an important product of Hawaii, use sugar cubes to play this game. Fill a glass with sugar cubes. Slowly turn the glass upside down on a tabletop. Remove the glass, letting the cubes land as they may. The player starts removing cubes one by one, trying not to disturb the other cubes in the pile. He continues removing cubes until the pile tumbles over. See how many cubes students can pick up!

American Bike Month

May Is American Bike Month!

Be a safe rider! Remember to wear your bike helmet when you ride! Design a bike helmet that all your friends would rave about. Create a bicycle safety slogan to remind kids to wear their bike helmets.

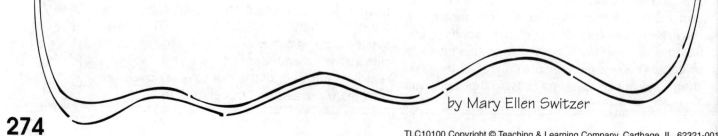

by Mary Ellen Switzer

Cinco de Mayo

Cinco de Mayo is a very special holiday in Mexico. On this day, Mexicans celebrate their important victory over the well-trained French army on May 5, 1862. Today, flags and banners decorate the streets for this national holiday. Festive parades and parties are held. Pinatas are a highlight for children at some of the celebrations. These papier-mâché containers are filled with candy, toys or presents. Children try to break open the pinata with a long stick. When it is broken, everyone scatters to pick up the goodies!

Pinatas come in a variety of different shapes. Some are animal-shaped, while others have seasonal or holiday shapes. Design a pinata that everyone would enjoy during Cinco de Mayo.

by Mary Ellen Switzer

Cinco de Mayo

Cut or tear discarded pieces of construction paper into irregular shapes to resemble a mosaic. Collect Mexican weaving, pottery, straw baskets and other artifacts made in Mexico. Cut the letters from bright paper for the caption. Gather a collection of books on Mexico or books written by Mexican authors.

Make your bulletin board look like a mosaic (a mosaic is a form of art using small pieces of broken tile or pottery to make pictures or patterns). Cover the board with newsprint, which serves as a base for attaching the construction paper. Glue the paper pieces over the newsprint.

Attach the letters. Staple or tack Mexican art to your board. Some items may be hung with yarn near the board. Place books on a small table in front as part of the display.

Clip Art for Cinco de Mayo

Celebrate
National
Postcard Week
with Hands-On Mathematics in May

From throughout the state, across the country and around the world, the postcards are coming . . . and coming . . . and coming as your class prepares for National Postcard Week. It promises to be an exciting, colorful celebration filled with a variety of challenging, hands-on mathematic activities.

Ready . . . Calling all postcards! Send home a letter to parents informing them of the upcoming celebration. Invite them to share any postcards that their family has received, as well as those purchased as souvenirs. Assure parents that all postcards will be returned in good condition at the end of the week.

Set . . . To guarantee the safe return of all postcards, you may wish to prepare a simple yet accurate record-keeping system. Write each child's name at the top of a 4" x 6" index card. When a child delivers a fist full of postcards, write a description of each on his/her index card. Use a capital letter *B* to indicate that the reverse side of a postcard is blank. Or perhaps you'd prefer to assign each child a number. Place removable number stickers on the postcards as they arrive. Both systems will keep teachers and parents smiling when the postcard celebration has drawn to a close.

Go . . . Keeping track: Before the first postcard arrives in the classroom, set three clear jars on a table or counter. Above the jars, post three signs: State, U.S., World. Beside the jars, place a large container of Unifix™ cubes. Challenge the children to estimate the number of postcards that will be gathered in each category. Discuss why one category may prove to be more popular than another. Record the estimates. Explain to the children that throughout this festive week, they will be keeping track of postcards that arrive from their home state, the rest of the country and the rest of the world. Each time a child brings a postcard to school, assist him/her in selecting the appropriate category and adding a cube to the correct jar. Daily, count the number of cubes in each jar. Invite the children to assist you in forming trains of 10 cubes to make counting easier.

Post the current number below each jar. Challenge the children to make true statements about the amounts. Depending on the age and ability of your students, these statements may range from, "More postcards come from our state than from the rest of the country" to "There are 13 fewer postcards from outside of the U.S. than from inside the U.S." List their statements on a piece of chart paper. After counting the cubes each day, review the statements made on the previous day. Ask the children to identify those that are still true. Place a tally mark beside these statements. At the end of the postcard celebration, you'll be able to see the number of days that each statement proved true.

Sorting It Out

The children will be delighted with the number of ways that the colorful postcards can be sorted. You may choose to work together as a class or have the children sort the postcards in small groups. Invite the children to offer their own sorting suggestions or choose from the list of categories below.

1. No writing on the front of the postcard—cursive writing on the front of the postcard—printing on the front of the postcard

2. People—animals—both people and animals—no people or animals

3. City scene—country scene

4. Message written in cursive—message printed—no message

5. Message written in blue pen or ink—message written in black pen or ink—message written in pencil—other

6. On or by an ocean—on or by a lake, pond or river—by another body of water—not by a body of water

7. Hot weather—cold weather

8. Mailed to a person in our class—not mailed to a person in this class

9. Color—black and white

10. Shows a method of transportation—does not show a method of transportation

11. Photographed inside—photographed outside

12. Mailed with one stamp—two stamps—three or more stamps

After the cards have been sorted, identify the number of cards in each group and calculate the difference between the amounts. Encourage the children to use the terms: *greater than, less than, odd* and *even* when discussing the amounts.

by Nancy Silva

Venn Diagrams Using Postcards

Create exciting Venn diagrams using your postcard collection! Form two large, overlapping yarn circles on the classroom floor. Choose two of the characteristics listed below, writing each on a 4" x 6" index card. Place one card in each yarn circle. Randomly pass out one postcard to each child. Invite the children to come forward and place their card in the correct location. Postcards sharing both of the characteristics should be placed in the overlapping section, while those with neither of the characteristics are placed outside of the yarn circles. When the Venn diagram is complete, identify the number of cards in each circle, in the overlapping section, and outside of the circles. Compare the amounts. Ask the children to make true statements about the postcards based on the results of the Venn diagram. Depending on the age and ability of your students, you may wish to reduce the number of circles to one or increase the number to three.

Venn Diagram Ideas

cards showing a person or people—cards with no writing on the front

cards showing one building or buildings—cards with writing on the front

cards showing the ocean—cards sent to a member of our class

cards showing one or more animals—cards showing clouds in the sky

cards with a message written in blue ink—cards showing one or more trees

Measuring Distance with Postcards

Challenge the children to estimate the number of postcards needed to create a path from the front of your classroom to the back, if the cards are placed vertically. Test their estimates by allowing them to arrange the postcards on the floor. Discuss: Were their estimates too high, too low or very close to the actual number? Now, invite them to estimate the number of postcards that will be needed if the postcards are turned horizontally rather than vertically. Discuss: Will the amount be higher, lower or the same? Why? Again, arrange the cards and then discuss the results. Ask the children: Was your estimate too high, too low or very close to the number needed? Were more or less postcards needed the second time? What was the difference between the two amounts? Your class will be eager to suggest other distances to measure using the postcards. The width of the classroom, the length of the hall or the distance to the principal's office are just some of the ideas that you're sure to hear!

Finding Area with Postcards

A postcard carpet? What a colorful way to remember exciting locations around the world! It's also a great way to introduce area to your students. Use masking tape to mark off squares and rectangles measuring 2' x 3', 4' x 4', 5' x 5' and 6' x 8' on your classroom floor. Explain to the class that you will be creating a postcard carpet to cover each of the four shapes, beginning with the 2' x 3' rectangle. Invite the children to estimate the number of postcards that will be needed to "carpet" the small rectangle. Volunteers will be eager to form the "carpet" with postcards. Compare the children's estimates with the actual number of cards needed. This is a great time to introduce the term *area*. Work together to cover the remaining three shapes. The children's estimates are sure to become more accurate each time.

Measuring Postcards

Invite your students to measure the length and width of standard 4" x 6" postcards using nonstandard units such as beans, pennies, keys, Unifix™ cubes or Cuisenaire™ rods. List the unusual measurements on a piece of chart paper. Challenge the class to compare the number of items needed. They'll be eager to find the area of the 4" x 6" postcards using color tiles or centimeter cubes.

V.I.P.s

Give the special postcards in your class the recognition that they deserve. Invite your class to assist you as you hunt for these V.I.P.s—very important postcards! Choose the categories that match the age and ability of your students. Select five award winners to hunt for, or work to locate all 14. Divide your classroom collection of postcards among four to six small groups of children. Identify the categories that you'll be hunting for. Allow 10-15 minutes for the children to sort through their postcards and identify the winners. As a class, compare the V.I.P.s from each small group, deciding on one winning postcard from each category. Prepare a V.I.P. bulletin board that identifies each category and the winning postcards. You may wish to have the children write about the V.I.P.s using mathematics vocabulary. Children and adults stopping by to admire the board will enjoy reading their tributes to these colorful cards.

V.I.P. Categories

Counting
Greatest number of people pictured on a postcard
Greatest number of animals pictured on a postcard
Greatest number of words on the front of a postcard
Most numbers or number words on the front of a postcard
Greatest number of letters on the front of a postcard
Greatest number of words in a postcard message
Fewest number of words in a postcard message
Greatest number of stamps on a postcard

Comparing Numbers
Greatest ZIP code
Lowest ZIP code
Greatest street number or box number
Lowest street number or box number

Time
Oldest postmark
Most recent postmark

Mother's Day

by Terry Healy

Teacher's Background

England first had a day which was called Mothering Sunday. In America, many individuals contributed to the holiday. Julia Ward Howe in 1872 suggested an observation of Mother's Day which would be dedicated to peace. Two other individuals, Mary Towles Sasseen and Frank E. Hering, also campaigned for the observance of a Mother's Day. Anna Jarvis, however, is recognized by most as the founder of a National Mother's Day. Her campaign for a nationwide recognition began in 1907. Seven years later, President Woodrow Wilson made the second Sunday in May an official national observance.

Mother Facts

1. Mother Goose, famous literature figure, was found in an early 1697 collection of Charles Perrault.
2. Virginia and Ohio are known as the Mother of Presidents. Virginia is also nicknamed the Mother of States.
3. Missouri holds the title Mother of the West.
4. Julia Ward Howe first suggested Mother's Day be observed on June 2.
5. Mother-in-Law Day was first celebrated in March of 1934.
6. The poem "Mother Hubbard" was written by Sarah C. Martin.
7. The Mother Lode was the name given to a mineral vein rich in gold in the Sierra Nevada Mountains.
8. The first wife of Feodor Vassilyev gave birth to 69 children.

Adopt a Mom

Not all families have a mom. Members of the class may choose to adopt another female member of their family, a neighbor or a senior citizen.

Oral Language

Mothers care for us in many ways. Help your students list those things which mothers and parents do to care for them. Write the list on chart paper.

Mom's Quilt

In years gone by, when clothes were worn out, the material from them was saved. The worn dungarees or fancy dresses would be cut into pieces for a quilt. A mother would choose the pattern to piece or applique and soon those old clothes were lovingly stitched into a warm quilt. The mother's love and care were remembered as the quilt gave comfort on cold winter nights.

Make your own paper quilt. On 9-inch squares, have students draw pictures of their moms in any setting they wish, or write *I love my mom because . . . .* Fasten the paper pieces together and place on a bulletin board.

Mother's Coupons

Discuss ways in which your students can help their moms on Mother's Day. Write out or draw coupons on 3" x 5" pieces of paper. Make three coupons to give to each mom.

Tea Mix

Make spice tea mix to send home as a Mother's Day gift. Combine $1/2$ cup instant tea, $1/2$ cup powdered orange drink, $1/4$ cup powdered presweetened lemonade mix and $1/3$ cup sugar. Mix and place in individual sealable plastic bags.

Marigolds for Mom

Approximately three weeks before Mother's Day, plant two or three marigold seeds in small paper cups filled with potting soil. Water the plants and let them grow to be sent home with the students for Mother's Day.

Stamped Stationery

Cut white writing paper in half. Using different rubber stamps, let your students decorate the paper for stationery. Matching envelopes may also be made by stamping on white envelopes.

Mom Math

Moms come in many different shapes, sizes and colors. Help your class graph mothers' different characteristics such as hair color, eye color and favorite color.

Games at Recess

In honor of Mother's Day, teach and play Mother, May I? with your class.

Creative Writing

Open up class discussion with answers to the question, "How would your mom like to spend her ideal day?" List the answers on the board. Ask each student to write and illustrate their mom's absolute dream day! Share the results with the students' mothers.

Stories to Read and Share

Eastman, P.D. *Are You My Mother?* Random House, 1960.

Galbraith, Kathryn. *Laura Charlotte.* Philomel Books, 1990.

Neitzel, Shirley. *Dress I'll Wear to the Party.* Greenwillow, 1992.

Waber, Bernard. *Lyle Finds His Mother.* Houghton Mifflin, 1974.

A Mother's Day art project can be found on the following page.

To the teacher: This project can be used as a reproducible or patterns can be made so that each child can make his own flowerpot using construction paper, glue, markers and crayons.

I love you because . . .

I love you because . . .

I love you because . . .

Happy Mother's Day!

by Veronica Terrill

Happy, Happy Birthday To . . .

Sally Ride
May 26, 1951

Who was the first American woman to fly in space? It was Sally Ride. Sally was born on May 26, 1951, in Encino, California. She went to high school at the Westlake School for Girls, and her favorite subject was science. In 1978, she received her Ph.D. in physics from Stanford University. Soon after that, she started working for the National Aeronautics and Space Administration (NASA). In June 1983, she made a six-day flight on the space shuttle *Challenger.* She resigned from the astronaut program in 1987 to accept a fellowship at Stanford University.

by Mary Ellen Switzer

5 . . . 4 . . . 3 . . . 2 . . . 1 . . . Blast off! Create a spaceship that could take a group of astronauts to the moon.

286

Memorial Day

Every year on the last Monday in May, the
United States celebrates this special holiday
to honor those who have fought and died in the
country's wars. Memorial Day first began during the Civil War. In 1971,
Memorial Day was declared a national holiday by President Richard Nixon.
Today, this holiday is celebrated with special events and parades. Flags and
flowers decorate the graves of people who were in the military. Special services are held at Arlington National Cemetery in Virginia, as well as other military cemeteries around the country.

*Design a special trophy to honor American soldiers who have given their lives for their
country.*

by Mary Ellen Switzer

The Count

The end of the school year is almost here. Students are looking forward to vacations and the lazy days of summer. Their thoughts are outside the classroom, and it is your challenge to provide a meaningful end to the school year. Here are some suggestions to help.

Summer Planning

Discussing summer vacation time is inevitable. Have students fold a large sheet of art paper into four boxes. This activity should be based on the theme of "This summer I would like to . . . ." Each of the four boxes should be labeled as follows: Try to do something I haven't done before; Try to visit some different places; Explore a new hobby or area of interest; Learn about something new. Papers can be shared with classmates and sent home as "clues" for parents!

"The Year in Review" Journal

Ask students to think back to the first day of school. What were their reactions? Did they know anyone in the class? Had they just moved from another area? What did they think this grade would be like? Provide several sheets of art paper for each student. Fold them in half and staple several places on the fold. Title the booklet *My Memories of ____ Grade*. Headings on each page can be: Early Memories, Favorite Stories I Heard or Read, Great Field Trips, School Events, Favorite Units of Study and a page for classmates to sign. More-able students can add a comment for each page regarding what they liked the best about each activity.

Who Is That?

Set up a tape recorder in a quiet area of the room. Tell students that at some time during the next few days, they are to tape their voices. They can tell a riddle, recite a short poem, tell something they enjoyed this year or tell about a favorite book. They are NOT to tell their name! After the tape has been completed, use it as a guessing game in the morning, before lunch or as a quiet time activity to see if students can guess "Who is that?" Can they recognize voices they have heard all year?

Very Special New Vocabulary Lists

Keep a running list on chart paper of all the new vocabulary words students have learned. They can enter the words themselves, or you can write the words for them. Students can be divided into teams for "word thinking" sessions.

A Summer Treat

Summertime is ice cream eating time. Ask students to create their own special "super duper" sundae or banana split. Have them give it a special name and list the cost to buy their creation.

Have a great last month

by Teddy Meister

down Begins

SUN	MON	TUES	WED	THURS	FRI	SAT
			~~1~~	~~2~~	~~3~~	~~4~~
~~5~~	~~6~~	~~7~~	~~8~~	~~9~~	10	11
12	13	14	15	16	17	18
19	20	21	22	23	24	25
26	27	28	29	30	31	

MAY

Summer Reading and Other "Unboring" Things to Do!

Parents look to us as professionals for ways to keep their children involved during the summer. You might "publish" a list of free and inexpensive field trips they can take, summer programs available in the community or at the schools, and of course, a suggested list of books to read. Check your public library for storytelling days and times, museums and art centers for schedules and perhaps suggest a few films appropriate for children to see.

Visitations

Talking about getting ready for "next year" is something that is ongoing during the entire present year! Give students a chance to eliminate any anxieties they might be feeling as they look ahead. Plan visits to classrooms with teachers at the next level. Student speakers in these classes could answer questions, show curriculum materials and talk about things to look forward to. After your students return from a visitation, they can draw or write about themselves and include some items that would help the next teacher get to know them before the year starts. Visit several classrooms if possible. Students can gain different perspectives and meet more than the one teacher who might be theirs.

It's Party Time

End-of-the-year parties can be organized and fun for all if everyone has input into the planning. Students can be divided into groups to plan such things as food, the kind of manners they should have, games to play, setup committee, cleanup committee and who they would like to invite as special guests for the festivities. If weather permits and space is available, the party can be planned as an outdoor picnic or a "pretend" visit to the beach. Themed parties are more creative and can be easier to plan.

Setting Goals for Next Year

Discuss with students that goals are something that we decide on an individual basis that will help us do things in a different way. Talk about conduct, study habits, manners, class participation, cooperativeness, academics and personal grooming. What areas do students need to set new goals for improvement? After discussion and possible solutions from the class on some of the topics, ask them to each select three goals for themselves they would like to work on harder next year. These can be drawn or written, depending on the level of your class.

nd a wonderful summer!

Summertime Fun

Getting Started

Summer is a time for having fun, learning new things and discovering more about life. Children are excited about vacation time and having more opportunities to spend time with family and friends. For these reasons, provide ideas for each child in your room that continues the learning you started. Encourage a creative summer filled with activities that produce fun!

Extend Language Skills

Collect pictures or photos of children having summer fun with family and friends. Display on a bulletin board. As you discuss each scene, draw from past experiences about last summer, such as: What are these children doing? Have you ever participated in this activity? Ask children to bring photos showing something they did on a summer vacation. Encourage each to talk about the events leading up to the photo.

Seashells, Rocks and Natural Wonders

As children travel this summer, encourage them to start a collection of things they might find in a new site. If they visit the beach, they could look for seashells; mountains, bits and pieces of rock; a farm, crops such as cotton, wheat, soybeans or corn that is grown on the land. A clear plastic box makes a sturdy container for their summer collections. This activity teaches organization skills.

Literature Connection

Visiting relatives is something children enjoy during summer months. Read the delightful story *The Relatives Came* by Cynthia Rylant.

In this story, the main character is a child who enjoys being part of an extended family. In this family, relatives come and visit. They bring musical instruments, share in the workload of cooking and gardening and sleep on the floor at night. It's a wonderful tale of love between aunts, uncles and cousins. After you read the story, ask these questions:

- Where did the relatives live? (Virginia)

- How did they come? (in an old station wagon)

- What did they pack for a lunch on the road?

- What happened every time the children saw their relatives? (They got hugged.)

- Why was it difficult to sleep with a house full of relatives? (They all snore.)

- Why was the main character sad when the relatives left? (She would miss their singing, hugging and being together.)

- Were plans made for a trip to visit the relatives in Virginia? (yes)

by Carolyn Ross Tomlin

Summer Weather

In most places in the United States, weather temperatures range from hot to warm. Use the chart on the following page for children to track the weather for a one-week period during the summer. Fill in the high and low temperatures, then check the appropriate weather conditions.

Cooking Up Summer

Invite summer to visit your classroom a bit early. Make a freezer of ice cream. Strawberries are usually available this time of year, or peaches may be ready. Young children can mix the ingredients for this simple recipe. Write the recipe on a chart tablet before you begin.

Ice Cream

- 1 can condensed milk
- 12 oz. container of whipped topping
- 1 quart whole milk
- 4 cups fresh ripe fruit (strawberries or peaches)

Stir ingredients together. Fill a gallon electric ice cream freezer. Pack with ice cubes and freezer salt. Turn until the mixture thickens. Serve and enjoy.

Summer Art Project

Encourage children to collect wildflowers for a summer art project. For best results, cut flowers after the morning dew has evaporated. Press between several layers of newsprint, weighted down with heavy books or a brick. Queen Anne's lace and goldenrod work well. Make children aware that some states prohibit the gathering of wildflowers. Instead, use flowers grown in home gardens.

After a week or so, the flowers will be ready to be placed in a glass picture frame. Use this project as a reminder of fun-filled summer days.

Color My World

Summer is a time of bright colors. Point out the different hues seen in flowers, vegetables and nature. Bring a selection of fruits and vegetables for children to match. For example, hold up a deep purple eggplant and ask: Can you name another food that is this color? Have students describe other fruits and vegetables they might find in summer produce markets or home gardens.

Weather Chart

	Temperature lows and highs ⬆ ⬇	Sun	Rain	Thunder-storms	Clouds	Fog
Sunday						
Monday						
Tuesday						
Wednesday						
Thursday						
Friday						
Saturday						

Working All Summer
A Story About Responsibility, Family and Fun

"Not too thin, not too thin . . . the filling will spill out and it will be a waste. Not good. Not good!" Grandmother Wong's voice gently nudged her eight-year-old granddaughter, Karen. At the long, white enamel table, Karen and her grandmother stood, rolling out wraps for egg rolls. Over and over again, Karen practiced her skill. "It is right to do things right," Grandmother Wong had said many times. Making egg rolls was not easy, especially for an eight-year-old girl who would rather be out roller blading than egg roll rolling.

Karen giggled at the thought! Roller blading instead of egg roll rolling . . . it was a pun. What fun! She giggled again.

"What's so funny?" demanded Grandma Wong. "Nothing, Grandma," Karen respectfully replied. Funny or not, it was not good to be disrespectful to one's elders. And Grandma Wong was certainly old. She was over sixty years old. Yet she and Grandpa Wong had been the owners of the Egg Roll Empire restaurant for twenty years, ever since they had come to America from mainland China. Grandma Wong believed in working hard. "Not to hardly work. Work hard," she would say. Everyone in Karen Wong's family worked at the Egg Roll Empire: her grandparents, of course, and her mother, her father, her two older brothers, their wives and now, Karen, too.

Karen kept rolling out egg roll wraps. Meanwhile, Grandmother Wong had disappeared into the deep freezer to bring out some small pink shrimp to mix into the egg roll filling. Karen took a moment to rest and think. She was tired of working every afternoon after school, and now summer was coming. "I'll be working all summer," thought Karen, and she was a little bit sad. "I wish I was like Rochelle. She has so much time to herself."

Suddenly, Karen heard a cheerful voice coming through the kitchen. "Karen, are you back here?" It was Rochelle.

"Come on back. I'm egg rolling. *Again.*" Rochelle appeared at the table. Her black hair was tightly corn-rowed and capped with yellow and blue beads. Rochelle's mom was a cosmetologist, "somebody who fixes other people's hair, you know," as Rochelle had proudly told her. Naturally, she took great care with her little girl's hair.

by Dr. Linda Karges-Bone

"Can I stay over here for a while?" asked Rochelle, hopefully. "Mama is working late at the shop. There's a big wedding at the Methodist Church tomorrow, and Mama is doing the hair on six bridesmaids. They all needed late appointments on account of they work late in the city, you know." Rochelle liked to add *you know* to many of her sentences; she liked the way it sounded.

Grandmother Wong answered, "Stay, stay . . . you can wrap these silverwares. Wrap them good in napkins. But wash your hands first. Hot water and soap. Move fast, little girl. Not to waste time." It was Friday night, their busy night. Many people ordered in on the telephone, or stopped by after work to pick up Friday night dinner from the Egg Roll Empire.

"Do you mind working?" Karen whispered to Rochelle as they bundled silverware into napkins. Grandmother Wong had scooped up the egg rolls to take to Karen's father, who skillfully dipped them into a deep fryer full of peanut oil.

"It is nice here," said Rochelle. "I like to help. Besides, your family is so much fun to be around."

"Fun?" asked Karen. "All we do is work. Every day, after school that is, after I do my homework and studies, I come back here and work. That's no fun."

"We go to Scouts over at the community center on Wednesdays," Rochelle reminded her, "and we went to the movies last Sunday afternoon."

"I guess so," sighed Karen. "But with summer coming, I'll be here working here even more. Everybody else will be having fun, and I'll be slaving away at the Egg Roll Empire."

"I wish I could work here this summer," said Rochelle. "Mama's going to put in a lot of hours at the shop this summer. She and her friend Louise are saving all the money they can to put a down payment on their own salon, you know. I can't hang around over there because of the customers. Mama says they come in to relax, not to watch somebody's children. I'll be by myself at the apartment. Baby-sitters cost too much, you know."

Karen thought about what Rochelle had said. Still, it sounded like an adventure, being by yourself in an apartment. You could do whatever you wanted to . . . with nobody around to say, "Work harder, not hardly working!"

A few days later, the girls arrived at the Egg Roll Empire with their report cards in hand. Karen's grandfather examined the report cards carefully, looking for good marks. He gave Karen and Rochelle a dollar for every "A" that they earned. Rochelle's grandfather lived far away, so Grandfather Wong had "adopted" Rochelle as part of the family. Between the two girls, they had nine dollars.

"What shall we do with it?" Karen asked eagerly. They were eating bowls of steaming soup with egg cooked into it. "Egg feeds the brains. Get smarter," Grandmother Wong would say every day, as she poured out the broth.

"I'm going to save part of mine, you know. For a rainy day," said Rochelle. "And then I'm going to buy a new book in the Mystery Girls series. I've already got fourteen of them."

"I read all the time," said Karen. "I'm going to get my roller blade skates off of lay-a-way. Mother put them on lay-a-way a month ago, and we have been paying some every week. With my dollars, there should be enough." Later that evening, after the dinner rush was over, Karen and her mother drove over to Discount City and carefully counted out the dollars to get the speedy new skates off of lay-a-way.

"I can hardly wait to try them," Karen bubbled. The next morning, Karen woke early and scooted out to the sidewalk to skate. She was surprised to see Grandmother Wong hurry out of their apartment across the hall. She was carrying a bag from Discount City.

"Wait. Wait, Child," called Grandmother Wong. "Put these on first. Not smart to break your head." She pulled a pink neon helmet and matching elbow and knee pads from the shopping bag. "Grandmother, these are the coolest!" breathed Karen. "How did you know?"

"I have eyes. I see things," nodded Grandmother Wong.

"Thank you," said Karen, and she hugged her grandmother awkwardly, tilting on her new skates and padded with her new gear.

Karen skated for an hour. She dipped and swirled and fell lots of times. Each time the padding and helmet protected her. She couldn't help but think of her grandmother who worked so hard at the Egg Roll Empire to earn money to buy these nice things.

She skated over to Rochelle's apartment building. Buzzing the intercom, Karen told her friend, "Come on down. It is eleven o'clock, time to set up the buffet for the lunch business."

"I don't believe it," Rochelle told her, as she walked and Karen skated over to the restaurant. "I thought you hated having to work all summer. No fun, you know. What happened?"

"All those eggs, I guess," replied Karen with a giggle. "My brain got fed, and I got smarter."

"Ah, my helpers," smiled Grandmother Wong as they entered the Egg Roll Empire. "Just in time for the lunch business. Good thinking. Time to work hard."

"Not to hardly work," finished Rochelle and Karen. And so they did.

Unit Activities for "Working All Summer"

Language Arts

1. Create a chart story titled "Ten Good Things About Work." Encourage children to brainstorm reasons why working is important and fun.

2. Read aloud the story: "Whitewashing the Fence" from *Tom Sawyer* by Mark Twain. Make a list of similarities and differences between Karen's experiences and Tom Sawyer's experience.

3. Write individual stories that begin with "I help my family by . . . ." Illustrate the stories with pictures cut from the newspaper or magazines, showing people at work.

4. Make a glossary of vocabulary words from the story. Put the words in alphabetical order, and write original definitions for them: work, family, egg roll, China, Grandmother, Grandfather, summer, skating.

5. Write a recipe for egg rolls. Practice putting the steps in order. Copy the recipe in your neatest handwriting on a recipe card, and take it home. (Use this with the egg roll-making activity from the social studies section.)

Social Studies

1. Locate mainland China on a world map. Locate your city on a world map. Mark both places with a sticker or stick pin. Connect the places with a string.

2. Make a list of similarities and differences in the geography of both places. (See the chart on page 298.)

3. Invite a parent or volunteer who can prepare egg rolls to do so at your school, or visit a Chinese restaurant t see them made. It is wonderful if each child can roll out his own. The deep fryer, however, should be used by adults only.

4. Discuss differences in cultures represented in your classroom. Use the chart on the next page to facilitate your discussion.

5. Set up a "restaurant" in the play area or housekeepin center. Bring in props to make the restaurant realistic cash register, tablecloths, a notepad for writing orders aprons and hats.

Math and Problem Solving

1. Using the string that was placed on the world map, estimate the distance between mainland China and your city. Be sure to record the children's names on their estimates. Compare the estimates to the real distance.

2. **Egg Roll Math:** Reproduce the shrimp and vegetable patterns and let children cut them out. Practice number skills by giving oral directions such as:

• If you want to make an egg roll with six shrimp in it, but you have only four, how many more will you need

• If you want to put two pieces of carrot and two pieces of cabbage in your egg roll, how many vegetable pieces will you have? (Count a whole carrot or cabbage as one piece, the same for shrimp.)

• Introduce money skills with this story. Use play money to role-play Karen and Rochelle earning $9 for good grades. Pair children to write their own "word problems" for spending the

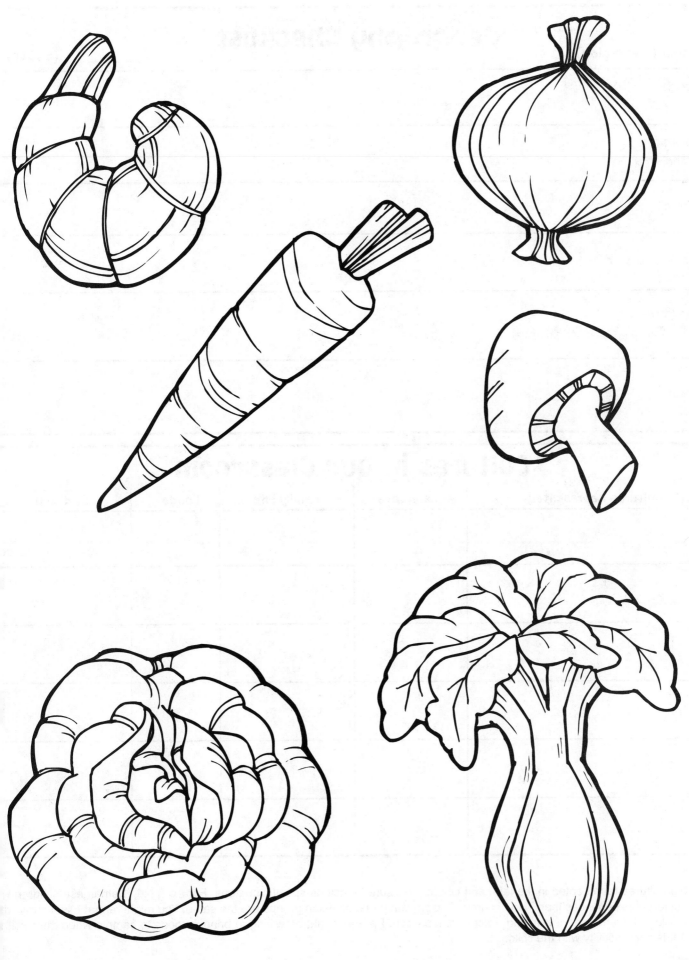

Geography Checklist

China (one region)   _____ (State)

Ocean borders	
Mountains in the area	
Climate	
Temperature	
Landforms (hilly, flat, plains, valleys, rivers)	
Other	

Cultures in Our Classroom

Cultures Represented	Language	Family Life	Foods	Traditions

List the cultures represented in the left-hand column. Be sure to include specific cultures. For example, Vietnamese children w
have different experiences than Thai children. Don't assume that all Asian groups are the same. You might repeat this activity wit
parents to get even more details and a richer perspective. Parents might be willing to bring in foods to sample when they visit
share this chart activity with the children.

Summer Catch!

Cover a bulletin board with bright colored paper. On the left side, place a small stick with a string and hook to resemble a fishing pole. Ask your librarian for book jackets that will catch the interest of your class. Make a list of titles and authors to send home before the end of the school year. Encourage parents to secure a library card for their child so they can check out these titles and others from the local public library.

Celebrate National Dairy Month

Without a doubt, cows are the source of most of our dairy products. Have students thing of all the dairy products they can. Write them on the board. Don't forget all of the food products that contain milk. Ask the students what would happen if we didn't have cows. What options would we have? What if there were no ice cream? What other animals provide milk? Have a classroom discussion on the benefits of milk and all other dairy products. Discuss nutrition, the benefits of calcium and dairy's place on the food pyramid. Prepare the following recipes to celebrate the wonderful world of dairy!

Make Your Own Butter

Talk about the different kinds of butter and margarines that are available today. Discuss the churning methods of the past and show children an old-fashioned churn if one is available. Then have students make their own butter using the following directions.

Provide a small jar for each child. Baby food jars work well.

Fill each jar $1/4$ to $1/2$ full with heavy whipping cream.

Have students shake jars as hard as they can. For younger children, another option is to use one jar and let children pass it around. It does take quite some time for the butter to form. However, the cream should eventually separate leaving a clump of butter.

Spread on crackers, muffins or bread. Refrigerate.

Milk Shakes

Mix 1 cup milk and $3/4$ cup ice cream in a blender. Add fruit, chocolate or vanilla. Blend until thoroughly mixed. Enjoy!

Fudge Pops

1 pkg. cook-and-serve chocolate pudding mix
 (3.4 ounces)
3 cups milk (whole milk works best)
$1/4$ cup cup sugar
$1/2$ cup whipping cream, whipped
wooden sticks or plastic spoons

In a saucepan over medium heat, combine pudding, milk and sugar; bring to a boil. Cook and stir for 2 minutes. Cool for 30 minutes, stirring several times. Fold in whipped cream. Pour into molds or small paper cups. Freeze until partially frozen; insert wooden sticks or spoons into center of pops. Freeze until firm, about 3 to 4 hours. Makes 13.

Moo Cookies

Heat oven to 375°F. In a large bowl beat butter with mixer til creamy. Add 1 cup of sugar until fluffy.

Beat in one egg and 1 teaspoon vanilla. Stir in $1/2$ cup dairy sour cream.

In a separate bowl, stir together $1 3/4$ cups flour, $1/2$ teaspoon baking soda, $1/2$ teaspoon salt. With mixer on low speed, gradually add flour mixture to butter mixture, beating til well mixed.

Divide dough in half. Stir 1 ounce unsweetened (melted and cooled) chocolate into one half of dough. (If dough is sticky, cover and chill in the refrigerator about 30 minutes.) To form cookies, drop a teaspoon of white dough next to a teaspoon of chocolate dough. Bake 12 minutes.

300

Design a picture of all the dairy products you can think of in the cow below. Draw a circle around your favorite one.

by Mary Ellen Switzer

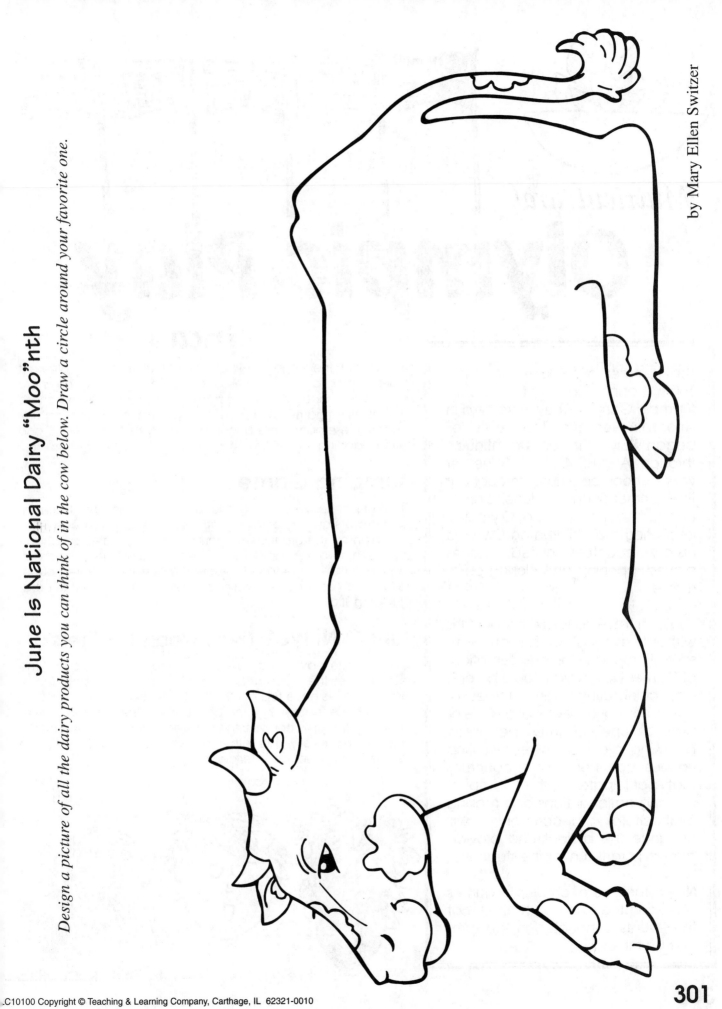

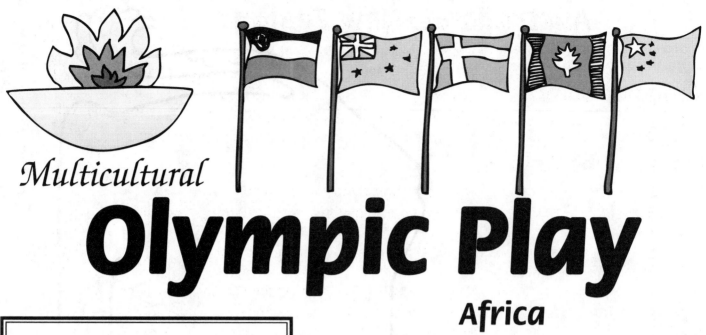

Multicultural
Olympic Play
Africa

The summer of 1996 marked the 100th anniversary of modern Olympic Games. They were held in Atlanta, Georgia. The festivities began July 19th and continued through August 4, 1996. Whether your school continues throughout the summer or ends in June, plan to conduct a unit on the Olympics, instructing the children on Olympic history, countries invited, games played, opening and closing ceremonies.

You can travel to faraway countries without even stepping off your school grounds. Plan an International Games Day, which could be one day celebrating many games or spread out over several days, celebrating one country per day. Following are games representing various continents and countries that participate in the Olympics. Painting national flags and making multicultural decorations will enhance the project and provide arts and crafts fun for the students.

Note: These are children's games played in the following nations, not the events conducted in the summer Olympics.

Throughout the large continent of Africa, there are different tribes and a variety of games played. Some popular ones are ball games, hide-and-seek games, "it" games, run-and-chase games, string games and games using items made from nature. Most of these games are accompanied by rhythms, chants and hand clapping.

Jumping Game

The Masii of Kenya play a game to see who can jump the highest from a standing position. With practice, children can jump very high off the ground. This game is accompanied by chanting. Each child has a stick that is used to thump the ground during the jumping and to help excite the performer. Store-bought dowels that are painted and decorated by children make great "jumping sticks."

Kini O Ni Iye? (Who Wears Feathers?)

Collect large leaves and pass them out to all of the players. The leader faces the group and starts to ask questions about feathers. "Do crows have feathers?" "Do horses have feathers?" "Do people have feathers?" If the answer is *no*, the children answer "Beko." If the answer is *yes*, the children shout "Beni." If a player answers incorrectly, the other children tap his legs with the leaves. Change leaders periodically.

Beni!

Beko!

by Tania K. Cowling

Australia and New Zealand

Australia is the world's smallest continent. New Zealand has two islands, North and South, and is located to the southeast of Australia.

Kangaroo Jump

Students line up and jump, one by one, from a stationary position. The jumping distance is measured and the winner is the person who jumped the farthest.

Game of the Animals

The Aborigines use their bodies to imitate animals in their environment:

Kangaroo—requires holding the hands in front with elbows bent and hopping on the legs.

Butterfly—requires flapping the arms to represent the fluttering of the wings and the graceful body movements of the butterfly.

Fish—requires twisting and turning the whole body as if moving through water.

Crane—requires high-stepping leg movement that represents lifting the long legs of the crane up and down as it moves on land, searching for food.

Canada

Canada is a vast country with a wide temperature span and a variety of ethnic groups. There are Eskimos, Native American Indians, French and English.

Ptarmigans vs. Ducks
(Eskimo Tug-of-War)

The Eskimos use a real seal skin rope, but you can use any kind of strong rope. The Ptarmigans represent those children who were born in the winter, and the Ducks are children born in the summer. Set up teams by birthdays and try to keep even lines. Line up on either side and pull!

Asia

Asia is a vast continent and is referred to by location. East Asia includes China and Japan. South Asia incorporates India and Sri Lanka. West Asia has Turkey and Lebanon. Central Asia covers Afghanistan and Bhutan. Southeast Asia covers Malaysia and Thailand. Indonesia is considered part of Asia. Northern Asia *was* the Soviet Union.

Crab Race Game

Divide the class into relay teams. The race is run on all fours–hands and feet backwards from a starting point to a designated finish line. Each player goes in succession until the entire team finishes.

Fukuwarai

Similar to Pin the Tail on the Donkey, where blindfolded children turn around three times and pin a tail on the board. In the game Fukuwarai, an outline of a face is made and placed on the wall. Children are given facial features to attach to the face. (**Note:** Each group will have a designated facial feature. See who comes the closest!)

Eastern Europe

Many countries make up eastern Europe; the most well-known are Finland, Greece, Romania, Hungary, Germany, Italy and Portugal, to name a few.

Nut Relay

Set up two teams of players. Each team needs a spoon and a nut. At a signal, the first player on each team must place the nut on the spoon, hold the spoon in one hand and walk briskly to a designated spot. The players then return to hand off the spoon and nut to the next player. During the relay, if the nut drops off the spoon, the player must scoop it up with the opposite hand and hold it in that hand while continuing the journey. The team to complete the relay first is the winner.

Wild Donkey Trail

The donkey who is "it" stands in the center of the circle of children. All players say this chant; the rhyme is like a ticking clock.

At 1:00 the donkey is asleep.
At 2:00 the donkey is asleep.
At 3:00 the donkey is asleep.
At 4:00 the donkey is asleep.
At 5:00 the donkey is asleep.
At 6:00 the donkey is asleep.
At 7:00 the donkey wakes up.
At 8:00 the donkey yawns.
At 9:00 the donkey washes.
At 10:00 the donkey dresses.
At 11:00 the donkey opens the door.
At 12:00 the donkey runs, runs, runs!

At the word *run*, the children scatter in all directions while the donkey runs and chases the players until one is caught. The one caught becomes "it" and the game starts over.

Latin America

Central and South America are represented.

Pahlito Verde

Pahlito Verde (pah-LEE-toe VER-deh) means "Where is the little green stick?" Children all stand around in a circle. The one who is "it" is outside the circle behind the players and holds in his/her hand a little green tree branch. (A painted green dowel can be used in the classroom.) As "it" goes around the outside of the circle, the players chant "Pahlito Verde" and "it" answers "Romero" (Ro-MER-oh), which means the herb rosemary. The players continue to chant and "it" answers. This goes on until "it" has made a complete trip around the outside of the circle. Then the chanting stops, and "it" runs around the circle and drops the branch behind a player, who must pick it up and chase after "it." If the person who is "it" can successfully return to the spot vacated by the one doing the chasing before being touched, the person with the branch becomes "it." Then the cycle of chant-and-chase begins again.

Father's Day Gifts

Wheaties® Frame

Ask your children to bring a box of Wheaties® to class to prepare a Father's Day Gift. If you send a note home to Mom, this usually works, if not, ask your grocery store to donate a few extra boxes. Also ask the children to bring in their favorite photo of Dad. Add paper to the front of the Wheaties® box where the athlete appears. Glue the picture of dad inside the paper. Add words to the bottom: *My Hero, My Dad* or *My Dad, the Real Champion.*

Promise Jar

There are many things a child can do around the house to help Dad. Make a list of them together and see how many you can come up with for your age group. Make them realistic and practical. Examples: Help clean the garage, never leave a bike in the driveway, carry in firewood, rake the yard, clean his golf clubs, etc. Write each one on a piece of paper and put them in an empty jar. On the front of the jar make a fancy label, and print this poem:

Dad,

> Promises I sometimes keep
> and sometimes I just don't.
> This time I wrote them down
> and forget them I won't.
> Just pull one out every day
> and that deed I will do.
> I promise not to complain,
> Happy Father's Day to you.
>
> Love, _____

Clip Art for Father's Day

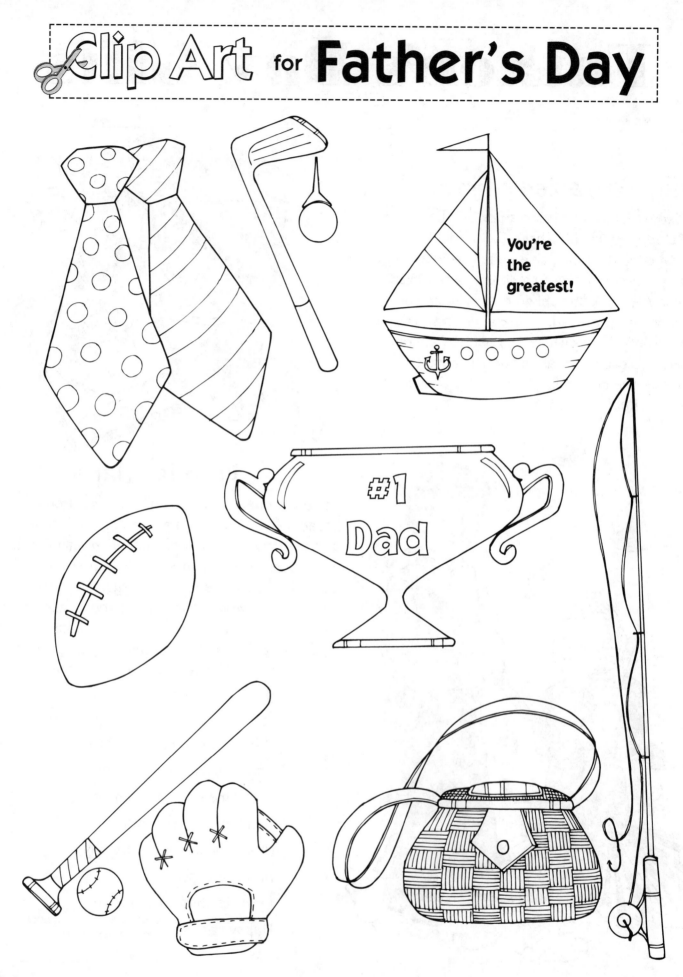

You're the greatest!

#1 Dad

Flag Day
June 14

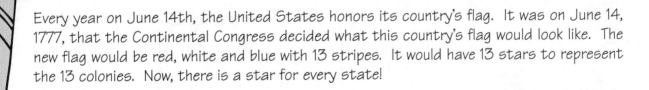

Every year on June 14th, the United States honors its country's flag. It was on June 14, 1777, that the Continental Congress decided what this country's flag would look like. The new flag would be red, white and blue with 13 stripes. It would have 13 stars to represent the 13 colonies. Now, there is a star for every state!

Design a flag representing your country or design a new flag for your country. Tell why you chose this design

Design a flag to represent your family.

Tell how this flag is representative of your family.

by Mary Ellen Switzer

Flag Matching

Draw a line to match each
country with its flag. Color
the flags.

1. United States

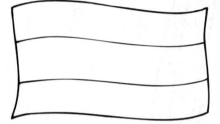

2. Canada

3. Mexico

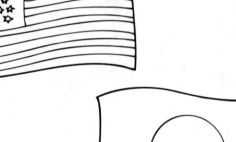

4. France

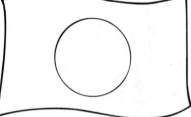

5. Germany

6. Japan

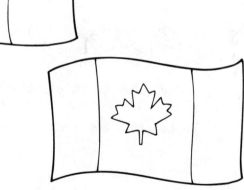

4th of July
Freedom Friend

Materials

Styrofoam™ drinking cup
red, white and blue tempera paints
paintbrush
potting soil
circle of sod to fill the top of cup

How To

A fun activity for groups of children during the Fourth of July holiday is to make a Freedom Friend. First paint a pace on the front of the cup. Add American symbols and other designs to the cup for the holiday. You can give your friend a name and print it on the cup if you wish. When the paint is dry, add potting soil and the sod to the top of the cup. Make the grass stand tall so that it appears to be the hair on your freedom friend. Water the "hair" and watch it grow. Braid the hair, comb the hair, put the hair in pigtails or give your friend a haircut. The children will have lots of fun with their freedom friends and can take them home and water them! Be sure to give your freedom friends some sunlight if you want their hair to grow.

Name That Tune Game

This game can be played in groups or individually depending on the number of children. Whatever the number of children, multiply it by three and cut out that number of red, white and blue stars equally. Pass them out to your groups or individuals. Play patriotic songs on a tape player or a piano. The child or group that names the tune correctly gives up a star. The team or person to lose all their stars, wins!

Clip Art for 4th of July

Bastille Day

Bastille Day is observed on July 14, commemorating the capture of the infamous French prison, the Bastille, by the French people in the year 1789. It held many of the political prisoners during the French Revolution. During the capture, the prison was destroyed and the prisoners freed. This triumph led to French democracy and independence from the King's absolute power in France.

The French national anthem, "La Marseillaise," observed the fact that it was the common people of France that stormed the Bastille. It begins with the words *To arms, citizens.*

Today, this holiday resembles Independence Day in the United States. It is a joyous celebration of parades, fireworks, carnivals and dancers.

Conduct a Parade

Children and families line the streets as they watch men in uniform wave French flags and listen to the music played by marching bands. In the classroom, work on flags and homemade instruments to conduct your very own Bastille Day parade.

Make a French flag starting with an 8 1/2" x 11" sheet of white construction paper. Cut a piece of blue paper 3 5/8" x 8 1/2", and glue this strip to the right side of the flag. Next, cut a red strip of paper 3 3/8" x 8 1/2", and glue this to the left side of the flag. Attach a pole replica made from heavy cardboard. Staple this in place on the blue side. March around the room to a recording of "La Marseillaise," waving the country's flag.

Construct a few musical instruments to use in your parade. A **milk jug shaker** would attract quite a bit of attention. Each child should bring in an empty milk jug (any size). Place a desired amount of beads (wooden or plastic) and jingle bells in the jug. You could substitute dried beans for the beads. Screw the lid on tightly (young children might need the lids glued or taped on for safety). The children can decorate this jug with colorful stickers, paints and markers. Shake the jug up and down and side to side for a variety of sounds. A **musical kazoo** is a fun instrument to use in a parade. Provide a cardboard toilet paper tube for each child and a 4" x 4" square of cellophane or wax paper. After decorating the tube, attach the paper to one end with a rubber band. The children can now hum loudly into the open end of a kazoo, making sounds that will surely cause giggles.

311

Street Fairs and Carnivals

During midday, the children of France enjoy the many festivities of fairs and carnivals. There are various rides to go on and races to watch. Boat and bicycle races are quite popular. Set up your own tricycle (or bicycle) races at your school. Decorate the cycles with crepe paper streamers of red, white and blue. Make a homemade obstacle course using rubber cones or empty cardboard cartons. Weave in and out of the track to the finish line. For a boat race, make sailboats out of foam grocery trays. Poke a plastic straw through the bottom of the tray. Slit the straw slightly on the bottom and secure it in place with heavy tape. You can decorate this mast with small triangular flags or small streamers taped on. Float the boats in a large tub of water.

The Left Bank in Paris is a famous place where artists display their works of art outdoors. In honor of Bastille Day, set up a miniature Left Bank in your classroom where the children can display their prize pictures. String clotheslines across the room and hang the pictures with clothespins. It would also be a good day to set up easels and paints. You could provide berets for students to wear to look like authentic French painters.

After Dark

In the evening, the skies are filled with colorful fireworks in France. Families spread blankets on the public grounds and picnic under the stars. Set up an area to picnic either inside the classroom or out on the school grounds. A typical French menu might include a slice of French bread or croissant, cheeses such as Brie or Camembert and a favorite drink, like hot chocolate.

Using a nontraditional brush method, create a fireworks painting with sprigs of parsley or baby's breath (found at the florist). Dip these sprigs into tempera paints and press a print onto black construction paper. Enhance the display with shiny glitter.

The end of Bastille Day is celebrated with much merriment, music and dancing. Colored lights adorn the streets and cafes. A replica of this tradition can easily be done in the classroom, ending the day with folk songs, dance and twinkling lights. String Christmas lights around the room.

by Tania Kourempis-Cowling

Bastille Day

In this unit, you will travel to France to spotlight Bastille Day, an important national holiday held on July 14th. This holiday commemorates the storming of the fortified prison in Paris—the Bastille—by a group of angry French people in 1789. The people wanted to free those inside who were unfairly jailed. This marked the beginning of the French Revolution.

Today, the holiday is celebrated with parades and other special events. French flags decorate Paris, and a big military parade is held. In the evening, fireworks light up the sky, and people dance in the streets.

Eiffel Tower

Connect the dots in the picture and create the famous French landmark—the Eiffel Tower.

Tower Tidbits . . .
Every year, tourists from all over the world flock to the fantastic Eiffel Tower in Paris. This well-known landmark is located near the Seine River in a park called the Champ de Mars. The Eiffel Tower, which stands 985 feet high, was finished in 1889. At the time, it was the tallest building in the world.

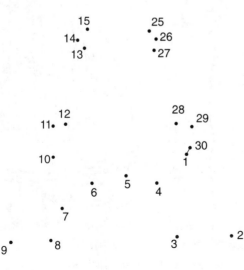

by Mary Ellen Switzer

Paper Pals Around the World

Here are two French paper pals for you to enjoy! Color the paper pals and the costumes; then cut them out.

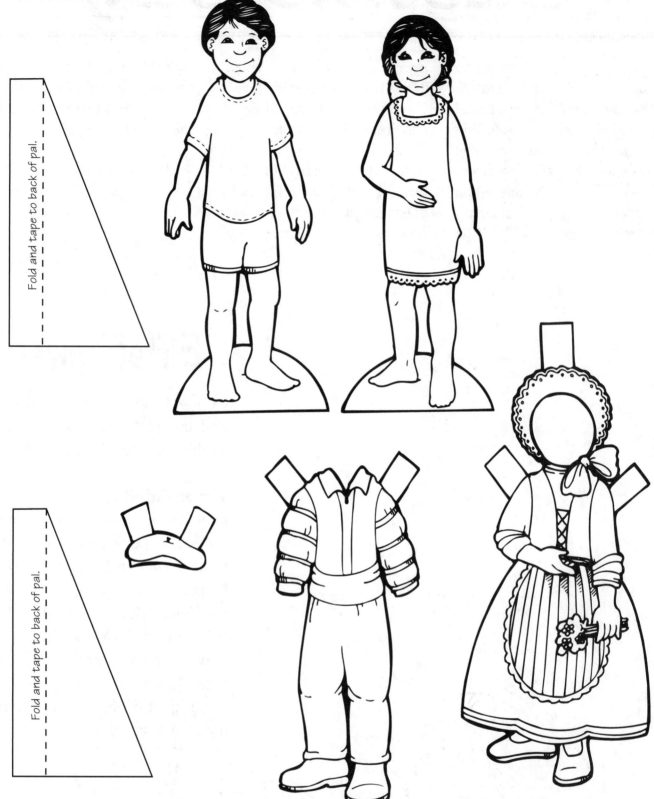

Fold and tape to back of pal.

Fold and tape to back of pal.

Bonus: Write a story or play that takes place in France, using your Paper Pals as characters. Draw a picture to show an event in your story.

France

Color the map of France and draw a circle around Paris, the magnificent capital city. Thousands of tourists visit this beautiful city every year. Add other cities, landmarks, etc., that you find notable.

Bonus: On the back of this page, write three facts that you have learned about France.

Ready, Set, Let's Count!

Can you count to cinq (five) in French?

1 (un) 2 (deux) 3 (trois) 4 (quatre) 5 (cinq)

My French Colors

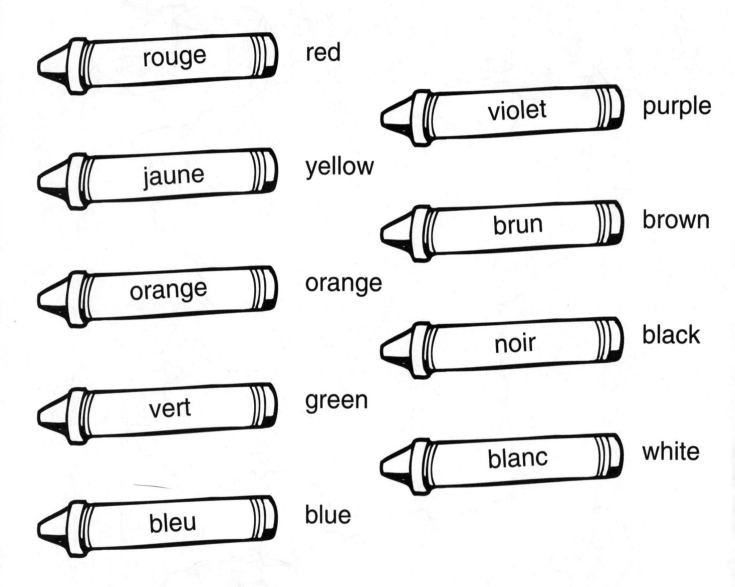

rouge — red

violet — purple

jaune — yellow

brun — brown

orange — orange

noir — black

vert — green

blanc — white

bleu — blue

Color all of the crayons above. Write your favorite color in French

_____

French Flag

Get your blue, white and red crayons ready—it's time to color the French flag. This flag is called a tricolor because it has three colors. Color the first stripe blue, the second stripe white and the third stripe red.

The Magic Suitcase

Calling all tourists! Let's grab our magic suitcase for a trip to France.

"Bonjour!" This is the way you would say "good morning" in France. Welcome to the beautiful country of France. When you travel around this country, you will soon see why it is called "la belle, la douce"—the beautiful, the sweet. Sunny beaches, snowcapped mountains, colorful vineyards and green forests are some of the places you will want to visit. You won't want to miss the famous monuments, parks and museums located in the capital city of Paris.

The important industries in France include aircraft, auto- mobiles, iron, steel, machinery, wine and cheese. Some of the food raised in France includes wheat, corn, grapes, apples, potatoes, barley, oats and sugar beets.

"Au revoir" (good-bye). Our trip to France is over for today!

Write a list or draw pictures of what you would pack in your magic suitcase for a trip to France.

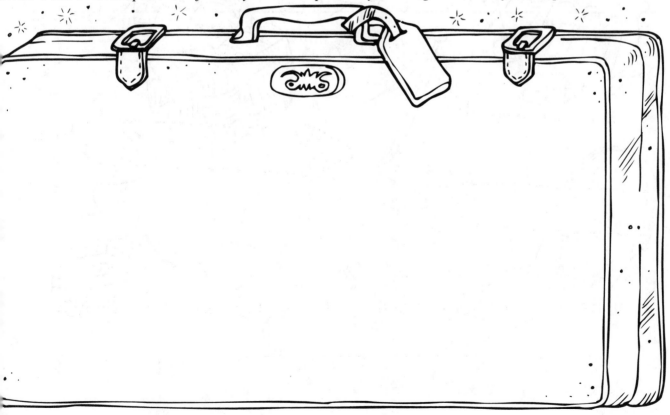

Clip Art for Spring and Summer

EARTH DAY

MOM

Clip Art for Spring and Summer

Have a super Summer!

Happy Spring

Hooray for Summer!

School will be dismissed

on _____

at _____,

Have a great vacation!

Have a Super Summer!

_____,

I've really enjoyed having you in class.

You were a great student!

Good luck in _____.

_____

Your Teacher

320